TWELVE YEARS IN CHINA

THE PEOPLE, THE REBELS, AND THE MANDARINS

BY A BRITISH RESIDENT.

With Illustrations.

SR Scholarly Resources Inc.
Wilmington, Delaware

DS
709
.S28
1972

SCHOLARLY RESOURCES, INC.
1508 Pennsylvania Avenue
Wilmington, Delaware 19806

Reprint edition published in 1972
First published in 1860 by Thomas Constable and Co., Edinburgh

Library of Congress Catalog Card Number: 72-79838
ISBN: 0-8420-1365-2

Manufactured in the United States of America

PREFACE.

In the absence of public information regarding late events in China, excepting from persons whose views would naturally, if not inevitably, be affected by the policy adopted by our Government, it seems to me a duty, in the present crisis, to narrate my experience during a residence of twelve years in that country, and the opinions I was led to form. In the light in which events appeared to me, they assumed a very different colour from that in which they have been painted by others.

The "Foreign Factories" at Canton, on my first arrival there in 1847, were enlivened by the presence of some of the troops forming part of the expedition hazarded by Sir John Davis to obtain the fulfilment of Treaty-rights. The chief results of that demonstration were the building of a church and parsonage, and the closing of a disagreeable thoroughfare called Hog Lane. More important advantages were obtained upon paper, but owing to the faithlessness of Chinese officials they remained documentary. The parsonage was blown up at the destruction of the Factories; the church was pulled down by the Chinese when the gardens were evacuated for the better concentration of the small force under Sir Michael Seymour; and Hog Lane was reopened over the site of the church, forming a melancholy pathway through the scene of desolation which marked the position of our famous old residences at Canton when I left China in 1859.

During the interval many interesting events occurred; some of these will be described in the following pages. In pursuit of business and health, or impelled by curiosity, I saw more of the country and people than has fallen to the lot of most foreign residents in China. As I give some account of my experience in the following pages, the reader will be enabled to judge whether my opinion is of value. It is quite possible for a person to reside long in China, and yet know very little about it: even the best informed has much to learn. Native society is so constituted, that the people themselves are very ignorant upon many points relating to their country.

I do not consider Government interpreters the best authorities on Chinese affairs; much of their time is taken up in studying old classics and official forms, and a great deal of their information is derived from native teachers, who are frequently spies of the mandarins.

During my residence in China, the empire has been disturbed by two distinct rebellions. Too little attention has been paid to these; the map which accompanies this volume will show how extensive they have been. One body of rebels proclaimed Christianity and the overthrow of idolatry, but as their doctrines were mingled with much error, and they pressed their religion by the power of the sword, it is natural that, however much Christian missionaries might hope for good to arise from the movement, they could not approve the acts of the insurgents. No attempt was made to remove their errors and to teach them truth ; the Bible they republished has therefore been left unheeded among the mass of rubbish by which it was surrounded. Neutrality during the civil war was proclaimed by the British Government, but has not been adhered to.

A British plenipotentiary, it must be remembered, had to take into consideration, that anarchy might endanger the vast revenue derived from tea-duties ; and that as the Insurgents at first punished opium-smoking by death, the large revenue derived from that source would have been lost had they gained the ascendency. Besides, our late plenipotentiaries have derived most of their information regarding political matters in China from one source. Mr. Wade has been their adviser and interpreter, and he cannot be considered impartial, having at one time held an appointment in the service of the Chinese Government. Lord Elgin availed himself of the services of Mr. Lay to assist Mr. Wade, though the former held at the time the post in the Chinese service vacated by the latter. I quite approve of the appointment they held in the Chinese service, but regret that Lord Elgin had not other assistance.

Our own advantage has been the regulating principle of our policy ; we make exactions when it suits us, and do not enforce them when inconvenient. Our diplomacy has resulted in confusion worse confounded ; we shall have probably now to overthrow a Government which we have been endeavouring to support. The empire is too weak to bear the double evil of foreign invasion and civil strife. Had we been more considerate in our de-

mands upon the Government, and tried to do some good
to the people, we should now have less to deplore. Little
can be said in favour of the mandarins; the people
deserve better rulers.

When I first thought of publishing my views on China,
shunning notoriety, I intended to let them go forth
anonymously; but I find that there are various matters
on which I differ from other writers on recent events,—
and that regarding events of such importance, that if
any additional consideration can be obtained for my remarks by adopting a different course, it is only right
that I should make them openly. I am confident in
my own opinion; and though I have such distinguished
men as Sir John Bowring and Lawrence Oliphant as
my opponents, I cast these notes upon the general current of public opinion, hoping that if there is truth
in them, it may drift into some powerful channel, and
lead to greater results than my efforts single-handed are
likely to attain.

As it is yet possible that the threatened war with
China may be averted, this does not appear to be the
time for discussing future operations should they ultimately be necessary. Publicity in such matters should
be avoided. When it was considered necessary that
Canton should be taken, as I was well acquainted with
the neighbourhood of the city, and knew the style of
defence adopted by Yeh when the rebels attacked the
place, I made out a plan of the environs, giving roads,
elevations, &c., on a large scale, described the whole, and
the best point of attack to two of the principal officers,
and placed the plan in the hands of the authorities,

taking care to mention nothing of the affair to any one else. The attack was conducted almost in exact accordance with the plan, and the loss of life, numerically, was very small. A different result might have ensued had the plan been publicly discussed.

These frequent wars in China are dangerous; the Chinese learn the art of warfare by experience. Every succeeding quarrel with them is likely to be more serious than its predecessor, and it must always be borne in mind that their climate is as powerful an enemy as their soldiers.

JOHN SCARTH.

EDINBURGH, *February* 1860.

Costumes, Mainland near Hong-Kong.

" THE PLAN TO PURSUE IN CHINA IS THIS : DARE TO ACT HONESTLY, AND DARE TO TELL THEM TRUTH."

Wingrove Cooke.

CONTENTS.

CHAPTER IV.

CHAPTER V.

FOOCHOW-FOO.

CHAPTER VI.

SWATOW.

CHAPTER VII.

NORTH-EAST PART OF KWANG-TUNG.

CHAPTER VIII.

RELIGION IN CHINA.

CHAPTER X.

CHARACTER OF THE CHINESE.

CHAPTER XI.

TRUSTWORTHINESS OF THE CHINESE.

CHAPTER XII.

CHAPTER XIII.

THE MANDARINS.

CHAPTER XIV.

PRISONS AND PUNISHMENT.

CHAPTER XV.

THE INSURRECTION.

CHAPTER XVI.

TAI-PING-WANG AND THE INSURRECTION.

CHAPTER XVII.

THE MARCH ON PEKIN.

CHAPTER XVIII.

THE AMOY REBELS.

CHAPTER XIX.

THE REBELS AT SHANGHAI.

CHAPTER XX.

THE FRENCH ATTACK ON SHANGHAI.

CHAPTER XXI.

SIEGE OF CANTON BY THE TRIADS.

CHAPTER XXII.

EVENTS ON THE COAST OF CHINA.

CHAPTER XXIII.

CHINESE EMIGRATION.

CHAPTER XXIV.

CRISIS OF THE INSURRECTION.

b

CHAPTER XXV.

THE DISPUTE WITH YEH.

CHAPTER XXVI.

LORD ELGIN'S MISSION AND ITS RESULTS.

LIST OF ILLUSTRATIONS.

LITHOGRAPHS.

WOOD ENGRAVINGS.

TWELVE YEARS IN CHINA.

INTRODUCTORY NOTICE.

THOUGH there have been many works published regarding China, very little has been told compared with what may yet be related concerning this extraordinary portion of the globe, and its still more extraordinary people.

The writings of Davis, Williams, Meadows, Fortune, Cooke, &c., have done much to bring the Chinese into notice, and the peculiar character of the principal insurrection has also attracted attention to the country. The dispute with Yeh brought Chinese affairs prominently forward, but public attention was still more strongly directed to China when the disastrous news arrived of the unfortunate defeat at Takoo. War with China, upon a more extended scale than was ever before contemplated, appears inevitable. As the subject is therefore likely to be interesting to many, and as I am not aware of any mercantile man having published any narrative of Chinese affairs, perhaps the views of such a one may, from this different light, form almost a new picture. Most of the books upon China have been written by men of official position—by missionaries and by persons who have seen but little of the natives in

daily general intercourse : the official stands upon his
dignity and goes through the tedious forms of stiff
diplomatic visits now and then ; most of his information
is derived from people who are devoted to the mandarins ; the missionary has better opportunities, mixes
more with the people, and his informants are less connected with the ruling authorities, but, from his position,
he sees the Chinese in a different light to most other
observers. He endeavours to impress upon his Chinese
hearers, in language which they often do not clearly
understand, maxims they care little for, and gospel
truths which they do not believe. Time, however, is
improving these things, and ere long, we may look for
some very interesting work from one or other of the
intelligent missionaries who have lately done much to
open up the country around Shanghai.

There is a great portion of the veil which envelops
China still unrent, and there is much to be said to
the good people of England regarding the position of
foreigners in China.

In treating of the Chinese people, I have been guided
chiefly by my own experience during a residence of more
than twelve years. In commenting upon public affairs,
I have endeavoured to make use of the most reliable
sources of information.

The sketches in the following pages are gathered from
a host of drawings made in different excursions ; their
only recommendation is that they are tolerably faithful,
though the costumes may often differ from pre-conceived
notions of the Chinese. It is with much diffidence I
place before the public my personal adventures, in the
hope that the book may lead some to think better of the
Chinese as a people, and less highly of the mandarins
and officials than they did before.

In my tours I confine myself chiefly to what I saw of the *people*, and purposely have not given descriptions of *places* which have already been visited and described by foreigners.   In such scenes as have not been previously described by others, I have given notes of what I saw.

Cotton Weeder.

CHAPTER I.

SILK DISTRICTS OF CHINA.

Departure from Shanghai—A metamorphosis—Province of Che-Kiang—Variety of boats—Peculiar mode of catching fish—Prodigious population—
A hint to high farmers at home—City of Kia-Hing—Mulberry leaves—
Large factories rare in China—Distrust of assemblages of men—Chinese
gambling—The author roughly handled—Reeling of silk—Various kinds
—Large exportation—Native manufacture defective—Its antiquity—The
wild worm—A French *savant*—Chinese children precociously sedate.

IN the spring of 1848, when few had extended their
journeys to any great distance, I set off from Shanghai,
accompanied by my Chinese teacher, a Singapore Chinese,
as interpreter in case of difficulty, and a barber, who
also acted as cook. My object being to see the country
as well as could be without interruption, and to penetrate
as far as possible into the silk districts, I adopted the
Chinese dress, and after getting fairly under way,
metamorphosed myself into a Chinaman, set the barber
to work to make a clean sweep of my hair, and, attached to my cap, wore a thorough-bred tail of some
son of Han, shaded the natural colour of my barbarian
eyes by a huge pair of tea-stone spectacles, and marched
forth without fear of recognition.

On entering the province of Che-Kiang, we came
upon the first line of mulberry trees. The leaves of
many had been partially stripped, and the stunted
branches bore a strong resemblance to leper's fingers.

It was here the tide appeared to end. The banks of

the canal were not much above the level of the water, except where mulberry plantations lined the margin of the stream. Wild strawberries were just beginning to bud, and the rich yellow of the vast fields of a species of pea enriched the view to a grand extent. The people used a different build of boat to what I had been accustomed to see ; and I have since noticed that in the various provinces there is a great dissimilarity in the craft employed on the water. In Kiang-soo, which is interlaced by a complete network of large canals, the boats are broad and roomy, most comfortable for travelling in,

perfectly snug ; and the better kinds make capital places of residence for a long trip,—it is like taking your house with you. I had two with me, that in case one were stopped I might get off in the other.

In Che-Kiang the boats are built narrow and flat-sided, to go through the sluices that are frequent in that province. The wide streams of Canton boast of many descriptions, admirably adapted for all purposes. In Fokien we get out of the cotton region, and find mat sails in general use. The rapid streams in the north of that part of China require the boats to be made of a peculiar form, and an immense plank is placed far out of the stern of each, to act as a powerful rudder to aid the helmsman to twist the boat quickly from threatened dangers in the noisy rapids. It requires no small nerve to steer them evenly through the gaps in the far-famed bridge of Foo-chow-fou, where the tide runs like a mill-race, and has often a drop perpendicularly of several feet. The Kwangsi boats that come to Canton have to pass sluices which must be very steep, for the bows are made long and flat, at an angle of 45° from the floor, so as to form a guard to the boats rushing bodily under the water when launched down the sluice. Before reaching the city of Kia-Ching the first bridge is passed since we left Shanghai,—a fine granite arch rising boldly far above the plain. The canal then takes a direct line to the city, the long perspective view being ended by a beautiful pagoda rising up at the termination of a long vista of mulberry plantations which line the water highway on each side.

In walking along the banks we came upon a man fishing in a most peculiar way. He was perched on a low bridge leading over a stream that joined the canal. At first I thought he had hooked an enormous fish, but on closer inspection found that it was merely a live decoy. Its dorsal fin was laced to two small sticks, one on each side; from these it was tethered to what I first took to be his rod. The poor fish sported about in the water, apparently doing its best to attract the attention of its finny fellows. The man held a small arrow-pointed trident, with which he dexterously struck any large fish that came wondering at the antics of the tethered decoy. The whole apparatus was so simple, that I wonder the same system is not applied elsewhere.

It would be a splendid thing for salmon in some of the clear streams in Scotland, and would give all the pleasure of leistering without the confusion attending torches and night-work.

Let any one sceptical of the immense population of China, pass between the towns of Kia-Ching and Kia-Hing, some eight miles apart, and his unbelief will be driven to the winds. There were boats in thousands, most of them employed in carrying mulberry branches; for the leaves are not picked, the *branches* are bodily lopped off. Some of the small craft contain men gathering the rich mould and decayed vegetable matter where the "ling" has grown in the water. They use long bamboos, formed like a pair of scissors, with oval baskets at the end; these baskets are shoved along at the bottom of the canal, and when full the scissors are closed, the contents drawn up, and deposited in the boats. The boat-loads are then heaped on the banks in large piles. The rich deposit undergoes a sort of putrefaction, emitting a most disagreeable smell. It is then used as manure, and greatly enriches the land. This may be a hint to "high farmers" at home.

It took as many hours to pass through the densely crowded suburbs of Kia-Hing, a large city on the Grand Canal, on the way from Hang-Chow to Soo-Chow, two of the wealthiest cities of China. I noticed on the sign-boards, "Mulberry leaves sold here," which leads me to suppose that the rearing of silkworms is not confined to the villages, but that there are filatures in the towns. It is strange that there are scarcely any large factories in China. Labour is not concentrated, but divided into small workshops. This may arise from fear of having large numbers congregated together, where there might be difficulty in having a direct supervision of the workmen. Where women and children are employed, such as in picking teas, sorting out the leaves, we find large groups working together. The same may be the case with the tending of silkworms and reeling of silk ; but where men are employed, it is rare that many are collected in one building.

I did not venture into any of the shops, but sent the old teacher to make some purchases while we anchored the boats at an island in the canal, on which there was a pretty summer-house, used as a sort of café. A party of gamblers were assembled in it, evidently enjoying themselves. One man held up his fingers, the others shouting out the number they thought would be held up. The one that guessed right was the winner ; but how he was singled out in the awful hullabaloo they made was a mystery. The old teacher had been directed to buy something as a memento of the place, and we anxiously awaited his return. When nearly dusk he made his appearance, bringing only a basket of green plums perfectly unripe, which, had I partaken of, would no doubt have given me reason to remember Kia-Hing. Perhaps he was afraid I might keep something that would have betrayed the visit, for in those days the Chinese were chary of taking us into the country beyond the prescribed limits.

The neighbourhood of the canal was comparatively barren. One side alone showed signs of artificial work ; it was for some distance flanked by a wall of stone. At intervals there were splendid bridges, high enough for the large grain junks to pass under, and these junks must be thirty or forty feet out of the water. In the villages we were civilly treated, though I was known to be a foreigner. At one place my boatmen wished to join in the spoil, and evidently tried to make the people tax

me for seeing the silk process.   When I was leaving, a
large crowd collected round me demanding money, but
I was determined not to give any.   We were some distance from the main canal, and up a narrow creek.   I
shouldered my way through the crowd, keeping in apparent good humour, though my dress was nearly torn from
my back.   A number of men had seized my boats, and
things looked by no means pleasant.   By dint of threats
I got on board, and had some difficulty in clearing the
people from the boat.   When out, they kept her fast to
the bank, and the crowd was fast increasing, until some
hundreds must have collected.   Being sure that the boatmen were at the bottom of my scrape, I set to work to
force them to move.   At last we got shoved off, but the
villagers kept one of my men, a rascally-looking fellow,
with a club-foot ; however, once free, we left him to his
fate, and I hope he got a good pummelling for his pains.
His colleagues insisted on waiting for him when we got
a mile or two away ; by and by he came limping along
in the rain, his club-foot *sucking* through the mud with
a loud report at every step.   It was fortunate the affair
ended so well, for I was very roughly handled, at one
time pinioned ; but keeping quite cool, no harm was done,
though I had a brace of loaded pistols under my dress all
the time.   Many foreigners have since made even more
extended tours quite unarmed, and in their usual dress.

The reeling of silk is very simple.   The Chinese adopt
several modes, and make various kinds of raw silk.
Books are published containing full directions regarding it, and are copiously sprinkled with superstitious
observances to insure success.[1]   The plan adopted in

---

[1] Translations of two of the best are published, one in *Chinese Repository*,
vol. xviii. ; the other in *Shanghai Miscellany ;* both give very useful hints.

Silk Reeling -- Che-kiang

the north of Che-Kiang, where the best silk is made, may be briefly told. After the proper season has arrived for hatching the seed (as the eggs of silk moths are technically called), the worm is brought forth by the seed being placed in the sun. The usual stages of voracious appetite and disease are gone through, and the worms, when ready for spinning, are placed on the "bush," which is generally made of a wisp of straw tied at both ends, and pressed slightly inwards so as to make it open and airy.

When the cocoons are finished, and the worm has spun its silken house, they are reeled off as fast as possible. This is a busy time for the industrious villagers; they all look happy and contented ; the women and children generally manage the winding off the silk. This is done on an oblong stand ; at one end is the reel formed by four bars fastened on an X frame, which is turned by a handle ; the cocoons are placed in a bowl of water, which is kept constantly hot ; the heat loosens the natural gum which keeps the silk in its place. A boy stirs round the cocoons with a slight splitted switch, which gathers up the ends of the thread of some seven or eight cocoons; these threads are passed over a guider, which has a horizontal motion given to it by an apparatus attached to the handle that turns the reel. This prevents the threads winding on to the reel one over the other at the same place, but crosses each thread when it is passed round the reel. The reason this is done is, that when the silk is wound off from the hank, or as we call it "moss," if a thread breaks it can easily be followed up, by turning the swift or reel on which it is placed, picking up each thread that is at the top of all the crossings, until the broken end is discovered, when it is again joined, thus preventing waste. When the

threads from the cocoons are gathered up, they are
united into one, and the natural gum of the silk makes
the whole number so collected pass onwards in one
thread. By the time it arrives at the reel it is sufficiently
cooled to prevent the threads sticking, except when there
is a slight pressure where it comes against the arms of
the reel.   When a cocoon is wound off, the thread from
another is dashed across the rest that are passing upward,
and it immediately unites.   The best raw silk is called
tsatlee, or more properly *tseihlee,* meaning seven threads ;
each of these is almost as fine as a spider's web.   There
is a class which is sometimes finer, and called *yuen-faa,*
or " garden flower."   This used to be beautifully fine ;
but of late years some very common kinds have been
introduced.   It is so fine sometimes, and consequently
so *wasty,* that there is difficulty in winding it off, on
account of the threads breaking.   Another sort is *taysaam,* or " large worm."   This is generally a coarse silk,
but is very useful, and the best kinds are often of beautiful quality.   There are different descriptions of it ;
some very long in the reel ; some made like *tsatlee* in
the *gum,* the distinguishing characteristic, irrespective
of quality, of the different classes.   Where the silk wraps
round the arms of the reel there is a pressure, and the
threads adhere slightly together, owing to the natural
" gum."   The arms of the *tsatlee* reel are made almost
sharp, so that the gum is very narrow ; in *yuen-faa* they
are nearly an inch wide, and in *taysaam* nearly two
inches.   The coarser the silk, the gum appears to require
a broader base.

No article of commerce is so clean and beautiful to
deal in ; few are so costly.   The price in England of raw
silk ranges from 8s. to 28s. per bound for China kinds ;
and the export from Shanghai alone in one year is now

over 8,000,000 lbs. to England and France alone, by far
the greater quantity going to England. This trade,
from the produce of mere worms, now equals in its
annual export to Europe alone, the value of the yearly
produce of the Northumberland and Durham coal mines.[1]

I found the people very willing to give information,
and after checking it at several villages, saw the cost of
production was nearly equal to the prices we paid in
Shanghai for raw silk. The making of this raw material
is open to great improvements; sufficient care is not taken
to keep the threads regular in size, a great desideratum.
Much finer silk can be made from the cocoons, and as
the bulk of Chinese silk is pure white, China could rival
all countries in the superiority of the article. The experiment has been tried on a small scale, and clearly
proved; but the difficulty of getting cocoons down from
the country prevents the improvement being extensively
made use of. I brought some back with me and reeled
them off, making *taysaam* of fair size but inferior quality,
as the cocoons were not good. However, I returned afterwards to the same village to see the silk the villagers had
made, and found that the small lot reeled in Shanghai was
worth nearly 2s. per pound more than the other. The
experiment, however, was on a very diminutive scale.

This valuable article is carried all through the country,
and from Canton or Shanghai to England, merely packed
in a cotton bag, covered with paper, oil paper, and
matting.

The finest silk is made in the north part of Che-Kiang,
to the west of the southern part of the canal. It has

---

[1] Within the last twelve years the export of China silk has increased
enormously, and probably might be still augmented. It must be noted,
however, that since the empire has been so much disturbed by civil war,
much of the silk which would otherwise have been taken for native con-
sumption has been available for foreign export.

been said that the search after the "Golden Fleece" may be ascribed to the desire to obtain silk. The priests who first took the eggs of the silk-moth to Europe most likely procured them in India, or, perhaps, in the province of Sze-chuen, the silk there being bright yellow or golden, as most of the European kinds are of that colour. But the generality of silks in China come from white cocoons; the rearing of this description may have been brought about by attention to improving the colour, but if it was so, the improvement must have been effected long ago, for we find in the "Tseën Tsze Wan," or thousand character classic, a work that has been a school-book in China for the last 1200 years, that an ancient sage of the name of "Mih," seeing the white silk coloured, wept on account of its original purity being destroyed.

We must not pass over the wild kind of worm which feeds upon a species of oak, and spins a coarse, hard silk which makes a strong useful material when worked up. Some of the eggs of this description were sent overland to Paris, proving a source of considerable anxiety to the different parties who received them during transit, the instructions on the box, instead of simply stating that it contained the eggs or seed of the *wild* silkworm moth, was couched in the following manner by the French *savant* who forwarded them:—" Must be kept far from the engines; this box contains *savage* worms." This species might be introduced with great advantage into Europe. There are many kinds of covered chrysalids that might be brought into use where a population is numerous; children and women can do all the work, as it is a healthy and profitable employment.[1]

---

[1] The Chinese say that eight acres of mulberry plantation can be made as valuable as one hundred acres of farming land ("Tsan Sang Hoh pien," by Wan Choo).

In China, the children begin to work very early, almost too young ; they get serious and sedate, are wonderfully old-fashioned, and think for themselves very soon. Though there is great respect shown to old age, juveniles are not snubbed for being precocious ; on the contrary, I have often noticed the little fellows give their opinions freely before their elders. It is by no means rare to see children under twelve years of age with full charge of a shop or stall, and even sculling ferry-boats, the large scull enabling young bairns to move boat-loads of people ; they fight their way independently through crowds of boats, and are sometimes as *cheeky* as cabmen.

Female Labourers.

CHAPTER II.

JOURNEYS IN THE COUNTRY.

Meeting with Mr. Fortune, the Chinese traveller, at T'heen-Tung—His
good humour and curiosity—Insect-hunting—Promise and disappoint-
ment—A priest and pale ale—The Temple in decay—Petty pilgrimages
—A laughing devotee—Silk-throwing in the Temple.

MR. FORTUNE has described the beautiful country
around Ning-po, and given a graphic account of the
Bhuddist Temple at T'heen-Tung, which is situated so
picturesquely among the hills that cover the eastern part
of the province of Che-Kiang. We had the good fortune
to meet this celebrated traveller there. He had taken
up his quarters in a pleasant part of the Temple, and
was busy securing botanical specimens, watching the
manufacture of tea in the neighbourhood, and picking
up all kinds of insects for the collection he was making.
It was most amusing to go through the villages with
him, he was always so good-humoured, and had made
lots of friends among the little brats that ran about the
cottages. They would run to meet him, crying out,
" chung, chung," meaning that they had got some insects, and they would upset a host of black dirty-looking
beetles out of the hollow part of a piece of bamboo. In
the ruck there might be a good specimen or two ; sometimes, probably, a new species. The children that
brought good insects were rewarded. I nearly spoiled
the market ; for one day, when shooting in the valley

near T'heen-Tung, a smart little fellow brought me a splendid elephantine-looking beetle ; I never saw one so large before. Thinking it a good prize for Mr. Fortune's collection, I sent the little urchin to him in the wood opposite, telling him what I thought would be given for it. The poor little fellow came back to me for a present, much disappointed at not getting his hundred cash,—a sum that would have been all very well for a person to give who fell in with a fine insect or two, but quite out of the question for one who was collecting hundreds in a day. Our friend the traveller had just exhausted his supplies, so that our arrival with a good stock of provender was most welcome.

It turned out that the old one-eyed priest had retained possession of some beer and wine that I had left here eighteen months before. We had posted up some doggerel verses, directing the next visitor to appropriate the liquor ; but it appears the priest had lost the verses, and not knowing what to do with the beer and wine, held firm hold of them, and would not give up a single bottle for any consideration. Mr. Fortune had discovered the store, but in the midst of plenty could not get a drop of the " Allsopp's Pale." The honest old priest was with difficulty persuaded even to give me back what was my own, as he did not recognise me until at last, when I pretended to sketch, to see if that would bring me to his recollection, he admitted my right at once, and faithfully handed over every bottle. This for a priest, one of a class that is the most degraded in China, was more than I expected.

The temple at T'heen-Tung shows no signs of the religion being very popular : it is fast going to decay. Its fine avenues and gilded josses alike bear witness to the fast-coming ruin. The priests mumble through their

B

chants in a dreary, negligent manner, and go faster to the beating of the wooden fish, the signal for dinner, than to the gong and drum, the sounds for prayer.   The main temple is very large—the Triune Bhuddah rising perhaps forty or fifty feet from the floor.   Numerous sparrows perch unceremoniously upon the idols, and plume themselves on the sacred nose of the great Foh, or build their nests in the ears of the God of War.   Whether it was with a wish to get rid of these little pests, or to see the effect of foreign fire-arms, I know not; but the priests pointed out to a pert little " sprug," perched on the shoulder of one of the chief josses, for one of the foreigners to have a shot at it.   Whatever his motive was, it said very little for his idea of the sanctity of the building or its monstrous images.

It is melancholy to see some of the old women that come to the temple on petty pilgrimages, rattling away at a box of bits of wood to get a lucky piece for their satisfaction,—the priests being able to interpret it in any way they like, probably according to the fee paid.   It is rare, very rare, to see China-*men* worshipping the idols, except on grand occasions: the women seem to be the chief frequenters of temples.   The wives of mandarins are prohibited from going to the joss-houses, it is said ; but from the number of elegantly dressed ladies that visit particular temples shortly after the New Year, there seems to be some doubt upon this subject.   I do not pretend to offer an opinion on the point.   I may state, however, that when at T'heen-Tung, a most beautiful and splendidly dressed lady, with a considerable retinue, arrived.   We met her again at another large temple some distance off, and when we were at the uppermost storey of the high pagoda at Ningpo, some days afterwards, were astonished to see her make her appearance.

She also seemed to be surprised at the coincidence, and was at a loss how to meet us, dropt all her reserve, and burst into an immoderate fit of laughter. Her features were quite Spanish ; fine eyes beaming brightly in her handsome countenance, and no Chinese characteristic in her face. We endeavoured to discover who she was, but only got some vague story that she was going the round of all the great temples *chin-chining* joss for a male child.

In the temple attached to the pagoda at Ningpo, and also in several other large temples at Foo-chow and elsewhere, silk-throwing is carried on. The process would astonish a Macclesfield throwster. The silk is hung in long lines from one end of the temple to the other, the end of the threads hanging towards the ground from a wooden framework. To the threads is attached a bullet-shaped weight, with a small iron pin to which the silk is fastened. The people employed take in each hand a flat piece of wood, something like but rather larger than the castanets boys play with in England. With the fingers of one hand at the wrist of the other, one piece of wood is pushed sharply forward, and the other drawn back. The bullet, being between the two, has thus a rapid rotatory motion given to it. It spins round for a long time, and twists the silk attached to it; but it does it too tightly for European notions, and the thrown silk brings a better price when the twist is less close.

CHAPTER III.

JOURNEYS IN THE COUNTRY.

Chapoo—Trade with Japan—A mandarin " know-nothing"—A beautiful
hawk—The sporting gentleman—Kite-flying—An empty shot—Adventure with a pirate-junk—Treacherous steersman—Trick with the compass
—The soup drugged—Aroused to danger—Presence of mind—Danger
averted by knowledge of the language—Necessity of encouraging its
study.

CHAPOO with its mud flats, city walls, strong tide,
and canals, has been described by others; in fact, one
Chinese city is very much like another; but Chapoo has
one addition, a trade with Japan. This, however, is fast
dwindling away, and two out of the four immense junks
that go yearly to Nagasaki, have been lost or taken;
and now that foreigners trade there direct from Shanghai
and other ports, the Chinese junks will have but little
chance in the competition. Some few Japanese articles
may be obtained in the shops; the bulk of the cargoes
appear to go to Soo-chow and Hang-chow. The trade
of the place is chiefly in wood and fish; the latter is
brought from Ningpo and the sea, preserved in *ice.*
The fish are distributed among it, laid on tiers of straw
mats; and the ice, though very thin, and frozen at very
little below the freezing-point, keeps wonderfully well,
serving with little replenishing for more than one
voyage. There is great difficulty sometimes in getting
boats here either to cross the Hang-chow bay to Ningpo,
or to go to Shanghai by canal. The difficulties arise

from the high prices demanded, and the payment being required before starting. Once or twice I nearly got into serious disturbances among vast crowds, and only escaped by threatening to take to Shanghai the old official who has charge of the passage-boats. We had upon one occasion to write to the mandarins, and to take the letter and the junk-man to the custom-house, but could get no other answer than that " they couldn't receive our communication at that office, nor even *know* that we were there." However, the sailor, seeing we were determined to go to head-quarters, at last consented to take us. There are a great many Fokien men here; they quite outnumber the Tartars, who form the garrison, and hold a distinct portion of the city. I saw a man here with a beautiful hawk, trained for hunting; it had jesses, and a highly ornamented hood fastened with beautifully coloured silk strings. The bird was small and had bright ruby eyes. Though there was a large crowd round me, they were all civil, so I made a sketch of the hawk. The man held the bird on his wrist, in proper style, and was the only sporting *gentleman* I have ever seen in China, unless you call paper-kite flyers sportsmen. It is strange to see sober, sedate merchants tugging away at a long string, guiding a kite very effectually in the air. Some are made in the shape of birds, and the hovering of the kestrel, or the quick dive of the sparrow-hawk, are beautifully imitated by expert guidance of the string. The first I saw in Shanghai appeared so real that I got down a rifle to try a shot, but was told it was only a kite: " To be sure it is; why not have a shot at it?" and it was some time till I understood it was a *paper* not the *bird* kite. The Chinese beat us hollow in these things, especially in the " messengers" that they send spinning up the string.

They send up prettily painted gigantic butterflies with outspread wings, at the back of which is a simple contrivance to make them collapse when the butterfly reaches the kite, and so soon as they collapse, down comes the butterfly, sliding along the string ready to be adjusted for another flight.

I look upon Chapoo with considerable interest, for once it appeared as if we should never get there alive. One fine September morning some years ago, J. C. S. and I started from Ningpo for the above place in a small junk; the distance is about 100 miles across the bay. The tide runs with perfect fury, so much so, that beyond Chapoo there is a " bore," and it is stated that the steamer " Phlegethon," with steam up and two anchors down, actually drifted. It is a famous place for pirates. We were well armed, however, having, without revolvers, fourteen barrels between us; these were all carefully loaded before leaving the Ningpo river. We had an unusually large crew for such a vessel, also a cook and two servants. Another junk kept company with us, but we had the better of it in sailing: it had two swivels in the bow. At noon, as they said the wind was contrary, we came to an anchor off Friendly Bluff, a high promontory on the south side of the bay. On inquiring what the other junk was, we were told that it had a mandarin on board going to Chapoo, and that he wished to keep near us *for protection*. We resolved to pay him a visit, as no time would be lost by it. I got out a bottle of brandy as a present, and we were just setting off, when one of the sailors whispered to me in Chinese, not to go. I asked, " Why ?"

" Because he is a pirate !" was the answer. We saw at once there was something wrong about our crew, and that there was some league with the other boat, but we fortunately kept cool and collected. It struck me, on looking at the land, that the wind was *quite fair*, and we had had no reason to anchor. I ordered the vessel to be put about ; no sooner did we round to, than about fifteen men rushed on deck on board our neighbour, and before we could think, bang, bang, went his two swivels ! All right ! he had to get up anchor and set sail, so we had a good start, and from what we had seen in the morning, we knew we could outsail him. Congratulating ourselves on our escape, we went to *tiffin*, taking the precaution to make our crew keep aft from the entrance to our cabin ; but, on again coming on deck, lo and behold ! there was the pirate junk fast getting up to us ; yet we appeared to be going faster than she did. Old Friendly Bluff was still visible far astern, and I noticed that the land " yawed " considerably, proving that our helmsman was steering badly to let the pirate get up to us. I drew a pistol and threatened to shoot him if he didn't steer right, or if he let the other junk get up to us. With the greatest coolness, but with rather insulted dignity, he pointed to the compass as his guide, and told me to watch if he didn't steer due north. True enough he did ; but stepping in front of it, and still getting a glimpse of old Friendly, there was no doubt about it ; the *compass* was steady, but the *land* appeared to yaw from side to side. I snatched up the compass, and, directly below it, in a right line with the ship, discovered a large iron nail, which had *nailed* the compass with a vengeance ! It seems a wonder to this day that I didn't shoot the fellow on the spot ! We were in a nest of pirates, and there was no use getting into a rage ; so procuring a bowl of rice, and sifting it through my fingers to guard against being *nailed* again, I placed the compass in it, and kept guard over it to watch the steering. We soon increased our distance, which was lucky, as night was coming on.

We were not done with our friend yet, but there seemed to be no harm in getting dinner, as everything was thoroughly prepared for a fight, if it came to the worst. Pillows and mattresses were laid along the side to guard us from shot, and all the arms and ammunition laid out: our plan of defence was settled, J. C. S. bargaining for first rifle-shot at the pirate's steersman, and my account was laid with the man at our compass according to promise. The soup was served in a large China bowl, we using tea cups as plates. I helped my companion, and then upon tasting the dish myself, didn't like it, and passed it away after taking a few spoonfuls. Dinner went on, but before it was over poor S. was nearly asleep, and soon went fairly off, no doubt thoroughly drugged. I could scarcely keep awake, but used every effort to do so—a good start gave me a help. On looking out, there was the other junk within thirty yards to windward and tideward, ready to run down on us in a moment: the front part was crowded with men. There was no time to lose. I hustled up S., who was on his mettle sooner than I had even hoped for: the start did him good too. Without a moment's hesitation, scrambling aft, I held the pistol at our helmsman's head, keeping well clear of him, and the crew, in case of accidents; gave him to understand, in the best Chinese I could, that he was a dead man if the other junk didn't pass round our stern to leeward, and certainly dead if she fired a shot. There was perfect stillness in both junks. Instead of hailing as I told him, our *lowdah* shouted out, " The two foreigners on board have a great many guns ;" then he went on jabbering more Chinese, very little of which I could make out, but it resulted in the junk going to leeward as directed. Right happy were we, for our fate seemed to be so nearly sealed, that we had actually at one time shaken hands as a last farewell before entering upon a contest in which God alone could save us.

It would not have been prudent to have remained aft to watch the steering with all the crew around, and the drowsiness by no means gone. It was difficult to keep awake, even resting on my gun, and I nearly went off when leaning against the mast. The sensation was curious : a sort of mesmeric slumber ; going to sleep against one's will ; feeling perfectly awake, but unable to prevent sleep coming on. We had determined not to give ourselves up. A short time before, in the same place, Mr. Lowrie, a missionary, had been attacked, got off, and then the pirates returned and pitched him overboard to drown—a miserable death, far away from friends and home ! The night was beautiful. A clear harvest moon shone softly on the rippling waves as we rushed quickly past some rocky islets ; the tide grumbling loudly as it dashed past their storm-rent sides. I remember distinctly our noticing this at the time, and saying what a fine sight this would be if it were not for the character of the junk in view, whose dark brown sails cast a long shadow on the waters as she still continued the chase, and how hard a lot it would be to be killed so far from home by a parcel of Chinamen, who, I believe, only wanted the large stock of arms, which was probably, under Providence, our main salvation.

At about ten o'clock the breeze freshened, our unpleasant companion gained on us, and soon took up his old position to windward. We could see the lighted matches in the hands of the men at the swivels, both of which were now on our side of their junk. We had a mattress against our bulwarks, and S. was ready to give them a barrel the moment they fired. I shouted to them to beware, and told our men to make them go right up to windward, the wind being a-beam, and I couldn't trust them with the chance of ranging past our stern again. There was a long parley ; they saw their plans had failed, and that we were ready to sell our lives dearly, so eventually sheered off into the wind. We watched their junk grow less and less in the distance. Notwithstanding the excitement we could hold up no longer, though we knew we had traitors among our crew. So after a strong warning that the first man who came forward would be shot, we barricaded the after door of the cabin, put our pistols handy, and in a moment were fast asleep.

In the morning we awoke and found our junk aground at Chapoo, where we had evidently been for some time, yet the bustle of grounding at the pier had not awakened us. I never slept so soundly before. Nearly all the crew had gone, and we took no steps against the others for fear of getting the man into trouble who had befriended us in the beginning : we were only too thankful to have escaped.

This adventure shows how very useful even a slight knowledge of the language may prove. There can be very little doubt that had one of us not known what was said, or how to speak a little, both would have ended their career in this world in Hang-Chow Bay : it is surprising how few foreign residents make any attempt to learn Chinese ; and most of those who do, soon tire, owing to the difficulties attending it. It ought to be a rule in all mercantile establishments, that any of the assistants who choose to devote their attention to the language in leisure hours, should have every facility granted them, and the expense defrayed. When the country opens up, this would prove to be of incalculable advantage ; and if Government would only offer pay that would induce more young men to come to China to study the language, and allow those that do come to devote their whole attention to it, instead of employing them as clerks in the Consulates, or in Hong-Kong, there would be more justice done to the public service in China, and to the young men themselves. It is a fact that the salary paid to the Government supernumerary interpreters, who have to provide themselves with board, and lodgings too, in some places, is less than the pay of the youngest mercantile assistants in China, who are provided with house-room and all table expenses. The teachers and books should be provided at cost of Government ; and facilities granted, and permission obtained, for the young interpreters to take long trips into the country.

CHAPTER IV.

Amoy, its forbidding aspect—The home of the missionary—Tradition of
the Rock—Relish for traditions—Ride by the gun battery—Marks left
by H. M. ship Cornwallis—Temple of Lampooto—Hospitalities—Dislike
of cold drinks—Rough riding—White graves—Temple of the White Stag
—Pony race upstairs—Fine view—Ruined villages—A washerman in
petticoats—Koolangsoo—Sad effects of civil war—Early deaths of British
chaplains—Trade of Amoy—Frequent disturbances—Aborigines of Formosa—Their ferocity—A Yankee exhibited by a Chinese Barnum.

A DRIZZLING rain is falling; fit weather to view Amoy
in. Why should sunshine visit such a forbidding-looking
place ? There is not much to be seen ; let us name it
over, and do it quickly. The horses are sent down to
the outer part of the town, and we go to meet them by
water, passing the long lines of junks, with their towering sides and uncouth sterns, over which the lazy tur-
baned sailors loll listlessly. We pass the foreign residences, giants to the pigmy Chinese houses around them.
The clean-looking houses of the missionaries have a
comfortable appearance, showing that *home* is not forgotten in this scene of their weary, almost unprofitable
labours. The telegraph on the hill signals a vessel in
sight, so we must make haste with our lionizing, lest
the ship be the one by which we are to leave. There is
a large rock near the mouth of the harbour, formed
between the islands of Amoy and Koolangsoo. It is
supported by a pile of large stones to prevent its falling.
Tradition says that when it falls the Tartar dynasty is

over. Why did not the rebels accomplish their wishes by this easy process ? Perhaps their attempts to destroy a neighbouring pagoda prevented them. Their efforts there failed. The pagoda ruled the destinies of the city of Chang-Chow : that city would be taken when the pagoda fell. A barrel of gunpowder was sent to hasten the decrees of fate ; but the rebels gained nothing but the loss of their powder. The pagoda still stands, though robbed of some of its height. Chang-Chow fell, but the people did not relish their new rulers, and speedily expelled them. Every Chinese city is full of tradition. The superstitious nature of the Chinese has a relish for such legends. Nor do they let real historical events pass unnoticed. At the mouth of the harbour at Amoy is another stone, with a long Chinese inscription, said to give an account of the expulsion from Amoy of the Dutch or other foreigners long long ago.

Leaving the boat we take to the saddle; three sturdy little horses wait for our party, and off we gallop, away past the long two-hundred gun battery, which the "Cornwallis" peppered severely when Amoy was taken. Away we go over the dismantled guns, their trunnion-less sides stamping clearly the signs of disgrace and defeat upon the powerful battery. Why do not the Chinese hide such signs of foreign victory ? There lie the guns on the inside of the battery exposed to view ; outside are the hastily made graves of the thousands that were massacred when the rebels lost Amoy. Would there have been rebels had the government been more careful of its honour, and not suffered the symbols of its weakness to lie unheeded ? There is much room for thought here ; the very graves of the rebels seem to form steps by which the fort wall might be escaladed. Onward we gallop away across the sands, dashing over little narrow stone bridges scarcely broader than the pony's back. At last we reach the Lam-poo-to joss-house, a fine temple, romantically situated beneath huge overhanging rocks, which look as black as Erebus after their drenching with the fast-falling rain. The temple is a capital model of Chinese architecture, the chief building in the centre especially. Outside are some large monumental slabs, with long inscriptions, each stone alternately in Chinese and Mantchoo. Leaving the ponies, we wander up into the grottoes at the back of the temple—capital places for a pic-nic; the cool rocky dining-rooms take the place of temples, and a clear stream of water is conveyed past them to the temple through a granite duct—a step in civilisation beyond the hydraulic apparatus met with at other temples in the north. The quiet old priests look quite contented and happy among their flowers in the little garden. Surely their camellias, strawberries, and oranges, their fan-tail pigeons, haverdevats, and pet white mice, give them ties to this life, ties which it is their religion to overcome. The march of civilisation has extended here; we were offered some excellent preserves, and the tea given to us was *sweetened* with beautiful clear lumps of sugar-candy. We, no doubt, have to thank some of the foreign ladies of Amoy for teaching the priests this luxury. I have heard of the Chinese, in some of the western provinces, using sugar in their tea, and of some who did eat the leaves, as the English did at first, as vegetables; but strangest of all perhaps is, that the Chinese in some places do not take tea at all; the poor people in the north of Kwang-tung seldom get it, and drink instead the water that rice is boiled in. It is kept hot; cold drinks, especially cold water, being considered unwholesome by nearly all Chinamen.

After a hurried sketch of part of the Lam-poo-to temple, we mount again and steer for the Telegraph Hill and the White Stag temple, in search of views. Away we go across the country, up the stone roads, down the stone steps—rough riding that would astonish a fox-hunter: never fear, the ponies are used to it; never mind the holes, the ponies see them; as for the steps, if they do not take them in their stride, they scramble up at a hand-gallop; who cares though the stones are slippery, the ponies are not shod. Away we dash through the crowds, past the orange-stalls, our stirrups nearly scattering the fruit among the host of expecting boys; round the sharp narrow corners of the streets, the people squeezing themselves flat against the walls as the harum-scarum cavalcade fly past. There is no time to wait, however, and the people enjoy the fun, if we may judge by their laughing faces as we pass them. No cry of " foreign devil" here; the foreigners are evidently feared, perhaps respected. We ride on through a part of the country covered with tombs—in this part of the world strange-looking objects, differing from any other graves that I have seen in China. The coffin is placed in the ground, covered over with earth, and then the earth is covered by a coating of lime—plastered in fact, so that at a distance the country has exactly the appear-ance of a large washing-green, or a links in Scotland : the graves look just like whins with clothes to dry hung upon them. The temple of the White Stag (the name is derived from a small stone figure of such an animal in a cave hard by) is approached by a high flight of stone steps. No ; I won't ride up these ; a fall would be no joke; but the ponies seem to think nothing of it, and run up the stairs like lamplighters. From the temple there is a fine view of Amoy : the business part of the town fills up the largest part of the picture ; the city is a small place, and of no great strength, yet the rebels

held it for more than a year, I think. A banyan-tree shades the White Stag temple ; it is a wonder how it grows in such a rugged spot,—

> " Crags, knolls, and mounds, confusedly hurl'd,
> The fragments of an earlier world."

The ponies pick their steps carefully down the stairs, and, after their rest, gallop on as briskly as ever. It seems a shame to ride hastily on the rest of our journey, through mournful-looking, desolate, ruined villages. The inhabitants of some were utterly exterminated by the mandarins ; a few houses were slowly being re-inhabited, but the bulk were roofless—speaking monuments of the cruelty of Tartar rule. The same system of wiping out the stain of rebellion seems to be carried

on here as at Canton, but the quantity of blood shed
only makes the stain the deeper. The roads, once
crowded with villagers, we now gallop along with scarcely
an interruption. Past the British Consulate (sadly in
want of paint) we enter the city, and in two minutes
are out again at the opposite gate ; there is nothing to
be seen inside. Always anxious to find out new costumes, I was surprised one morning while at Amoy by
seeing a Chinaman clad differently to the usual custom ;
down I posted, sketch-book in hand, to the well where
he was. A closer inspection only confirmed my curiosity ;
there was no making out the dress ; at last, upon examination it proved to be an emblem of his calling : he
was a washer-man. His head was covered with a turban ; his body was enfolded in a comfortable English
jersey, and his nether extremities were protected from
the cold, keen north-easter by—a lady's flannel petticoat.
There was no mistake about it ; the name was legibly
written thereon ; and, horror of horrors ! he held in his
hand a beautiful lace bertha (is not that the name ?),
which he alternately rubbed with soap, then scrubbed it
upon a hard piece of rough granite. I wish the owner
had seen him ! These fellows play sad havoc with
foreign wardrobes ; one would require almost two wives
to keep an adequate supply of buttons. We caused no
little excitement among the foreign ladies upon reporting the occurrence, giving no clue to the name ; but
they quickly singled out the unhappy owner of the lace
as the latest arrival ; the older residents were too wary
to run such risks.

What would the old British residents at Koolungsoo
think of the place as it is now ? I don't mean those old
adventurers who were there at the beginning of the
last century. Their tombstones on the island are all

C

that is left to tell of their strange wanderings in those bygone days. Some good follower of Old Mortality has kindly cared for these mementos, and cleared away the intrusive grass that had well-nigh brought the stones to as dark an oblivion as the memories of those they tell of. What would the old residents, the officers and others who lived at Koolungsoo after the war, think of the place of their former sojourn if they saw it now ? War is a strange affair. The English held Koolungsoo; quartered some troops there ; repaired the buildings, and left them in good order. The people re-occupy their dwellings ; some are fairly built, substantial houses, not much the worse of the barbarians' visit. Yet the regimental letters which still point out the old quarters, frighten away some of the householders ; the barbarian devils have left their spirits there, and these alone shall occupy some fated houses till war again brings a change upon the scene. The civil war came ; it passed away, and Koolungsoo was covered with ruins. The houses left standing by the foreign foe are now made desolate by the vengeance of civil strife. The people, who were left unmolested by the western barbarians, are massacred by their own natural protectors.

'Tis a sad sight to walk through these deserted villages, and melancholy to think of the miseries they have witnessed. There is even a feeling of satisfaction, a congenial sensation, when we turn from such scenes into the neat burial-ground allotted to the unfortunate foreigners who end their days at Amoy. The quietness is a relief after visiting the wreck caused by the unrelenting power of the mandarins. We wander round the tombs, and sketch some of the gravestones of those who are known to some of our party ; slight sketches, that friends at home may see the last resting-place of those they are never more to welcome. Death has played sad havoc in this part of China. Out of the small community of Amoy, since 1843, we find tombs to three different British consuls. There is also one to the first chaplain. Strange that the first chaplains brought out by the foreign residents at Canton, Shanghai, and Amoy, should all have died almost immediately after their arrival. Those who were to point out the proper way to meet death were the first to suffer.

Enough of this dismal subject. Let us cross the harbour again to Amoy. It is a miserable-looking city, dirty in the extreme, surrounded by arid hills, burnt up, dry, and desolate. The rocks stand out roughly from the rugged mountains, reminding one of the plums in an over-boiled plum-pudding. The ground has much the appearance of the treacly paste of sailor's " duff." The town is well situated for trade; its harbour is easily made, and few dangers surround it. What seems most wanted is wealthy native merchants to trade with. Cotton, cotton-yarn, and opium, as well as a fair quantity of Straits' produce, form the chief imports. The exports are unimportant so far as foreign trade is concerned. Considerable quantities of rice and sugar are exported to other parts of China.

The city of Chang-Chow, thirty miles distant, up a partially navigable river, is the chief place of trade connected with Amoy inland, but the trade with Formosa is probably of more importance, and is rapidly being opened up by foreigners. The junk men are against this interference with their trade; but the cupidity of the mandarins, and the natural trading propensities of the Chinese there, as elsewhere, lead to business in spite of prohibitions. The Formosan ports to which trade is directed, are Apes Hill, at the south; Cok-si-

Kiang, a little farther north; a sort of port to Taiwan, the capital (difficult of access); and Tamsuey, at the north-west part of the island. Sugar, rice, camphor, and sulphur, are exported from Formosa, the prices being generally very moderate. Civil commotions on the island keep it in a state of constant turmoil, and troops are always being sent over from Foochow; the soldiers having the promise of being brought back again to China—a promise fulfilled to the letter, for even their corpses are returned. A Chinaman thinks it of more importance that his dead body should rest in China than that his living one should revisit it. The east side of Formosa is still held by the aborigines, a tribe similar in many characteristics to the Malays; but little is known of them, as their side of the island is seldom or never visited, and such foreigners as have fallen into their hands have been murdered or grievously maltreated. The Chinese in Formosa had not, until recently, much to boast of in their treatment of foreigners. During the war two ships' crews were murdered by the Chinese officials; the officers were tortured, and most of them died; but this was the work of the mandarins. The chief actor was promoted by the emperor; the people, however, seem to be less bloodthirsty, and are civil, though sometimes extraordinary.

A stout gentleman, well known in China, was lately fêted at Taiwan for two or three days, the " observed of all observers," he being an immense man, and a good specimen of a Transatlantic Anglo-Saxon; but the series of crowded visits he received at last became troublesome, and he found he was being made too much of. The fact was, he was *being exhibited!* a charge being made for the exhibition.

Foochoo.

CHAPTER V.

FOOCHOW-FOO.

Foochow-foo—Its important foreign trade—Chinese honesty—Beauty of the city—A quaint old chronicle—Taking portraits—Good female sitters —Small feet not general—Tartar women—Tartar soldiers inferior to Chinese—Bow and arrow practice—Feats of strength—Fishing with cormorants—Its dangers—Poetical names of places—British consulate— Obstacles to foreigners obtaining land—A mandarin and his tail—Processions shabby and grand—Places worth visiting—Hot springs and tea-houses—Hot baths—Scanty ablutions.

Foochow-foo, the capital of Fokien, and residence of the governor-general of that province, is rapidly gaining great importance as a place of foreign trade. The interruptions occasioned to the inland transit of tea to Canton and Shanghai, owing to the disturbances in Hoonan and other parts of the empire, led to this port becoming one of the chief stations for procuring teas that otherwise would have been destined for the above cities. Foochow should naturally be the principal place to obtain tea ; but either the restrictions caused by the native officials, the difficulties of the port, or its small trade in imports, left it comparatively neglected till the rebellion broke out, and even then great risks had to be incurred on the part of the foreign merchants in sending funds into the tea districts in charge of Chinese,—risks not being limited to the honesty of those employed, but extending to dangers arising from disturbances, not to say anything of the quality of the produce purchased by

the men sent to procure it. Much to the credit of the
Chinese, however, so far as honestly taking care of both
produce and money was concerned, they proved very
faithful to the trust.

Canton may well boast of its Pearl River, with its
numerous branches, bearing the products of a teeming
commerce past many wealthy cities ; and Shanghai is
even more favoured in its position, placed as it is at the
confluence of a series of navigable streams, winding like
veins through the richest provinces of the empire to an
extent unequalled in the whole world. Foochow is not
so happily situated. Standing some distance from the
mouth of the river Min (a large river, but difficult of
navigation, and passing through a mountainous country),
Foochow can never become an important place for imports. The Min leads to few large cities, and does not
extend beyond the Fokien province ; but the hills past
which it winds its tortuous course, and the mountains
from whence its waters flow, besides bearing large
quantities of timber, are dotted with innumerable plantations of tea, which will always make Foochow an important station for the foreign trade, now that it is at
last fairly opened.

It is a large and beautifully-situated city, surrounded
by fine mountains. It is built around three small hills,
and the line of its walls forms a plan in shape something
like the ace of clubs. A long suburb extends from the
city to the river, which is about two miles off. The Min
is here crossed by the celebrated stone bridge of about
100 arches,—not arches exactly, the piers being joined
by large slabs of granite. It is a very rough piece of
work, and numerous petty hucksters' stalls upon it de-
tract from the utility of the structure, as well as from its
appearance. The tide rushes through, and the shallow-

ness of the stream prevents large vessels coming up within ten miles from the city. The residences of the foreign merchants are situated on the south bank of the river, Foochow being on the north. The population is estimated at 600,000, but I think it is scarcely so great. If we are to take all for truth that the first missionaries who visited it say, it must have fallen off amazingly. These old accounts are so quaint and amusing, I cannot resist giving some extracts :—

"They were a good houre and a halfe before they coulde come vnto the citie, and seemed vnto them that they had trauelled two leagues in the suburbes; the which was so well peopled, so fair houses, and many shoppes full of merchandise, that if it had not beene told them, they would not haue beleeued it to be the suburbes but the cittie itself.

"This cittie is the richest and the best provided that is in all the kingdome, &c., &c. The people that were at the windowes and in the streete, betwixt the houses and the soldiers, were so great a number, that it seemed to be doomes-day, and that all the people in the worlde were there ioyned together in that streete.

"In the cittie of Fucheo there is a towre right against the house of the king's chiefe receiver, and it is affirmed by those that have seene it to surmount any building that hath beene amongst the Romans; the which is raised and founded vppon fortie pillars, and everie pillar is of one stone, so bigge and high that it is strange to tell them, and doubtful to the hearers to beleeue it; for which cause *I thinke it best not to declare it in particular !*

"They sawe a bridge all of mason's worke, and the stones verie well wrought, and of a mightie biggnesse; they measured some of them that were 20 and 22 foote long and five foote brode, and seemed vnto them that it was a thing impossible to be layde there by man's hands."

And writing of an adjacent city, Chin-chew :—

" All things that you will desire to be eaten be so good cheape, that it is almost bought for nothing !" [1]

In looking about for information regarding the trade of the place, and seeing all the sights, I spent six weeks very pleasantly ; found the people remarkably civil, especially in the villages at some distance from the city : making a point of always going into one of the public eating-houses in order to see as much of the people as possible, my sketch-book began to fill rapidly. It was amusing to see the conceit of some of the fellows as they set themselves in attitude, or stroked down their moustaches when they saw their faces appearing on paper. The women were by no means bashful, and their fine sturdy figures, prettily decked hair, and peculiar costume, made capital subjects. They do most of the carrying work, and, considering their occupation, are remarkably neat and clean in appearance. The folds in their little white aprons were carefully puckered out, and the fine healthy bloom on the faces of some reminded me of the girls about a farm-steading in the Lowlands. Don't imagine that all deserved such praises ! Some were poor miserable wretches, earning a scanty subsistence by cutting grass on the hill-sides ; and any of you who have depicted to yourselves the women of China toddling about upon small feet, should see the firm, free step displayed by the female peasantry of Foochow, as they walk off with a burden of more than 100 pounds weight, making nothing of it. A woman will carry two chests of tea at a time from the city to the river, each chest weighing about 100 pounds.

[1] *Mendoza,* vol. i. p. 27 ; vol. ii. pp. 60, 80.

Torturs

Fr. Schenck Lith. Edinburgh, 56 Geo. S.

In Canton, it is a rarity to see a woman with small feet compared to those who have their natural " understandings ; " and as for the small feet at Shanghai and Ningpo, as well as through all the country districts that I have been in, they are swaddled up in a host of dirty cloths until they appear larger than they would naturally have been. Few things look so disagreeable ; the wrappings have an old look about them, as if the women always slept in them, which indeed they probably do. Chinese ladies by right, ladies by courtesy, and courtezan ladies, have the real small feet, and wear the diminutive shoes that are wondered at in England. But in Foochow, there are a good many Tartars ; they have a quarter to themselves, and their wives have all natural-sized feet. These women dress differently from the Chinese. The hair is all drawn back from the forehead and fastened in a knot behind, with a sort of skewer stuck through it, at the end of which is a flower ; their robe is a long affair, something like a man's dressing-gown ; they wear unmentionables, which appear to be tucked into wide, loose stockings, generally very dirty, and their shoes are thick flat-soled affairs, often worn down at the heels. I know nothing of their gala dresses ; but the above answers to the description of all I saw, and I frequently went into the Tartar quarter to get sketches of them. There was a peculiarity in their faces which was very striking ; they all had square, sensual-looking *jowls*—an appearance which I did not remark in the Tartar men.

The men, who form the Tartar garrison, are a dirty, lazy-looking set, have a slip-shod, forbidding sort of look, and would stand a poor chance with some of the Chinese soldiers we saw there. In one of the guard-houses on the walls we frequently stopped to see some of the Chinamen practising with bow and arrow, not for aim, but for strength of arm to pull the bow. They had a target consisting of several thick sheets of soft leather hung from a beam, and fired at this with the arrow-point within a yard of the target, the arrow merely throwing the leather back, then falling. One of the men could draw the bow-string to his ear, with the bow outstretched in his left hand ; we could not get it half the distance.   This man exercised his arms by lifting up and twisting about over his head a heavy beam loaded at each end with two large pieces of stone ; some of our party, stout men too, could not lift the beam from the ground.   The Canton Coolies amuse themselves in this way, but I never saw them use an instrument nearly so heavy as the one above described.

One of the strangest sights at Foochow are the cormorant fishermen, standing erect, each on a little raft of bamboos, not over two feet wide, directing their birds and propelling their raft with a long bamboo, in a fierce tideway, with eddies surrounding them, that threaten almost certain death in case of accident.   They appear to be wholly intent on the work of their sagacious birds, who dive about in all directions after their prey.   But the best place to see the fishing cormorant is in the clear streams in Che-Kiang.   It is very pretty to see the birds chasing the fish under the water—the pace they go at is wonderful ; and when they are swimming along near a rough, stony bottom, it is quite marvellous to see the rapidity with which they crane their necks from side to side in the crevices of the rocks as they rush through the water.   They seem quite proud when they get hold of a good fish, and bear it triumphantly to their master.   He generally has a pet bird, and places relative values on each of his flock ; for some, less than a dollar is asked.

I think the ring placed round the neck of the cormorant by the fishermen is not to prevent their swallowing the fish, but to distinguish the birds belonging to each fisherman ; for when several boats have been together, I have noticed that each lot had different marks, and sometimes a boat-load had no rings. They know their masters readily, and rarely make a mistake in taking the fish to a wrong boat. I once got four or five lots sent into the water at once, all together, and the men being told to call back their birds, they returned without a mistake. When in the boat they are disagreeable, stupid looking birds, and being fed upon fishes' entrails, have a disgusting smell. When they reach the side of the boat the men shove a bamboo under them, on which they perch, and are lifted on to the boat. It is only at Foochow that I have seen rafts used by the fishermen.[1] This is strange, because the wood that is used to build the boats elsewhere nearly all comes from that place. The chief native trade of Foochow is in timber ; huge rafts are brought down and are guided under the bridge with surprising cleverness, by very few hands for such cumbersome contrivances.

The timber junks go to sea from Foochow with wood lashed on each side, and piled up, making the vessel look three times as broad in the beam as she really is. Some of the timber brought down to Foochow is very finely scented, and a rich gummy oil exudes from every pore when it is cut. The Chinese set great value on this wood, which they use for coffins, giving as much as a thousand dollars for a single coffin ; judging from the grain of the wood, it appears to be a kind of pine.

The Chinese are full of poetry in their names of places. Foochow is known by them as the " Banyan

---

[1] Subsequently, I saw rafts used *at sea*, near Swatow.

Tree City;" it is quite green with these trees; there are some beautiful specimens in the courts of a temple near the British consulate in the city. Though they send down shoots, these do not take root, but form light-looking pendants which are very graceful. The old consulate is beautifully situated on a wooded rocky hill within the walls, and commands a splendid view.

Mr. Alcock laid out the grounds with great taste; but the sporting ideas of one of his successors have allowed the gardens to grow into jungle, as cover for a carefully preserved brood of pheasants. There were many inconveniences arising from the consulate being within the city, and far away from mercantile establishments; so when the trade increased the consulate was removed. The shutting of the city gates at sunset was a great drawback to a residence there, as it was no joke to clamber over the walls at night. When the tea trade opened out, some difficulty was experienced in getting houses; the missionaries for a consideration turned out of theirs, but still they were very inferior sort of places, and roughing it was then the order of the day. Fine houses and spacious warehouses are now erected.

The authorities raise great hindrances in the way of foreigners buying land, excepting in a situation which would be inconvenient for business. They certainly had right on their side, as it was a local regulation that no warehouses should be built below the custom-house; but thanks to the activity, firmness, and perseverance of Mr. Acting-Consul Gingell, the difficulties were removed. His Excellency Sir John Bowring, when he visited the viceroy at Foochow, had hosts of promises made to him; but promises in China, like lovers' vows elsewhere, are made to be broken.

I saw a good many processions when at Foochow,

chiefly official. A mandarin never moves about without a "tail" of followers at least equal to a Highland chieftain, and very likely as ill paid. There are lictors, soldiers, messengers, secretaries, pipe and standard bearers, &c. &c., as dirty-looking fellows as you will see in any country, but still they must be there. Some of them look as if they had just been borrowed from the jail, and ragged official dresses thrown over them for the occasion. The pictures sent from China give a very *fine* idea of a procession here ; the originals generally give a very different notion. The only really grand procession I ever saw in this country was one in Canton in honour of Shangte. It was splendidly got up, and a number of children dressed as mandarins of different ranks were a very interesting part of it. Some unfortunate women, who were dressed up in grand style, seemed to take the part of *tableaux vivants.*

There are some beautiful places in the neighbourhood of Foochow ; the Pih-Ling range of mountains at the north contains some fine, bold, well-wooded scenery ; and the great temple at Koo-Shan is well worth the climbing needed to reach it. The monks in China, like " the monks of old," generally manage to pick out good sites. From Koo-Shan the valley of the Min forms a beautiful panorama ; the priests are remarkably civil, and offer comfortable quarters to foreigners seeking the temple as a sanatarium—a purpose for which it is admirably adapted from the coolness of its situation, and the " shadowy walks" in the adjacent woods. We were conducted into a fine airy apartment appropriated to visitors, and I was rather astonished to notice the caution written in Chinese at the entrance, " Beware of the Dog !"—rather a damper to the hospitality-seeking stranger, forming a striking contrast to the European notion of the monastic dog,—St. Bernard's, for example.

At the east side of the city are hot springs which the Chinese use for baths, and believe to be efficacious in curing skin diseases. The water is very hot, but clear, and not only rises from the ground, but bubbles up out of the beds of streams in the neighbourhood. There are tea-houses built over some of the largest of the springs, and a number of bathing-rooms are attached, but these have a seedy, deserted appearance. The baths most used are square tanks in the open air; the poor people take the benefit of them. They are sometimes thickly packed with naked celestials being parboiled into a state of cleanliness, if not of healthfulness. There was some satisfaction in seeing Chinamen being made thoroughly clean, for nine-tenths of them are contented with a hot damp cloth being passed over their face and necks as the sole ablution.

The baths are near the Tartar part of the city outside the walls. There is no division between the Chinese and Tartar quarters, as in Canton and Chapoo, but the streets of the former have quite a different appearance, no trade being carried on, and a general idleness prevailing.

The Loo-chooans have a factory at Foochow; their residence is a miserable broken-down sort of barrack; they do a small trade in grain, soy, paper, &c.; their dress is in the old Chinese style; some wear chintz pattern robes, and have the hair drawn up into a small knot at the crown, fastened by a silver or gold pin, like the Japanese. They have an underhand, deceitful expression of countenance that does not contrast well with the Chinese. I asked one to write his name on a sketch of himself; he wrote it in Chinese characters.

Country Women – Foochoo.

CHAPTER VI.

SWATOW.

Swatow—Its late rise into importance—Numerous wells—Primitive sugar-
making—Waste and loss, yet extraordinary cheapness of production—
Rival clans and predatory expeditions—Excess of males over females—
Fine appearance of the men—Eating mandarins—A sketch—Shaking
hands—A little rebellion and a great tragedy—Differences in manners
and customs—Theatrical entertainment—A peep behind the scenes—
Second visit to the theatre—The audience and the actors—An agreeable
family—A Catholic missionary.

Swatow is, strange to say, a new place in China. A
few years ago it was merely a small fishing village with
a fort. Then the foreigners had an opium station at
Namoa; but when the receiving-ships moved over to
the island of Masoo at the entrance of the Han, the
village of Swatow, about five miles up the river, gradually
assumed the proportions of a town. In the early part of
1856, I found it growing into a place of trade, new
buildings springing up along the banks of the river, and
land being reclaimed; more than a hundred large junks
were anchored off the place; and though it was not legally
a port of trade, the enterprise of foreigners, in conjunction with the commercial propensities of the Chinese,
had brought about a thriving trade, and seven foreign
vessels were at anchor in the harbour.

The local mandarins finding this a source of increased
revenue for themselves, raised no objections, but quietly
pocketed all they could get, and permitted the foreigners

to appropriate the island of Masoo as a place of residence, which speedily became covered with dwelling-houses and godowns. The worthy officials receiving a ground-rent, paid sometimes by the potent medium of opium balls, the seductive nature of the drug attracting their cupidity, while its narcotic effects, perhaps, let them watch with apathy the irresistible progress of the wedge which is being daringly driven by foreign influence into the very vitals of the empire.

The right bank of the river is rugged and mountainous for some distance from Swatow ; but the north, or left bank, is a fine delta-like plain, richly cultivated. Rice, sugar-cane, and wheat are the chief products, and the low land is easily irrigated. In the valleys on the south side, where water is not so abundant, every field has its well. The water is drawn up by a lever placed at the top of a high pole, and the bucket is suspended by a long straight piece of bamboo. These wells have a strange appearance ; the numerous poles distributed throughout the valleys, give them the appearance of stunted decayed forests. The same mode of raising water is employed in Syria, and I have noticed it also in Egypt. The end of the lever is weighted with a stone.

Every village has its series of sugar-mills, rude, but efficient constructions. The cane is pressed between two perpendicular granite cylinders, one being turned by oxen, giving a motion to the other by means of cogs cut in the granite, and shod with hardwood at each cog. The cylinders are supplied with cane by a man who stands in a hole cut in the ground ; this hole is stuffed with straw, and makes a comfortable warm berth for his legs. The cane is passed twice through the cylinders, and the juice expressed is collected in a tub sunk into the ground at the side of the press. Four bullocks are yoked abreast to the lever beam which turns the press,—the largest animal being on the outer part of the circle, the smallest inside. Teams of assorted sizes wait in readiness as relays. The sugar boiling-house is close by the mill, and the fire is fed by the refuse cane. There must be a great loss of sugar from the cane being so imperfectly pressed, owing to the rudeness of the machinery; and much might be made out of the *begass* or waste. The Chinese do not appear to make any spirits from the sugar; at any rate, none is offered for sale, perhaps the best criterion in China.[1]

Let us enter a boiling-house. In a low cottage building we find a cloud of steam filling the room, though it has a means of escape by a large hole in the roof. The place would be unbearable if the fire were inside, but the Chinese know their climate too well for that, and supply the fuel from the exterior. The stout muscular-looking fellow with a long-handled colander sort of ladle, stops his skimming to watch the barbarians, and the troop of little boys (the foreigners' pest in China) crowd round to watch the progress of the sketch, as I put down the triple boiler; each of the pans spreading from a common centre like a clover leaf. The first pan nearest the door receives the sugar direct from the tub at the press. It boils fiercely up, and is carefully skimmed from time to time by the jolly Herculean-looking fellow. When he is satisfied with this part of his work, he takes up a little of the sugar in the third or last pan upon his finger, much to our astonishment, as it is boiling, struggling, as it were, to get away from the fire below. One application is not enough; he watches

---

[1] In the account of Lord Macartney's embassy a sort of rum shrub is mentioned as being made from sugar.

intently the caking of the sugar, as he blows the end
of the finger on which it is ; and after two or three
attempts at this strange ordeal by touch, he seems to
think the boiling is complete. " You can't carry water
in a basket," we say in England ; but the Chinese not
only carry liquids, but will even carry oil in their well-
made baskets, and our sugar friend ladles out the hot
syrup with one, pouring it into a wooden shallow case,
about six feet by four, until he has nearly emptied the
pan.   Before all is out, however, he replenishes it from
pan No. 2, filling it from No. 1, so that the sugar juice
undergoes three successive boilings.

The syrup spread out on the shallow case is of a rich
dark brown, and is covered with a lot of small lumps
just now.   What are they ?   The little boys are intent
upon them.   We saw the man put a little lime into pan
No. 1, but that was to correct the acidity in the sugar ;
and he put some grease into No. 3, but it was to keep
the boiling down, perhaps to make it boil more strongly
below the grease ; and we did not notice him put in
any lumps of any kind, though we watched the process
intently.   The little urchins had been after something ;
they wanted their tit-bit, and took advantage of the
boiling syrup to cook something for themselves.   How
they rush at the lumps with their chop-sticks ; the
syrup is too hot for their unpractised fingers ; they must
be cautious even with the chop-sticks.   One fellow has
a small basin filled with the lumps ; they look like
beans ; but as he picks up one on his chop-sticks, and
crams it almost into my mouth before I can see what it
is, I notice that it is a large grub, just like a beetle with
its skin boiled off,—perhaps it is one.   How the rascals
enjoyed them !   They had brought them here to cook for
their evening meal.

Now comes the Herculean work of our strong friend. He seizes a spade-like implement, and bending over the hot mass of syrup, begins to spread it about and mix it in all directions. As it cools it thickens; his work gets harder and harder; over the side, up the middle and down again, backwards and forwards he works the stiffening sugar until it loses its liquid state. Then he takes up a short thick piece of wood with two upright handles; holding these, he commences to rub over the sugar hard, very hard. You see the labour by the working of his powerful muscles. Gradually the stuff assumes a sand-like appearance, its colour gets lighter and lighter; and within an hour from its being merely sap in the cane, the juice is expressed, boiled, cooled, and made into sugar,—real Muscovado. The sugar-boiler turns round his happy-looking face, streaming with perspiration, evidently proud of his work, and glad to see himself and apparatus all jotted down in the sketch-book. Everything is most primitive and simple: well need it be so. There is first the sugar to be planted, after the cane-ends have been soaked in water till they sprout. The Chinese give all their seeds this soaking before planting them, and it seems to answer well with rice, wheat, and cotton. I wonder it is not more frequently done at home. The ground has a week longer for its old crop, or to lie fallow, or can be worked up while the seeds sprout.

Well, there is the planting, cultivating, cutting, bringing to the mill, and all the above process to go through, and the sugar produced only brings about three-farthings the pound sold wholesale! so the worker of the sugar probably only gets about a half-penny the pound for it. The white kinds, which go through a sun-drying and a lot of other processes,

is worth about twice as much; but it is made from
better cane, and also loses a great deal of weight in
the drying.

I believe that the sugar-cane of the south of China is
different to the *Sorghum saccharatum*, which has lately
been grown with some success in different parts of
Europe for sugar, as well as for food for cattle. The
seeds are now procurable in England. Sugar-cane is
well adapted for giving as extra food to horses, to bring
their coats into fine condition, and to put flesh on the
bones.

Hard work is not all that the sugar-boiler in China has
to encounter. Why are these long spears at his door?
The place does not hold out strong inducements for any
one to attack it; everything is old, common, and rude;
and who would care to steal and carry off sugar that was
only worth about two dollars the hundredweight? But
there are the spears. Perhaps the sugar trade is a bad
one at these prices, and the strength of our friend is
sometimes applied to other purposes. The fact is that
this northern portion of the Kwang-Tung province is
occupied by hosts of rival clans; predatory expeditions
are made from one village to another; we meet men
returning from their work, one of the party generally
carrying a spear or long knife, perhaps both. Each man
holds his own by the strength of his arms. The male
population predominate; the women form a fruitful source
of plunder; and there is little doubt that to save trouble,
or perhaps to prevent misery, many female children
hereabouts meet an early death from the hands of their
natural protectors. But everything goes by contraries
in China. Strange as it may appear, this desperate state
of clannish anarchy has proved to be the sole safety of
this part of China from worse anarchy at the hands of

the rebels. The people were so given to quarrelling that they would not agree to fight. At one time the rebellion seemed ,likely to prosper here, if we may judge of the fact by the decay of the mandarin power. The people are a fine race ; splendid men, big burly fellows, especially the fishermen on the coast, and larger than any other men I have seen in the East. They would make capital grenadiers; but unfortunately, though very good fellows, they are sometimes wild and intractable. It is said when one city in this neighbourhood was taken by them, they killed twelve mandarins, boiled them, and ate them ! The mandarins seem to have no power. I met with a lazy jolly-looking fat one the other night (I am writing from Masoo) ; he puffed and blew, and looked quite complacently on the foreign devils that were about him. What did he care for save to make money while he had a chance. There is a big Malakoff-looking fort on the hill. He is supposed to be living there in command of 100 men ; but the barracks are roofless, the fort is breached in two places from sheer decay and neglect, and he lives snugly in a temple ; his body-guard consists of two very pretty Namoa girls, and perhaps he bought them with the money that should have paid for the 100 soldiers. He pays for his berth, and must make money out of it. His superior paid $7000 for the office he holds, though he knew he was only to have it for ten months ; but no doubt the fat centurion and his fellows aided in making up his pay. The other day we were at the town of Swatow, and got a glimpse of this superior. He had held a review ; for there are rumours of rebels and rebellion not far hence. But what a set the soldiers were ; what arms and what dresses ! One sailor-like fellow, with a turban on, could not be persuaded to take

it off, for the weather was bitterly cold ; so he popped
his soldier's cap on the top of the turban, and shivered
in chattering concert with his cold-looking comrades.
We marched right into the fort, not one of us armed,
among a set of rapscallion soldiers—the three mandarins
were standing waiting by their baggage ready for a
start—and, " shaking hands" *at* him, paid our respects
as if we had a right to be there.   In China, people don't
shake each other's hands, each man shakes his own ;
not a b'ad arrangement in a country where skin diseases
abound.

The mandarins in this part of the country are to be
pitied.   Their resources are drained at head-quarters,
and disturbances progress ; in fact, the people get independent before the mandarins can prevent them.   One
fellow, called Heng-Soon, an opium smuggler, was chief
of a clan at Go-swa (I give local names).   He had heard
of rebellion, and thought he would try it too ; so raised
his clan, and marched against the neighbouring places.
The other clans did not aid him, and he had to fortify
himself in Go-swa, a town about ten miles from Namoa.
The mandarins for some time could do nothing against
him.   They had no resources in themselves ; could get
no assistance by the coast, as it was in the hands of
rebels or pirates ;[1] and the mandarins inland had enough
to do to hold their own.   At last the Governor-General
was made aware of the necessity of doing something, lest
matters should get worse.   The people, too, in some of
the large cities aided, and eventually a British ship
brought up a lot of dollars, and a few men and some

---

[1] A paper on the Sinoan district was read before the Asiatic Society in
Hong-Kong : it stated that the mandarins there let out their "men-of-war"
to hire, and that not long ago one junk belonging to the Imperial navy
was actually taken as a pirate !   The pirates again are often bought over
into the Imperial service.

arms, for the mandarins at Foo-Seah, as the people here call the prefectural city of Chaou-Chaou. Then, the Government, having the sinews of war, made a demonstration, and collecting men, marched against Go-swa, but feared to go further than Masoo for some time, and ran out of provisions there ; but getting a supply through a foreign source, proceeded, and after letting the rebels escape, took the place. The chief and his brothers made their way through foreign interest to Hong-Kong ; his wife did not escape, and perceiving that she was likely to be taken, collected her children around her, and placing a barrel of gunpowder in the room, when the soldiers arrived at the door, blew herself and the whole family to atoms. The town was rased to the ground, and the people of Go-swa, numbering now only a few hundred families, live in mat huts near the sea. Those who were in arms have all dispersed, some in fleets which were classed as pirates, and killed in hundreds by British men-of-war. Such is the history of a small rebellion. It was begun by foreign connexion, quashed by foreign aid, the leaders rescued by foreign connivance, and the followers destroyed by foreign power. Who says we have no influence in China ? But does our influence predominate for good or evil ? Two years afterwards the foreigners at Masoo had to protect themselves from threatened attacks of the Go-swa people and their neighbours.

The Chinese are a curious puzzle, and it is difficult to solve the riddle of their character. There are, too, so many varieties in their manners and customs at different places. The people of the Chaou-Chaou district, though sometimes so troublesome among themselves, are very friendly to foreigners. This may arise from many of them having been abroad. It is this district, in con-

junction with Fokien, that supplies most of the Chinese
settlers in the Straits settlements. It is curious to be
addressed by a labourer in the fields in the Malay language. He sees a foreigner, and thinks he should know
that foreign dialect. Numbers of the people here speak
Malay. There was a grand *sing-song* or theatrical entertainment going on one day at Masoo. Crowds were
admiring the performance ; all civil and even polite to
us when among them. I was anxious to see behind the
scenes of a Chinese theatre, and scrambling up a ladder
in the dark, at the back of the pavilion that had been
erected for the performance, was at once face to face
with the actors in their green-room—a very dirty,
dingy place. We were received by a knowing-looking
fellow, with his face strangely painted all red, with a
blotch of white across the eyes ; he gave us a hearty
reception *in Malay*. My companion and kind host,
being well acquainted with that language, commenced a
conversation with him, and we were standing at ease on
the boards of a Chinese stage. The actors had seen me
sketching them when I was in front, and were anxious
to see the product of my pencil. It was long before I
could get my book back ; at last I discovered it in the
midst of " the band," the leaves being turned over by one
man, while the others examined the pictures as they
went on with the music.

True to their usual contrariety, the Chinese have
their orchestra at the back instead of the front of
the stage. Banging and clashing went the drums and
cymbals, making a terrible noise, especially when the
striking or fighting scenes were going on ; for, in
order to give force to the blow, whenever a man was
struck, bang went the drum, and another crash of music
was given as the victim fell on the ground. It was

curious to see the pompous mandarin, in all the glory of
satins, silks, and golden ornaments, strutting on the
stage, and then on his retiring come hastily over to see
what we were after. I got crushed up in a corner, and
had numerous applicants pushing their strangely-decked
heads forward to be sketched, all at the highest pitch of
good humour. Here are some of my theatrical friends,
and a sketch of their little theatre. It was a roughly

got-up affair, as the temple was not large enough for a
first-rate " sing-song." The actors were really very good
in their way, and doubtless had performed in many finer
places. The dresses were capital, and the wardrobe extensive. Three performances were given every day for
three days in succession, and were in honour of the
Mother of Heaven, the presiding saint over the welfare
of sailors,—the contributors of the entertainment being

three merchants, who had just received the returns of a
lucky venture. Most of the actors could speak the
mandarin dialect. Their heroines were, of course, men,
and made very fair specimens of Chinese beauty. One
in particular acted remarkably well ; and the studied
attitudes, even to the position of the fingers, were admirable when seen from the front, but from behind the
scenes, or rather, where the scenes should be (for there
are none in Chinese theatres), we were let into too
many secrets of dress, &c., to give full credit to all the
glitter and sentimentality. In one furious scene, where
the heroine had been going through a terrific piece of
fierce declamation, in a high falsetto, she threw herself
(or rather himself), in the height of injured innocence,
into a chair, and hiding her face from the spectators, as
if in the deepest grief, quietly expelled her quid, invisibly
to them, but bringing the sublime too near to the
ridiculous as seen from our side of the house.

Unfortunately some of the players, appearing next
day in the garden of the house at which I resided,
and being in *mufti*, were taken to be trespassers,
and were pelted out. This was a great pity, after their
civility. I had promised to colour the sketches I had
taken of them, and show them to the actors next evening, but was rather doubtful of my reception. However,
thinking it only right to try to explain, I resolved to
repeat my visit, at the risk of a disturbance. So I went
alone, putting full confidence in the fellows. It was
very dark, and I was not noticed till I was fairly among
them at the back of the stage. I was not disappointed.
They received me politely, but at once assailed me with
questions about the stone-throwing, and were satisfied
when told that being in plain dress they were not recognised, but that I was sure, had they appeared in their

" Ta-ming " hats, no one would have troubled them. The comic genius got so interested in his portrait, and a cigar, that he had to be called twice to take his place on the stage, the play hanging fire meanwhile. He soon set matters right, and gave me a knowing wink from the stage when he had appeased the audience. There is no use attempting to describe a Chinese play. Grand dresses, marches, processions, *kotowing*, fighting, and love-making are jumbled up in inexpressible confusion. The actors, in absence of play-bills, coolly walk forward and proclaim who they are ; sometimes even hold up a placard with their title on it ; make no difficulties about distance ; pretend to get on a horse, no horse being on the stage, and then say, I am now arrived at such a place. Most of the plays relate to old Chinese times, the costumes being almost invariably such as were used prior to the Tartar invasion. Their travelling apparatus is well arranged. The wardrobe and property are all packed in large gaudily painted boxes. The boxes form seats behind the stage, and one I noticed was fitted up for cooking; another as a dressing-stand for washing and painting the face. Some of their faces are most curiously painted to represent demons or some other terrible creatures.

This theatrical performance apparently made a great sensation. The position was beautifully chosen in front of a small temple, surrounded with magnificent banyans stretching widely around, covering a space that might encamp a regiment of cavalry ; the fine dark foliage of the trees being relieved by the long, graceful, slender stems of a grand clump of giant bamboos, rearing their tops far higher than the flagstaff that bore the yellow banners in front of the little joss-house—the yellow contrasting pleasingly with the trees around. Then there were the little mat sheds, put up as private boxes for the female portion of the spectators. But by far the best of the whole affair were the people and their varied costumes ; the men,—fine sturdy fellows most of them, in turbans of dark-blue nankeen ; and the women in most picturesque dresses, all of the gayest colours. The head-dresses are charming, especially those of the young girls—many very pretty—their hair plaited in a long tail, which is wound round and round the head, terminating in a tassel behind. A broad black silk or velvet band encircles the upper part of the forehead, and has generally a gaudy jewel in the front. A fine flower jauntily placed at one side of the head, completes one of the prettiest head-dresses imaginable. Others have the hair curiously worked up into shape. Handsome gold ornaments, and flowers tastefully placed about them, give the head of a pretty girl a fine appearance. Sketches give but a faint idea of the effect which I would wish to describe, but the accompanying may aid the description. The old women that have small feet have strange ways of dressing them. Some cover them with a sort of white flounce at the ankle ; others wrap the whole ankle and calf tightly with red bandages, making them walk as if they were going on razèed bedposts. But the variety of fashions would be tedious to enumerate. The dresses of the women and children show great ingenuity, and yield a whole budget of sketches. The ladies are rather bashful and difficult to be jotted down, but the children are delighted to have their pictures taken.

I paid a visit to a large town, Tai-hop-po, on the seacoast, between Breaker Point and a promontory which

Costumes Swatour.

Fr. Schenck, 50 Geo. St Edin^r

rejoices in the name of the Cape of Good Hope. We were invited into one of the best houses in the place. The owner had a large family of good-looking sons, all handsomely dressed. One was a remarkably sharp little fellow. Upon his being called down to see the barbarians, he marched up to us just like a grown-up man. He looked very precocious, and made the prettiest salutation or *kotow* that I ever saw. He was scarcely nine years old, but came in with the air of a perfectly polished gentleman. His father was evidently greatly pleased at his manner; I begged to be allowed to put the little fellow down upon paper, and did so. Of his brother, a delicate child with beautiful soft eyes, I also took a good likeness, and coloured it on the spot, much to their amusement. They were all kind ; and so pleased with the little pictures, that I could not help leaving the sketches with them. A large crowd had collected at the door as we went out ; but though we walked more than a mile through the town (a poor, miserable sort of place, with a riff-raff sort of populace), not the slightest insult was offered. Fish, rice, and cotton shops denoted the chief trade of the place.

On our way to the town we passed a small village, where a worthy Catholic missionary resided. He had about 200 converts. His house was just like the other cottages in the village,—all the villagers being of a poor class. Chinese Catholic calendars decked the walls, and a small altar-piece (apparently) was hid in a niche in the wall. Poor man ! he had just got out of prison, yet had returned to his flock. He seemed to be much respected, but was too delicate-looking for his task. He was about to proceed some thirty miles off to visit a sick man. His intelligence had at once given him an ascendency among the poor ignorant villagers ; and he seemed bent on doing good. It is a pity that all missionaries are not equally self-sacrificing ; but it is hard to call upon intelligent men to tear themselves from civilized European habits, to plunge into poverty and obscurity in a Chinese village.

CHAPTER VII.

NORTH-EAST PART OF KWANG-TUNG.

North-east part of Kwang-Tung—Chaou-Chaou-Foo, a Quixotic expedition
—Stuck fast in mud—Mocking Birds—Eel-fishers—Sledge-racing over
mud—Launched again—Disturbed appearance of the country—Fighting preparations—Hoong-lo-Chee—Poultice *versus* Precipitate—Young
Braves and ladies—Opium-smoking—Civility of the people—Their surprise at first seeing foreigners—Predominance of males—A beauty—Uses
of a sketch-book—Mountain view—Opium-dealers.

I WAS disappointed with the general appearance of
the country near Chaou-Chaou-Foo, and had been greatly
misled as to its importance as one of the rich districts of
China. In the far distance we saw from Swatow a
high range of blue-looking hills; the prefectural city
was at their foot, and a long day's journey, with a fair
wind, would bring us nearly to it.

The question was, how far was such a visit practicable ? The country was by no means quiet, the people
always at war with each other, and noted as the greatest
rascals in China. As for the government, it had no
power, no control over them. For this latter reason I
thought it would be safe to go as far into the interior as
possible, until, in fact, we got to where the government
had real power.

We were told that the river at Swatow was navigable
nearly to the Tung-Kiang, which leads into the Canton
river below Whampoa; that it had many fine cities upon

it, among others, the prefectural city Chaou-Chaou-Foo ; the boats that now and then arrived at Masoo brought people from that place.   So we were determined to go there, or, at any rate, as far as we could.

A boat was put at my disposal, with a dozen men for a crew, and well armed with small swivels.   I had the good fortune to get two gentlemen to accompany me, both of whom knew something of the local dialect, one speaking it well.   Our cabin was about seven feet square and four feet high, barely room enough for us to lie down in ; however, we made up our minds to rough it, and off we started, after having first made the attempt in two pleasure boats, a Quixotic expedition which nearly ended in the wreck of both vessels in a severe gale.   How it blew ! We beat up under close-reefed mainsail and jib, until the water made clean sweeps over us, and it was with no small danger we got the boat round and back as far as Swatow, where we got good quarters in a Chinaman's house for the night.

The native boats are far the best to travel in, especially in rivers, they draw so little water.   The Han is deep, and is a broad fine river, excepting about six miles from its mouth, where it widens into a large lake, with several outlets to the sea.   This lake is about thirty miles in circumference, and is shallow, except in one channel. This we missed in the night, and after we saw the crew prepare the guns, each man hang his powder-horn round his neck, matches lighted, and all ready to meet pirates at a noted place for them, we had the satisfaction to find that we were hardly moving, and shortly after midnight we stuck hard and fast.   The cabin was so wretchedly small that I got quarters in the hold among the crew, but one of them snored so loudly there was no rest to be had.   It appeared as if daylight would never come ; at

last, slowly and sadly, we arrived by the growing light
at the melancholy certainty that we were *somewhere,* but
where, we could not tell. There was no water in sight!
mud, mud, nothing but mud for miles. By our minutest
calculation we had gone aground on the great mud flat
at the very top of high water. The wild geese, curlew,
teal, and long-necked cranes were in flocks, just *out*
of gunshot, and when a bird flew past within shot, it
was sure to be only a gull. I could have sworn the birds
chuckled at our position as they hooted apparently at us.

We turned all our crew overboard to find the nearest line to the deep channel; and as the sun rose, we
could make out we were about a mile from it, and likely
to lose the day before we had a chance of getting off. In
desperation I double-charged my gun for a long shot at
the geese, but even that did no good. Soon, however,
our attention was attracted by specks in the distance,
coming quickly to us. These proved to be men; eel-
fishers, a queer race; they flew along the mud, though
it was so soft that a man sank above his knees. Each
of these eel-hunters had a sort of sledge, the size and
shape of the stave of a large cask; in the middle of this
was a small railing, about eighteen inches high; he had
a small basket for his fish, and an adze-shaped spade
with a handle about two feet long. With one foot, or
sometimes kneeling with one knee upon the sledge, and
holding on by the rail, with the hands well down,
"jockey fashion," the man propelled the sledge forward
with the other foot. On the fellows came at racing-pace.
It was quite wonderful to see the speed at which they
progressed. The mud is so soft, that when the men
kneel with one knee on the sledge, their toes hang over
the stave, dragging in the mud. It is as soft as hasty-
pudding, and twice as slippery. To catch the eels or

E

other fish that are in the mud, the men appear to watch
for air-bubbles, and then dig about them. They are very
quick at their work, and it employs a large number.
We shouted until about a couple of dozen came to the
boat, and after a great deal of bargaining we arranged
that they should make a sledge of our boat, and push it
until they got into the river. The men were evidently
accustomed to find people in a similar fix ; for no sooner
was the bargain settled, than they surrounded us, and
after a good shout, walked away, slipping the boat along
the mud quite easily ; we might have been sailing.
They stopped once or twice to try extortion, but that
would not do ; and eventually launched us into the river
just as a shoal of large white porpoises rolled past.

The channel was wide and deep, passing at one side
of the extensive flat, a great part of which had apparently
been reclaimed. The river then divides two small
ranges of hills, guarded by forts on each side. No guns
were visible, and the forts were falling rapidly into decay.
Within twenty miles we counted eight forts. The posi-
tions chosen in most cases were very favourable for defence against an enemy on the river ; but on land the rear
could be easily battered. This, however, would not be a
correct way to fight, according to Chinese notions : the
British did not fight fairly, they say, when they got into
the forts at the Bogue by the back. There seemed to
be very little for the fortresses to guard ; we saw no
trading boats on the fine river, except at one town where
a few were at anchor. Dyeing was the chief trade of the
place ; but very little trade could be comfortably carried
on. All the neighbouring country was in a state of
chronic anarchy ; the villages, towns, and hamlets were
all walled, and each seemed prepared to fight with its
neighbour. There were villages, certainly not a quarter

of a mile distant from each other, both surrounded
with distinct walls about sixteen to twenty feet high,—
the house-tops inside were just visible ; the walls generally formed a square ; there were no butresses or places
from which a flanking fire could be directed along the
walls, nothing but architectural fortification in its most
primitive form.

After proceeding about forty miles up the river,
the scenery in some places being pretty but not grand,
we discovered that there appeared to be good cause
for the means of defence each place had provided itself
with ; for, on branching off into the stream which led
towards Chaou-Chaou-Foo, we found the people rushing about with guns, spears, and flags in great excitement, evidently making ready for a fight. Some shots
were fired, and at one time we thought the intention
was to stop us. We waited patiently to be fired at,
being quite prepared to return the compliment if need
be ; but they were so intent on their own squabble that
we moved past almost unheeded, and shortly afterwards
stopped at a village where the stream again divided.
The people were quite civil, and invited us to land.
We now began to skirt some small hills, which lay like
islands in the midst of the flat lowland that stretched
around them in all directions. Some of the villages
were beautifully situated in bamboo groves at the side
of the hills ; but they all bore a poverty-stricken, deserted look, an appearance rather increased by the melancholy droop of the bamboos over the rugged walls.

It was a fine warm day in spring ; the land on the plain
was bleak and fallow, waiting for the rice to be planted ;
now and then there was a gloriously bright green patch
where the grain was thickly sown with a view to trans-
planting ; but these bright spots only made the rest look

more sad and gloomy. The dark-looking walls of the
numerous villages had a forbidding appearance, especially
those that were at some distance from the river; for
the heat rising from the ground created a mirage which
hung over the land just about the height of the walls,
and while it made them look dim and darker, seemed
to drag them out in line till one village joined another,
and a long hazy-looking wall apparently surrounded the
foot of the hills, marking as it were the boundary of our
journey. It would have taken something having greater
powers of resistance, however, to keep us back, and on
we went until we arrived near a place called Hoong-lo-
Chee. The chief man there had been doctored by my
companions, and fortunately had recovered, more by good
luck than good guidance. One pinned his faith upon
poultices for sores; the other swore by red precipitate.
Fortunately, when this worthy chief was at Masoo, he
got into the hands of the red precipitate doctor first, so
that the poultice came in afterwards to cure; but there
would perhaps have been a different story if the red
precipitate had followed the poultice. The Chinese
have great faith in Europeans for any surgical operation
or for sores: the man above alluded to had gone to
Masoo to try if he could get his foot cured. Ship captains are generally doctors, and they and their officers
have good practice, often very successful, among the
Chinese. We found out the patient by sending in my
card with a flag painted upon it, the well-known St.
Andrew's cross, and at once were hailed as friends.

He took us through several villages, where we were
fêted in the chief houses, got some excellent tea, and
were squeezed almost flat in the crush of natives who
flocked to see us. The kindness was too pressing.

One part of the chief village was a good deal damaged

by shot. We asked the head man how that happened, and he coolly pointed to the next village, saying in Chinese, "These fellows did it." He could command 15,000 men, and from what we saw of them they would make a formidable force at guerilla warfare. There was not a man that had not the matchlock mark on the cheek, caused by firing with the butt against the cheekbone. In some cases the mark was fresh and bleeding, for these fellows appear always to be firing. In every village there were targets marked off against walls and joss-houses. The *hits* were not generally what would be called good shots, and the distance fired from was short. The young "braves" had a dashing hap-hazard style about them; and their hair, being plaited with a third of scarlet silk or thread, mixed with the hair, and hanging in a large tassel at the side of the head, added to the jauntiness of their appearance. The men all remarked upon the gun my Scotch friend carried, and the women seemed to be chiefly attracted by our mode of dress. Their own attire came in for a good deal of my attention, and I noted their costume in my sketch-book whenever there was an opportunity.

The chief peculiarity in this district was a sort of leathern shoe worn on the head, to protect the hair probably, but perhaps to save the trouble of making it up every day into the fantastical shapes that are in vogue in China. The people were poor-looking, and on the verge of squalidity; the houses had few comforts in them, except the opium-pipe and a bed in the best of them. This drug was openly smoked among the surrounding crowd in nearly every village we visited, and was offered to us as the chief act of politeness. In the three days we were in this part of the country we must have passed through thirty villages; some were equal to

large market-towns. We stopped at shops, went into
temples, stood in the crowd at theatres, and never met
with a single term of abuse. When we went from one
place to another where the people were not on good
terms, we were passed on by a neutral party ; and at one
place, where we were advised not to enter, and even to
have our arms prepared in passing, the people came out
and asked us to go in. Entering these walled places is
rather like going into a trap ; however, though the guide
we had that morning told us not to go, I thought it was
better to show the people that we trusted them. The
women were at their doors, which was a sure sign that
no mischief was intended ; so in we marched and passed
through, with thanks from the people. No foreigner
had at that time ever been in this part of China, so that
we were quite a show ; in fact, we drew away most of
the people from a theatre in one place, and when M—,
who was a capital shot, brought down a swallow on the
wing, we evidently rose greatly in the estimation of the
young village "braves," and they came with us further
than usual towards the next village. It was rare that
people from one place followed us to the next. The
clans keep themselves very distinct, and their chief
battles arise from kidnapping women and children.
The proportion of males over females was quite remarkable. We had good opportunities of judging; and it
was the more extraordinary, as this district supplies a
great many soldiers, a great number of emigrants to the
Straits, &c., nearly all males, and the women do not get
such hard labour as in other parts of China.

As this poor district is essentially a fighting country,
male children must necessarily be looked upon as the
greatest gift, and I have no doubt female infanticide
is carried on to a large extent. This is a point that

is not readily ascertained ; and although in a book of Chinese dialogues, for the use of Englishmen who study Chinese, there is the question, " Do the people of this place kill their female children or not ?" I did not consider that my curiosity should master politeness by asking the question in a place where I had been so civilly treated. So far as we could judge by appearances, the *pretty* girls must all have been made away with while infants. I only saw one that was really good-looking ; she was certainly very handsome, quite a child, and, for a wonder there, had large feet,—I mean they were not bandaged into deformity. We got her imprisoned in a crowd of little boys at a temple, and succeeded in running off a sketch of her as she nestled up in a pretty group of flowers with which the old joss-house was ornamented.

A sketch-book is the best weapon to travel with in China. In the first place, it at once gives the people your motive for wandering about ; and as it keeps them in good humour, there is nothing to fear. It is advisable to use a bound book for drawing in ; the sketching-blocks are ill adapted for the purpose, because the loose sheets are asked for, and the drawings have often to be handed about among a crowd of people, whose cleanliness is near akin to their godliness. It is difficult to refuse giving a man his own portrait after he has patiently sat for it ; so that, without the excuse of the leaves being bound up in a book, many sketches are apt to be lost. There is a degree of harmlessness associated by the Chinese with an artist's handicraft, and I often found that women and children would come up to me when sketching, who would certainly have run away had I been otherwise employed.

When we reached the end of the navigation of the

stream that led towards the prefectural city, we left our
boat, and were kindly provided by a fine old fellow, the
elder of the township, with a shallop to proceed farther.
We eventually reached the foot of the mountains, which
were to be the limit of our journey, and being joined by
a few men from a village near which we landed, made
for the highest peak. The mountain was bleak, bare,
and uninteresting—no easy one to ascend ; however, in
course of time we got to the top; it might be about 2000
feet high. All the difficulties of the ascent were amply
repaid by the view. In the far distance to the east we
could just distinguish the high peak of Namoa towering
out of the sea ; to the south and north were wild ranges
of fine hills ; and towards the west, the chain of mountains, at the end of which we were, piled themselves up
peak upon peak in rugged grandeur to the far distant
clouds. We were upon the Ow-Ling range, or the eastern
part of the Meiling mountains : I had never seen such
desolate-looking hills. There was not even a bird in
view,—not a bush, not a tree, only a burnt-up, coarse
sort of grass ; even wild-flowers seemed to shun the
place, and the scanty stream which oozed out of the
hill-side exposed not even a pebble to reward our search.
We could not expect much *on* the mountain, when it
granted such a glorious view *from* it ; but its barrenness
was so striking, that I should not wonder if some hidden
mine of coal or gold were some day brought to light from
beneath its bleak exterior. We counted five pagodas in
sight from the summit; one at Chaou-Chaou-Foo, at Kip-
chooey, at Umpo, at Keih-Ying, and at Ta-Chea. The
plain below was abundantly watered by the numerous
branches of the Han, some of which appeared to join
with the river which passes by Chaou-Chaou, and forms
swampy ground between the sea and that city. The

Chaou-Chaou river is a large and important stream, and if it is navigable must form one of the best routes by which to reach the province of Kiangsi.

Opium is conveyed from the above city into that province. We saw it being unpacked, and put into pillow boxes, rice-baskets, &c., quite openly, ready to be carried into the city. We were asked to go in by the opium-dealers, but did not relish making our entry in such doubtful society. They appeared jolly, respectable sort of men, and were very civil.

After our pleasant trip we returned to Swatow in safety. The Rev. Mr. Burns, who visited Chaou-Chaou-Foo the following year, was taken prisoner by the mandarins and sent to Canton. Mr. Burns has since returned to Swatow, where his philanthropic exertions have been of service in mitigating some of the evils of the coolie emigration trade.

CHAPTER VIII.

RELIGION IN CHINA.

Religion in China—Statements of Huc and Meadows—Enlightened Chinese not idolaters—Taouist traditions regarding the Messiah—Rise of Buddhism—Belief in Supreme Being—Religion founded in fear—Injudicious proceedings of missionaries—Buddhist priests—Three classes of Buddhists—Idols—No State religion under existing dynasty—Supremacy of the Emperor—Taouist priests—Pretty temple—Religious offering—An emperor's definition of worship.

" FROM all that we have said concerning the present condition of the various modes of worship recognised in China, and the position of their ministers, it is allowable to conclude, that the Chinese are living absolutely without religion. There remain among them a few superstitious practices, to which they yield, rather from habit than conviction, and from which they are very easily detached. No account whatever is taken of religious belief by the legislature ; and the magistrates only speak of it to turn it into ridicule."[1]

" M. Huc asserts that the Chinese are destitute of religious feelings. If by this he means nothing more than that the Chinese show no ready aptitude to embrace his form of Christianity—no alacrity to desert the Confucian tablet or the Buddhist idol for the images of the saints and the Virgin, I fully and thoroughly agree with him. And if Protestant writers mean, when they 'endorse'

[1] *The Chinese Empire* (Huc), vol. ii. p. 210.

such opinions, that the Chinese display little intellectual or moral promptitude to adopt their several creeds, which less enforce the great truths of Christianity, as ' Peace on earth, and good-will towards men,' than they plant repulsively before the unprepared mind of the heathen the bare results of some centuries of doctrinal disputes and sectarian bickerings,—then with them likewise I am fully agreed. . . . But if by 'want of religious feelings' they mean to assert that the Chinese have no longing for immortality,—no cordial admiration of what is good and great,—no unswerving and unshrinking devotion to those who have been good and great,—no craving or yearning of the soul to reverence something high and holy ; then I differ from them entirely, and emphatically contradict their assertion."[1]

I have headed this chapter with two extracts from the works of Huc and Meadows. The opinions of both are in some respects correct, though differing from each other in material points. I shall endeavour to show that enlightened men amongst the Chinese are something better than mere idolaters.

The Taouists, it is said, heard of the birth of the Messiah, and sent some of their " wise men of the east " to learn something of the new religion. Their emissaries, it is supposed, never reached Jerusalem, but on their way picked up the principles of the Buddhist doctrine, and returned with them to China. These new principles, Frankenstein-like, grew; they usurped the Taouist doctrines of their introducers almost entirely. The Buddhists have now commenced their decline. The number of their demigods crowd upon the principal deity, crushing it from the influence it originally had. Shall

[1] *The Chinese and their Rebellions* (Meadows), p. 66.

we see the same revolution continue, and pure Christianity triumph over the tottering dogmas of existing religions, by the pureness of its simplicity, or by the avenging hand of a jealous God ? Shall we see the Chinese as a nation discard their auxiliary deities which they scarcely worship even in form, and earnestly turn to the Supreme God, whom they already acknowledge in spirit ?

In asserting that those Chinese who think at all about religion are not idolaters, in the real sense of the word, it may be right to state the reasons from which the assertion is drawn.

There is no doubt that the majority of the Chinese of any intelligence believe in a Supreme Being. Some may have a lingering superstition of the power of idols, but it is only as auxiliaries to a higher worship, when they worship at all. Their religion is not one of *love*, but solely of *fear*. Believing that sin draws down misfortunes, they are kept under moral obligations, without which society would be intolerable. In fact, such a belief is necessary to the wellbeing of a people. It has been said by Chinese scholars, that the misfortunes which befall them are attributable to accidental sin, and not to any wilful act. But do not multitudes of proclamations, in which the wrath of heaven is invoked to punish the disturbers of public tranquillity, prove the contrary ? What old resident in China could not point out hosts of instances where the Chinese profess to be deterred from bad actions by the fear of heaven, or where they reason on man's misfortunes being sent by heaven deservedly for his sins ?

A vast proportion of the Chinese do not worship images at all, and are perfectly open to the belief that their Supreme Being is the same as ours ; but while we try to persuade them against their theology, and endeavour to debase it in their eyes, and substitute what we call a new doctrine, or perhaps, like one distinguished missionary, think we do good by physically overturning the images, we can expect to see little good arise from the labours of foreigners. The whole number of Protestant missionaries in China probably exceeds the number of converts who are not actually in their pay. This I think is traceable to their way of introducing religion.

The Buddhist religion, as it is understood in China, is a mere blank in the present day; most of the priests are ignorant of the mummeries they go through in a language foreign to their own. We rarely see the people congregated together in the temples for any other purpose than to see a theatrical representation, excepting on a few days in the year, when the priests lay out the sacrifices. We never see a priest exhorting the people to any other good deed than to give contributions. A worthy missionary at Shanghai tells us, in a small work printed at the mission-press there, that " the chief priest at the monastery of Tsing-leang-sze, was found to be a very intelligent and agreeable old gentleman. He readily understood our object, conversed with us freely on the subject of religion, and entered into a discussion on the differences which existed between us, without the least loss of temper. He maintained that Buddha was before all things, and superior to Heaven, while his appearance in our world was merely his taking upon himself a body, for the purpose of enlightening and saving the host of human beings. His statements were, however, not based on evidence, and had to be received by those who believed them on his assertion only. It seemed to be a pure matter of faith. . . . We asked him about image-worship; whether the prayers he offered were to Buddha or the image? He said, 'To Buddha.' 'Why, then, was the attention directed to the image?' 'Only to fix the mind; as soon as the thought was once fixed, the image was no longer of use.' 'All,' he said, 'rested with the heart; if that was right, all was well.'" At another Buddhist monastery, when the conversation turned upon the real object of worship amongst the Buddhists, whether it was Buddha himself, or the image that represented him,—the priests asserted that Buddhists were divided into three classes. The superior class worshipped Buddha without the intervention of any image; the middling class worshipped through the medium of images; and the inferior class never worshipped at all. "For themselves," they said, "they could worship without any image, and they thought it best to do so. We asked them what was the need of images?" They said, "For the vulgar who could not be induced to attend to religion without such aids." [1]

It has been said that Buddha rather represents the Saviour than the Almighty. Sometimes he is figured with numbers of arms, all ready to stretch forth to save

[1] The Rev. Joseph Edkins, in his interesting little work, *The Religious Condition of the Chinese*, published since the above was written, states, "They have not been led to look at religious truths and duties as communicated and enjoined directly from God. This renders it hard to persuade them that idolatry is a sin, as forbidden by Divine authority. They consider idols to be symbols, and nothing more."—Page 115, chap. vii., on "Confucian and Buddhist notions of God."

"We have seen Buddhism attempting to subvert the faith of mankind in God, placing as a substitute on His throne a self-elevated, self-purified sage called Buddha; and yet it could not prevent this personage from becoming dehumanized, clothed with Divine attributes, and so coming to be worshipped as God by the multitude in all Buddhist countries. So far is this the case in Mongolia, that in the Protestant translation of the Bible into the language of that country, Buddha, or, as it is called, Borhau, is used for God."—Rev. J. Edkins' *Religious Condition of the Chinese*, page 168.

his followers. By a gradually increasing complication of the Buddhist heavens and Buddhist deities, the religion has become so confused it is scarcely understood at all even by many of the priests. But take some of their idols as they are understood. Kwan-Yin represents *Mercy;* Wen-Chu, *Wisdom;* and Pu-Hien, *Happiness.* These three gods are frequently in the chief position in the temples, and each is prayed to as representative of the separate attribute of the high power believed in by the devotee. In the same way there are pet deities for different diseases, and even for certain trades and occupations. The sailors are very particular on this point; their protectress is the " Mother of Heaven." There is " Wy-do," who represents the protector of the temples : this is artistically the handsomest of all the images. No one who has entered a Chinese Buddhist temple when " service" was being performed will forget the continued muttering of the priests, and the constant recurrence of " O-me-to-foh, O-me-to-foh !" this is the name of the image which represents one of the highest divinities, the one who has charge of departed souls in their future paradise. At Pootoo, I saw engraved on a stone some writing which I believed to be Sanscrit, with a sentence in Chinese characters meaning, " Disquiet me not, Amida Buddha :" a sort of Chinese " *requiescat in pace.*"

Under the existing dynasty there is no settled religion of the State ;[1] the people are enjoined to keep the laws

---

[1] The Chinese State doctrine is this :—" The Emperor is the Son of Heaven, nobles and statesmen are the sovereign's children, and the people are the children of nobles and statesmen. The sovereign should serve heaven as a father, never forgetting to cherish reverential thoughts, but exerting himself to illustrate his virtue, and devoutly receiving from heaven the vast patrimony which it confers ; thus the emperor will daily increase in felicity and glory. Nobles and ministers of state should serve their

of the empire, and to cherish reverential thoughts towards the *nobles* and *ministers of state*. It is only the emperor who is considered exalted enough to serve heaven directly ; but this rule is merely a political one to raise the emperor in the eyes of his people. Just in the same way, and for the same purpose, Tai-ping-wang, of whom we shall speak more hereafter, assumes a direct relationship with the heavenly Father ; but the usurper declares a religion of the State, and calls upon all people not to worship any other than God Almighty.

It may not be a difficult thing to introduce a State religion when its place is not pre-occupied. The Tartars, it is true, have the Grand Lama as the chief of their religion, but this is not prominently brought forward in China. The Emperor goes first to one temple and then to another, not to worship certain deities, but to pray to High Heaven. He is even superior to the images in the temple, and has recently conferred higher titles upon some of those who are supposed to have aided the Imperial cause. We cannot, therefore, look upon these deputy-spirits, who are represented by images, as anything more than auxiliary saints or representative demons.

In Shanghai, besides a large number of Roman Catholics, there are many missionaries of other denominations—Protestants, Lutherans, Calvinists, or Calvinistical Seceders, Baptists, Sabbatarians, &c. It may be doubted whether they could be brought to adopt

sovereign as a father, never forgetting to cherish reverential thoughts, not harbouring covetous and sordid desires, not engaging in wicked and clandestine plots, but faithfully and justly exerting themselves ; thus their noble rank will ever be preserved. The people should never forget to cherish reverential thoughts towards the nobles and ministers of state, should obey and keep the laws, should not excite secret or open sedition, nor engage in insurrection or rebellion ; then no great calamity will befall their persons."

the opinion of an old Buddhist priest in the monastery at the top of the Hwa-ting hill, who laid it down that " the differences between religions he considered to be a species of denominational diversity, something like that which he had observed between the Romanists and Protestants at Ning-po!"

Some of the best parts of Chinese morality may be traced to Confucius; no wonder he has had so many followers, and been almost deified by them.

The Taouists have but little power, though they profess that their doctrines are founded on *reason*. The Taou-sze (Taouist priests) are generally a dirty-looking set; they seem to be absolved from shaving the head, or wearing the hair after the manner of the Tartars; they have it drawn up to a knot on the crown, not unlike the ancient style of Chinese head-dress, or the one which the Loo-Chooans adopt. There is a very pretty Taouist temple between Canton and Whampoa, on the south side of the river. The situation is charmingly chosen; the temple and an observatory are perched on the top of a small rocky hill, commanding a beautiful view across the valley of the Pearl River. The place is neatly decked with shrubs, and some fine specimens of the dwarf bamboo, and is almost entirely shut in by a large plantation of high trees which surround it; the tops of the trees reaching just to the roof of the temple, so that the view from the entrance is through the wide-spreading branches—a lovely and appropriate situation for religious retirement.

It is difficult to define the religion of the Taouists; it is largely connected with astronomy.

One of their chief divinities is Yuh-Hwang Shang-te, the God of Heaven. During a very severe flood at Shanghai, when the waters were at their height, a Taou-sze came down to the banks of the river close to our house; he made a small offering, then knelt down, prayed most earnestly, and, with his face turned to the rushing waters, bowed to the ground in the most abject supplication. The tide never passed the ashes of his offering, and, doubtless, he thought that his prayers for the stay of a public calamity had been kindly answered.

This was the only act of apparently real religion that I ever saw performed by an unconverted Chinese. The purest act of unmitigated idolatry that ever came under my notice was at a short distance from Canton. An old woman knelt on the ground half wailing, half praying, before a paltry paper figure not eighteen inches high. This figure she had placed at the side of the path, at some distance from any house; in front of it burned three wretched little candles, the position of which she changed from time to time—for luck: not content with this, however, she left the extraordinary shrine at which she had been worshipping, and tried her fortune by tossing up some copper coins, watching the manner in which they fell upon the ground, and again reverted to her genuflexions before her paper god.

We should be more correct, perhaps, in believing that the Chinese have no real religion they care for, than in giving them credit for caring for any at all. Huc[1] tells us of the funeral of a mandarin where Buddhist, Taouist, and Lama priests were invited to officiate. Yet a supreme being is not only acknowledged but worshipped. The emperor, Kang-hi, who was the most tolerant of all the rulers of China, and paid some attention to the different systems of religion, told the Roman Catholic priests that the sacrifices he offered were to the creator of the universe, and not to the visible and material heaven.[2]

[1] *Chinese Empire*, vol. ii. p. 220.   [2] *The Chinese* (Davis), vol. ii.

A really intelligent Chinaman is as rational a being as any other man, quick to observe, clever in reasoning; he is not to be imposed upon by gods that he can see manufactured. Even the pet point of many Chinese, the worship of ancestors, which would not be unnatural among a people whose rule of life and government is founded upon filial piety, is accounted by many missionaries, perhaps sometimes correctly, as one of the most conclusive evidences of their idolatry. We are indebted to M. Huc for information on this point; information which can be verified by any one in China:—" One day we asked a mandarin, a friend of ours, who had just offered a sumptuous repast at the tomb of a deceased colleague, whether, in his opinion, the dead stood in need of food ?"

"How could you possibly suppose I had such an idea ?" he replied, with the utmost astonishment. " Could you really suppose me so stupid as that ?"

" But what then is the purpose of these mortuary repasts ?"

" We intend to do honour to the memory of our relations and friends; to show that they still live in our remembrance, and that we like to serve them as if they were yet with us. Who could be absurd enough to believe that the dead need to eat ? Amongst the lower classes, indeed, many fables are current, but who does not know that rude, ignorant people are always credulous ?"

" We are inclined to think," says the experienced missionary, " that all tolerably well-informed Chinese, a little accustomed to reflection, would be of the same opinion as this mandarin, with respect to the practices to which the multitude attach superstitious ideas."[1]

[1] *The Chinese Empire,* vol. ii. p. 220.

Armed with the instances herein given of some of the
ideas of Chinese regarding religion, and without compli-
cating matters by entering into the details or forms
taught by any particular sect, I hold to the assertions
I have made, that the Chinese are not such determined
pagans as they are generally imagined to be. Consequently, there may be less difficulty in making them
Christians, by whatever means so happy a consummation
shall be brought about. The more we try to make them
believe themselves to be pagans, the less likely are they
to become Christians.

We have purposely abstained from including the
worship of Kwang-te, the god of war ; the sacrifices
made by the mandarins to propitiate this canonized
general are merely political, and may be considered in
the same relation to the empire of the Mantchoos, as the
annual sacrifices offered by the local officials of each city,
are to the tutelary spirit which is supposed to preside
over it. The Greek and Roman Christian churches have
saints which may be classed in a similar category.

The Chinese are as little likely to imagine that their
graven images *require of necessity* the sacrifices offered
to them, as they are likely to believe that the mortuary
feasts set before the tombs of their ancestors will be
partaken of by the mouldering remains.

The *mock* silver and gold which is so lavishly scattered
by the Chinese to propitiate good or evil spirits, is so
palpably unreal, that the requirements or discernment of
the spirits addressed, must be held in very light estimation by the distributors.

The only religion inculcated by the State, is obedience
to the Emperor and his officers.[1] The emperor is the
great high-priest who supplicates heaven. His officers

[1] See Note, p. 79.

publicly sacrifice only to the lesser divinities or saints; the Supreme Being governs all, but is thought too high to be publicly worshipped by the people ; and special edicts have been issued against the Chinese indulging in any other religion than the one above stated.

The commentary to the Shing-Fu, sacred edict, says, " All these absurd tales about keeping fasts, collecting assemblies, building temples, and fashioning images are feigned by those sauntering priests of Buddha and Taou, to deceive you; still you believe them, and not only go yourselves to worship, but also suffer your wives and daughters to go. . . . I see not where the good they talk of doing is : on the contrary, they do many shameful things that create vexation, and give people occasion for laughter and ridicule."[1] But these edicts neither keep the people from attending the temples, nor prevent them from thinking that their actions are under the supervision of the most high Power. The ignorant are doubtless imposed upon by the priests, but when we look into the position of a people, and their standing among mankind, we must not judge of their enlightenment by taking the lower classes for our standard.

It would be of very little interest to an English reader, were I to give the Chinese names of all the different festivals set apart for propitiating the various good and evil spirits on their respective birthdays : such as " Fuh-hoo Heuen-tau," the tiger-quieting spirit; the " Too-shin," gods of the ground ; half a dozen spirits that are supposed to have influence with thunder ; there is, in fact, scarcely a day that cannot boast of its being the birthday of some canonized personage, the seasons being cleverly fixed upon, so as to happen at appropriate times. Hwa-Kwang-ta-te, the genie of fire, has his day

[1] *Chinese Repository*, vol. i. p. 307.

in November, just when the Chinese begin to dread the fearful fires that ravage their slenderly-built dwellings. Tsew-seen, the spirit that presides over wine, has his festival in the autumn. Shang-te, is, of all their deities, so far as I can learn, the only one that is honoured (and it is an honour in China) by having devotions paid to his supposed progenitors ; for the Chinese must have a reason for everything, and they seem to think that even this supreme being must have had a father and mother ; festival days are granted to them a few days previous to the grand one given to Shang-te, but none of the three, father, mother, or the high ruler, are *represented by any image*, but deified in spirit only. The term *Teen* (Heaven), perhaps has even a higher signification than *Shang-te*. When the Jesuits first came to China, they used both these terms, but eventually quarrelled with other Roman Catholic missionaries about the correct one. Affairs became so troublesome, that the Emperor Kang-hi wrote to John v. King of Portugal, to get the Pope to interfere, and the Roman primate settled the point, by ordering the priests to use the term *Teen-choo*, or Lord of Heaven.

Before concluding this subject (which I have entered upon with much diffidence, and which would have been better conducted by a clerical man), and having unintentionally been drawn so far into it, I offer some of the quotations given by Morrison from the Chinese classics, as having been used when the Roman Catholic controversy was at its height, to prove why *Teen* and *Shang-te* were proper words to be used for the Deity. "When Heaven (Teen) created mankind, it made them princes and teachers, and said to them, Assist the Most High Ruler (Shang-te) in showing loving-kindness to every region." "Heaven (Teen) produced all things to nourish

man." " If Heaven (Teen) calls me to live, man cannot
hurt me.   If Heaven calls me to die, man cannot save
me." " A good man Heaven will no doubt reward. A bad
man Heaven will no doubt punish."   " Whether man's
heart be good or not, man does not know ; but no doubt
the Lord of Heaven knows."

For God the supreme and sole Ruler, both *Shang-te*
and *Shin* are used, Shin apparently meaning the Great
Spirit *par excellence*.   When the terms for gods are
used, neither *shang-te* nor *teen* are made use of, but genii
have the expression *shin* attached to them ; for instance,
the gods of the hills are called *shan-shin*.   The Buddhists have the term *poo-sa* for their divinities ; and the
common classes in some districts employ this, even giving
it the sound boo-sah, which may be derived from Buddha.   The country people call many things by this term,
not only the images, but even the sun and moon ; yet
all acknowledge Teen, Heaven.

Among a people like the Chinese there are, of course,
many strange and superstitious traditions, some of which
are partly verified by existing materials. Canton is sometimes called the " City of Rams."   Five genii, clothed
in robes of five different colours, and riding on rams of
five different colours, met together at the place now oceu-
pied by Canton.   Each ram carried a stalk of grain,
having six ears, and presented them to the people of the
district, to whom the genii said, " May famine and death
never visit your markets." Having uttered these words,
they immediately disappeared, and the rams were changed
into stone. A temple in the city was called after the
five genii ; it is near one of the gates, which is also
named after them, and in it are the five stone rams to
be seen to this day ! Certainly not very good representations of these animals.

In this temple there is the sacred place, from which it is said that the genii ascended, and the footprint in the rock of a gigantic Chinese shoe is exhibited as the exact spot !

The wishes of the genii, however, were not accomplished. Canton has several times suffered from famine, and been dependent on other places for its supplies.

In looking at the " Chinese as they are," we cannot but contrast their present position with some former periods of their history. Before the Sung dynasty ascended the throne, the condition of the people must have been debased in the extreme. In Kwang-tung, men were sacrificed to demons ; witches, wizards, and sorcery existed, and temples were erected for the practice of superstitious rites. The courts of justice were, if possible, more cruel than we now see them. " Criminals were boiled, and roasted, and flayed, and thrown on spikes, and were forced to fight with tigers and elephants."

On the other hand, we find that under the reign of emperors for nearly two centuries, perhaps the most prosperous era of the empire, the Nestorian Christians were not only tolerated, but the State actually built their churches. The Nestorian monument at *Sin-gan-foo*, gives an account of the Christian Church in China in the seventh and eighth centuries, and it was only when the Christian priests apparently took part in politics, that their church first fell to the ground. Whether it was the Nestorians or the Romanists who endeavoured to aid the Mongols, or whether it was both, I cannot say ; but it appears pretty certain that Christianity was driven out of China with the Mongols. How strange will it be if it again gain power at the expulsion of the Mantchoos !

The Emperor alone addresses *Hwang-Teen*—the imperial heaven ; the people can pray to *Shang-te*. Is the first expression to be considered more honourable than the second, or are the two denominations different ? We find the Chinese say—"When Teen created mankind it made them princes and teachers, and said to them, Assist Shang-te in showing loving-kindness to every region;" but again, we find Confucius says, "For him who has sinned against heaven (Teen), there is none to whom he can pray."

It appears that we may class the terms as those of State etiquette, and that the individual ideas of different emperors cause changes which are difficult to follow. The Emperor Kiang-hi declared that "Teen means the true God, and that the customs of China are political." After the English war, the French procured permission from Taou-Kwang, the last emperor, for Christians to carry on their worship unmolested, but certain clauses in the edict granting this permission, apparently limited it exclusively to the Roman Catholics. It was only granted to the followers of *Teen-choo*, the lord of heaven. As the Protestant missionaries did not use this term, the French Plenipotentiary was asked whether he intended his application to extend to all denominations of the Christian religion ? The answer was satisfactory, and Kiying, the Imperial Commissioner, explained it. "Originally, I did not know that there were among the nations these differences in their religious practices. Now, with regard to the religion of the Lord of Heaven, no matter whether the crosses, pictures, and images be reverenced or not reverenced, all who, acting well, practise it, ought to be held blameless."

In a future proclamation from the emperor himself, restoring various properties belonging to the Roman Catholics, that body is not treated with the respect they might have expected, if we may judge from the following sentence : " If after the promulgation of this decree, the local officers persecute and seize any of the followers of the religion of the Lord of Heaven, *who are not bandits,* upon all such the just penalties of the law shall be inflicted."

Of the Jews at Kai-fung-foo, apparently the last remnant of the Israelites in China who formed a synagogue, Williams mentions, that " they pay homage to Confucius as the Chinese do. They say Adonai for the ineffable name, and render it in Chinese by *Teen,* and not by *Shang-te.*

With all these different terms, we may surely grant that some of the Chinese use one or other as expressive of the Supreme Being. Let them use them as they will according to court etiquette, it is very evident that the difference is merely one of denomination alone, and that their highest Deity is the Almighty Ruler. Why, then, should we endeavour to rake up their demi-gods from the depths of their mythology, and search through their accumulating pantheon for fresh subjects wherewith to tax them with idolatry ? But beyond all, why should foreign missionaries add to the confusion by multiplying in their various sects the terms used to designate the one God Almighty ? If the rebellion is unsuccessful, is the *Shang-te* of the rebels to be cast aside ? It is no small matter to tamper with the Holy Name. We use many different terms for it, why should not the Chinese ? It is the multiplicity of their various demi-gods that has led them into a state of wild confusion, ending at last in a species of apathy, perhaps the most favourable condition for the propagation of true religion, which might be rendered as simple as possible in the outset.

If we turn to the early days of Buddhism, or the first flashes of reasoning of the Taouists, or Rationalists, we

find a simplicity and even goodness that doubtless led
to many converts ; and it was only when superstition and
error were heaped up that a settled decay commenced.
Disengaging Taouism from the imaginary traditions
which beset it, and which doubtless have been added
from time to time, their god, Yuh-Hwang Shang-te, is
denominated " The Pure and Immaculate One, self-
existing, of highest intelligence ;" and they believe that
the virtuous, when dead, are rewarded by being reunited
with their Maker.

Buddhism is lost in traditionary legends. It admits
the absolute mystification and obscurity of every legend
anterior to the close of the sixth century before Christ,
when Prince Siddhato, son of the sovereign of Magadha,
or Bahar, began his reign of righteousness and wisdom,
under the name and character of Gotama Buddha;[1]
and it was not till 400 years after that time that even
his tradition was put into writing. Some Chinese believe
in Buddha's worship of a Supreme Being, something
higher than Buddha (say, *Teen* or *Shang-te*), because
at Pekin, in the chief Buddhist temple, there is a relic,
Williams tells us,[2] of a curious nature, proving this. It
is a *scab* from the forehead of Buddha, caused by his
earnestly bowing down his head to the ground when
worshipping !

The Sabbath, or rest on the seventh day, so necessary
to the wellbeing of man, is unknown in China, unless it
is still observed in the insurgent camp, where at one
time it was strictly kept. A Chinese, who had once
been my teacher, was at Nankin with the American
Plenipotentiary : he told me, that while riding there, the

[1] Sir J. E. Tennant's *Christianity in Ceylon*, page 202.
[2] Williams' *Middle Kingdom*, a book full of the most valuable information regarding China.

party passed a Notice in Chinese—" To-morrow is the Sabbath !" The rebels requested them to dismount and walk respectfully past the simple announcement. The Chinese people, however, have no day of rest, and but few holidays, except at the time of the Chinese new year. Yet the people have gone on multiplying for ages, and though they have not advanced much in civilisation for hundreds of years, I do not believe they have degenerated. Their minds, however, do not expand and soar to the high regions of thought of Christian philosophers. A Chinaman thinks of little but what concerns himself individually, or his own peculiar employment. History is comparatively a blank ; science finds few disciples and scarcely any encouragement ; the fine arts, such as they are in China, are a mere matter of trade ; not one in a thousand knows the correct geography of the empire, or even of his own province. Politics are a sealed book to all except such as hazard their existence in the dangerous study, or aim at promotion under the fickle will of a despotic monarch. Oratory in a country where the spoken language is so varied is almost impossible. Even education is kept at a fixed standard, aiming only at the excellence of bygone ages.

May not this backwardness in civilisation, and the decline of the Chinese as well as other empires, be traced to this want of a day of rest to the mind, and account for its inability or unwillingness to trouble itself with affairs which do not immediately concern it ? I leave others to reply, as I bring forward this and other remarks in the present chapter with much diffidence ; my object in alluding to them is chiefly to show the Chinese in a different light to that in which they are generally pre-sented, thinking, as I do, that they are entitled to more consideration than has hitherto been granted to them as a

people: most of their faults are attributable to their rulers
and authorities.   There may be objections to the judgment I have formed of the Chinese character, but I claim
the indulgence of critics, as my observations are thus
made public in the hope that if they be fortunate enough
to meet with attention they may do good.

I have mentioned that a small sect of Jews existed in
China : there are also followers of Mahomet considerably
more numerous than the Chinese Jews.   Taking these,
and many of the disciples of Confucius, we count up a
goodly number of Chinese who are not idolaters ; but in
reality, many of the natives, probably the majority, no
matter whether they believe in a Supreme Being or not,
pay so little attention to religion that they may be classed
with one who, reasoning with me on the subject, said,—
" I think many men are fools ; suppose one is a *good* man,
what is the use of his praying to God ? suppose he is a
bad man, what is the use of his praying, God won't care
for him ! "   However, there is not such a bad groundwork
to build upon as most people imagine ; and in addition
to what I have stated, I quote from Williams' *Middle
Kingdom* a few remarks with which I thoroughly agree.
He says,—" Although they are a licentious people in
word and deed, the Chinese have not endeavoured to
sanctify vice, and lead the votaries of pleasure—falsely
so called—further down the road of ruin by making its
path lie through a temple, and under the protection of
a goddess.   Nor does their mythology teem with the
disgusting relations of the amours of their deities, which
render the religious stories of the Hindus and Greeks so
revolting ; on the contrary, they exalt and deify chastity
and seclusion as much as the Romanists do, as a means
of bringing the soul and body nearer to the highest excellence.   Vice is kept out of sight as well as out of

religion, in a great degree. . . . If the irresponsible authority of the Governor of the world be acknowledged in the establishment and removal of the kingdoms of the earth, and His declared detestation of these things be regarded as one reason for destroying those who practised them, then may not one reason be found for the long duration of the Chinese people and government, in their comparative freedom from these abominations ? . . . One pagan nation has come down from ancient times, and this alone is distinguished for its absence from *religious* slaughter of innocent blood, and the sanctified license of unblushing lust." The same author is also disposed to connect the long existence of the Chinese as a nation with their general regard for filial piety, and the promise made to the observers of the fifth commandment : " Honour thy father and thy mother, that thy days may be long in the land which the Lord thy God giveth thee."

There is much food for reflection in all this ; and when the true gospel of salvation gains a favourable entrance, and is sown throughout the length and breadth of the land which God has given to the Chinese, I think there is reason to hope for a speedy harvest.

Great responsibilities attach to the governments which are now entering upon a war with China. If extreme prudence and caution be exercised, we may yet see good results grow out of an apparent evil.

CHAPTER X.

CHARACTER OF THE CHINESE.

First impressions corrected—Chinese character opposite to that of Europeans—Chinese school-book—The new religion taught by the Rebels—Fundamental principles of the old faith contrary to that of Christianity—Official rank open to all—Rule regarding mandarins—Indifference to circumstances—Potted ancestors—Coffins for the living—Hired mourners—The famine at Shanghai—Stories of infanticide exaggerated—A tower full of bodies—Disreputable nuns—Canton fire-brigade—Stoicism of Chinese undergoing sentence of death—Suicide by order—Strange mixture of qualities.

On my first arrival in China, thirteen years ago, the contrariety of the native modes of doing anything struck me as most amusing, and a long list of the " opposites" of the Chinese manner and character to ours was soon made out ; but on giving deeper study to the subject, there is less reason to be proud of the general superiority of the European means than to feel abashed at our ideas of vaunted perfection.

The Chinese character is the exact opposite to that of Europeans generally. It is, however, changing from its old stereotyped existence, owing to circumstances that formerly could not have influenced it ; but even in the reason for changing, there is much cause for wonder. If a new plan is adopted, it is from contrary reasons to those which would affect the mind of an European.

It takes a long time to learn the native character, and

much study is required to do it full justice. We are far too apt to judge it from our own standards of civilisation, education, and morality, instead of doing the Chinese the justice of looking upon them according to their own ideas as much as possible. Few foreigners have had patience to take the trouble to do this, nor will I attempt to make you believe that I am able to study them as they deserve to be. To give a fair idea of the Chinese mind, it may be well to tell what they are taught when young, before we criticise their acts or customs. Let us look at the first Chinese school-book : the work is universally used throughout the empire. Every child is taught it by rote, even before it is understood ; and the maxims it contains have been learned by the Chinese youth for bygone ages. This Chinese Primer, called the *San-Tsze-King*, or Three-Character Classic, is composed in rhyme, probably to assist the memory, and begins with the bold announcement :—

> "Men at their birth are by nature pure !"

But qualifies the assertion,—

> "In this all are alike, but they differ in practice."
> "If left uneducated, nature deteriorates."

In thus looking upon the train of Chinese thought, we find, at the very commencement, the whole structure resting on a perfectly different foundation to our ideas of human nature. We believe that we are born in sin, and that we are improved by education. The people have no knowledge of any direct laws proceeding from God (it is only in the camp of Tai-ping-wang that God's commandments are proclaimed). Now, let me ask those who have rashly judged of Chinese character, if they have ever taken this matter into consideration ? What a vast difference there must be in the whole tenor of the thoughts of men so brought up from those educated like the English ! Many Chinamen, unless they actually break the laws of the empire, do not acknowledge that they are sinners. The Chinese compare man to an unwrought *gem*, and say—

> " A gem unwrought is a useless thing ;
> So a man unlearned is a senseless being."

Filial piety, of course, forms one of the earliest portions of the lesson :—

> " First practise filial and fraternal duties, next
> See and hear."

But perhaps the most difficult to understand of all their teachings is the trijuncture of what they call " the Three Powers,"—

> " Heaven, earth, and man."

What the power of the earth can be, I am at a loss to comprehend, and man being put upon an equality with heaven seems strange to European ideas ; but the ancient sages are classed in the equality, " because they teach men more than heaven or earth do !"—

> " There are three ties (or regulators) :
> That of prince and minister,   Justice.
> Of father and son, ...   Affection.
> Of husband and wife,   . .   Kindness."

" The upright prince in his palace is the regulator of his ministers ; the upright father at home is the regulator of his children ; and the upright husband is the regulator of his wife : these three being upright, then the prince will be immaculate, the minister good, the father compassionate, the son dutiful, the husband kind, the wife submissive, the empire quiet, and nations at peace."

The Chinese are taught that the earth is one vast

G

plain, and that the points of the compass indicate its centre.   Not content with this alteration of the universal economy, they transpose the " airts" themselves, and believe that the needle points to the *south*.   Confucius says east is *left*, and west *right !*

> " South and north, west and east,
>   These four points converge to the centre."

They say east-north for nor'-east, &c. &c.

The Classic points out a course of study, and gives a summary of Chinese history.   The whole forms a perfect example for an educational work, and one that might be followed with advantage in some points in other countries. One of the first books published by the Tai-ping rebels was a trimetrical classic, to take the place of the original *San-Tsze-King*.   A translation of the rebel pamphlet appeared in MM. Callery and Yvan's *History of the Insurrection*.   The original classic containing many points that did not agree with the new religion the insurgents attempt to propagate, they set it aside, and had the boldness to publish a new one,—probably the most daring innovation they could have made.   This commenced :—

> " The great God
>   Made heaven and earth,
>   Both land and sea,
>   And all things therein,
>   In six days ;"

and continued with a brief history of the Israelites according to the Bible, but omits any mention of the first fall of man.   A clear account is given of the escape from Egypt, and God's favouring protection to the Israelites, doubtless to inculcate the belief that similar protection would be vouchsafed to the believers in the new faith. It makes mention of the Ten Commandments :—

> " He himself wrote them,
>   And gave them to Moses :
>   The celestial Law
>   Cannot be altered."

After this, as a warning to evil-doers, the fall of man, who " was endowed with glory and honour," is first mentioned, and in the following terms :—

> " In after ages,
>   The celestial Law was sometimes disobeyed
>   Through the devil's temptations,
>   When men fell into misery."
> " But the great God,
>   Out of pity to mankind,
>   Sent his first-born Son
>   To come down into the world.
>   His name is Jesus,
>   The Lord and Saviour of men,
>   Who redeems them from sin."

These extracts will show that the original pure nature of man is not confined to the first parents, even by those Chinese who have adopted a species of Christianity, and that inborn natural sin is not one of their beliefs. The rebel classic goes so far as to state, that

> " The Chinese, in early ages,
>   Were regarded by God ;
>   Together with foreign states
>   They walked in one way,
>   From the time of Pwan-Koo
>   Down to the Three Dynasties,
>   They honoured God,
>   As history records."

It will be seen how the chiefs considered it necessary to make the new religion appear to be ancient, so as to suit Chinese prejudices ; and some trouble is taken to point out that idolatry was more modern than the new religion practised.

To arrive at a proximate insight into the Chinese, we must not only look at their education while children, but likewise at the doctrines they are taught and study as men. The Taouist and Buddhist faiths may be passed over for the present, as they seem to be tottering under the bad guidance of debased priests. The followers of Confucius, however, include many zealous students of the works of this great sage ; his maxims and doctrines are treasured, and their author almost deified ; in fact, almost worshipped : doubtless they have had an immense influence on the Chinese character. Sound and good as they must have been, to form the guiding-star for millions during many ages, they are void of some essential ingredients to constitute what we would call really good men ; for Confucius, the greatest oracle and standard of virtue, not only omits to teach forgiveness of injuries, but actually preaches revenge. Dr. Morrison says, that Confucius and Choo-Tsze were doubtful of the existence of gods, and these sages leave their followers under similar doubts ; and Mencius writes, that " none of the good principles are infused into us from without : they are inherent to ourselves."

Why wonder, then, at the arrogance of the Chinese ? Why be astonished at the small progress of Protestant missionaries, when one of the first things they have to teach these self-proud unbelievers is the sinfulness of man ? Every Chinese who can procure an education is theoretically entitled to aim at the highest position, but practically, it is generally great interest or bribery that leads to official rank ; however, it is open to all, and some of the best judges give this as the reason why the empire has been so long maintained.

" A prophet hath no honour in his own country," and a mandarin is not allowed to hold office in his native district. It is the pride of an Englishman to be a magnate in the place of his birth ; but the English trust to a

man's honour until he is proved unworthy of confidence.
The Chinese, on the contrary, proceed upon the assumption, that clannishness, or family instinct, must lead him
to partiality.

There is nothing in the Chinese character more striking than the apathy with which they undergo afflictions,
or the resignation with which they bear them. There is
so much elasticity in their disposition, that the most
opposite changes in their condition produce but little
effect. A coolie can admirably ape the dignity of the
mandarin when promoted, and a disgraced official, or
ruined merchant, who formerly had lived in luxury,
appears little to regret the change he has undergone.
There is no fear of death amongst them, though they
have a character for cowardice. It is true they have the
relics of the dead constantly before their eyes. The
country is covered with graves, and in many places about
Shanghai the coffins are openly exposed in the fields.
They are even kept in the houses till a propitious day
arrives for the burial, months passing by sometimes
before the body is removed. When the coffin is decayed,
the bones are carefully gathered ; and in a country walk
one very often comes upon jars containing " potted ancestors." Money is saved for the purchase of a coffin,
and it is put by till ready for use. The first time I saw
this was in a little cottage near Shanghai ; there was an
old cob-webbed coffin in the corner ; I asked a young
lad why it was there ; he quietly pointed with his thumb
over his shoulder to his grandmother, standing close
by, and said it was for her ! She was very old, and was
nearly wearing out the coffin before she was put into it.

At funerals, females are hired to do the " inconsolable
grief" parts of the performance. It seems very ridiculous
that such a custom should be kept up when it is known

by everybody that the mourners howl for hire; they certainly work hard for their money, and their piteous moans would be heart-rending if they were real.

During the famine in Shanghai, after the rainy years of 1848 and 1849, the poor people were reduced to the greatest misery. The women from the villages in the neighbourhood flocked daily in large numbers into the city, there to be supplied with food from the soup-kitchens that were established. They begged tickets during the day, and if they got more than they wanted, sold the balance to others, apparently caring little for the morrow. It was a wretched time; people died at our doors. One morning two poor women were passing down the road; one staggered and fell, and her companion left her: she was dead. The hand of Providence was against them; and calmly and solemnly they waited their fate. There were no robberies, no disturbances of any kind, except at one place, where the taxes were attempted to be levied during the distress. The mandarin got his house pulled about his ears. Much was done by foreigners,—by the missionaries especially, to alleviate the afflictions of the people. The wealthy natives subscribed largely to the " benevolent society." They carried bundles of soup-tickets at their girdles to give away to the poor; but a single ticket was merely for a meal of thin rice and water, and perhaps it only protracted wretchedness. I shall never forget the look of a poor widow, with a little daughter by her side, when I threw her a whole bundle of tickets in riding past; it seemed to break the spell of her fortitude, for, perhaps, she had made up her mind to die.

Much has been said of infanticide in China, but it appears to be exaggerated. Children are generally worth something; parents might sell them, or at any rate could

take them to the foundling hospital, of which there is
generally one in every city; but during the famine
alluded to, there were doubtless many mothers who were
unable to supply the natural nourishment to their offspring, and the infants died, or perhaps were put an end
to. It struck me at the time that many infants must be
destroyed, and I went to
the small tower, not far
from Shanghai, into which
the bodies of children are
cast. The tower covers a
well, and stands about
twenty feet high; at the
upper part are two small
arched windows, through
which the children are
thrown. On climbing up
to look down through the
windows, I was horrified to
find, that not only was the well full, but the tower piled
to the top with bodies! The keen frosty weather prevented putrefaction giving earlier notice of the dead pile
there accumulated. The infants were wrapped in mats
or old clothes; but there was nothing to lead to the belief
that they were thrown there alive, or that they had been
killed; and without better evidence than exists, the
Chinese at Shanghai should have the benefit of the doubt,
and we may believe that most of the children died a
natural death, and were deposited in this recognised receptacle for their corpses, to save the expense of a regular
burial. At the foot of the tower remains of small fires
were visible, showing that offerings had been made to
" joss" through that most glaring of cheats, paper *sycee*.
The strongest evidence against the tower is its proximity

to a Buddhist nunnery; these are often most disreputable places. There was one at Foochow, in which the nuns behaved so grossly, that they were put to death, and the funds of the nunnery confiscated to the government. The nuns may make use of the tower to get rid of illegitimate children, which they dare not possess; but bad as the Chinese mothers may be in selling their own offspring, I don't think they often destroy them. If you saw the hubbub in the Canton river when a child falls amongst the boats, though it may be protected with a gourd tackled to it as a life-preserver, or be tethered to the boat, you would not say that none cared to save the poor little wretch. Deformed children may perhaps be made away with, and it is said that many of the poor blind girls that go in strings along the streets of Canton are purposely deprived of sight; but considering the disease, filth, and poverty existing in many parts of that city, we may readily believe there would be a large proportion of blind children without such diabolical practices being resorted to. It is extraordinary to see how these poor wretches thread their way through the narrow crowded streets, none of which are broader than the pavement in the Strand, and are nearly, if not quite, as much crowded, besides being roughly paved.

In 1854, trade was sometimes quite at a stand-still in Canton. The shopkeepers sat lazily behind their counters, seeming rather to be taking advantage of the quiet that reigned, than regretting the loss of business. The fact is, the Chinese can live upon so little, bad times don't affect them much. There was a large fire in the suburbs of Canton one day, in a most dangerous neighbourhood—the houses and their contents were so inflammable. The streets were barricaded, the roofs were covered with people looking on, but very little ex-

ertion was made to remove property, though the benefits
of fire insurance were not known. We got the soldiers
to let us pass, and pushed our way up to the burning
houses; passed through several shops, in which not an
attempt was made at packing up. Certainly the fire
was being got under; still there was considerable
danger, and a good deal of excitement among some of
the people who feared incendiaries. The rebels were
besieging the city at the time, and all mischief was
laid to their account. In this case, however, the fire
was accidental; nor is it likely that men who were trying to gain the favour of the people would think of
burning their houses. Four hundred were destroyed.
The fire-engines and brigades were admirably managed,
but there was more fun than serious working among
the Chinamen—they worked with such a will; and
though it is rare for foreigners to move about on such
an occasion, my companion and I got on capitally,
and were received very good-humouredly, though many
around us must have suffered loss. We got hold of a
fire-engine, and pumped away for a short time; and as
we returned were recognised by the brigade. They set
up a shout, and redoubled their exertions, till, just as I
put my hand on the engine for another spell, the force
was too much for the hose, and it burst right over their
heads, drenching the whole of the men. A new hose
was attached in a moment, and they worked away as
briskly as ever. The fire-brigades in Canton are admirably arranged: the men wear distinguishing uniforms,
work with a will, and understand their business.

But the Chinese character when under suffering, is
best seen at executions. The victims are carried, bound
hand and foot, in baskets, and tumbled out into the
blood of the last sufferers, hustled up on their knees in

long lines, and in five minutes a hundred headless bodies lie weltering in their gore. Not a murmur or a groan to be heard, though none are gagged. Mr. Meadows, in his *Notes on China,* a most interesting book, mentions the cruel execution of an innocent man, and states, that as he was carried to the execution-ground, the people heard him proclaiming his innocence, and warning them from interfering with him, as the mandarin would only ruin them too. This is the only instance of the kind I have heard of. Out of a large number I saw beheaded, more than half of whom were stated to be perfectly innocent, not one uttered a cry. They may have been drugged. A striking case is related of a man that was being flayed alive railing at his tormentors to the last ; and one of the rebels at Shanghai, who was being cut to pieces, got his death-blow sooner than was intended, owing to his bearing before the executioners. He was a Canton man, and his countrymen at Shanghai spoke of it with pride.

After the rebels were unsuccessful in the Canton province, the mandarins erected pavilions at different places, supplied with every convenience for people committing suicide according to their individual taste. Those who had taken part in the rebellion were invited to destroy themselves, and thus have the privilege of a burial by their friends, which would not be permitted if they were caught and beheaded, even if their friends could pick them out from the mass of headless trunks that covered the execution-ground, after one of these brutal displays of the mandarins' vengeance. Suicide is the usual resort of a luckless official after a defeat. The history of the first English war in China proves this too clearly. Wells were found with whole families drowned in them ; and many people drowned themselves before the eyes of the soldiers.

Macao.

There is a curious mixture of cowardice and fortitude blended in the Chinese character, with a sort of half fatalism, that is peculiar to the sons of Han. They have courage without bravery, and pride mixed with servility; excessively clannish, but this feeling is only second to selfishness. In a gale of wind their sailors bear themselves boldly for a time, until an accident befalls them, when their courage fails, and they will give themselves up to their fate. Yet pirates have been known to blow up their junk rather than be taken.

At a large fire which occurred at Macao early in 1856, burning nearly 1000 houses, there was a good opportunity to watch the difference of character of the Chinese and Europeans. While the fire was raging, and there was little chance of their property being saved, the Chinese got away all they could, and set to work in a business-like manner, as if there was something to be done. There was no tearing of hair or dread of farther misfortune; the accident had happened, and they had to make the best of it. The Portuguese, on the contrary, frightened themselves with all sorts of rumours of incendiaries, piratical attacks, &c., called out the militia, guarded the streets, not letting the Chinese move about, and by some bungling managed to have a lot of Chinese shut up in a *cul-de-sac*, occasioning the loss of many lives. Some passenger-boats were landing their passengers on the wharf near the fire. "The Ladrones! the Ladrones!" was at once the cry. Down rushed the valorous militiamen to greet them with a volley, but as the supply of ammunition served out happened to be limited to the single cartridge that was fired, and this fact suddenly striking the brave Macaoese, they did not wait to see the result of their fire, but bolted as fast as they could to a place of safety.

CHAPTER XI.

TRUSTWORTHINESS OF THE CHINESE.

Cheating honestly—The compradore—Honesty of servants—Mercantile integrity—Chops of tea—Coolies, their fidelity—Open exposure of property—A pickpocket—Pawnbroking—No native gold or silver coin—Unwritten agreements faithfully observed—Rarity of drunkenness—Eyes and tails—Costumes—Chinese cotton goods—Dress of coolies—Fishermen—Perfection in matters of utility—Cooking by steam—Healthiness of the people—Medical treatment—Monkey-soup.

AFTER many years' experience in the north and south of China, I may state with safety that the greatest contrariety to ourselves marks the Chinese in their ideas of honesty and cheating. They cheat honestly! It is a paradox solved.

You engage a compradore as chief of the Chinese in the household. He is generally supposed to be accountable for the honesty of the other servants; he is thoroughly correct in all his transactions,—often has very large dealings himself. You know he came to you not worth a hundred dollars perhaps, yet he is soon worth thousands. The system is recognised: he gets a bonus some way or other on all payments, and in some transactions pays a percentage of it to all the other servants in the house.

I knew a man, nominally in receipt of $25 per month, who, after six years' servitude, on being asked to become security for a relation of his own, replied, that he would guarantee him—a fellow only worth the clothes upon his back—for $10,000 ! !

I have seen instances over and over again where there was positive inducement for undiscovered fraud, but the ordeal was passed through with most perfect honesty. Some of the compradores conduct most of the transactions in the sale of opium and other highly valuable produce during great fluctuations in the market.

In Canton, the compradores' quotations for gold and silver, in which the transactions are immense, have scarcely any check ; and yet in some houses and banks they conduct nearly all the purchases. They pack up the money, and I never knew a single instance in which the weights or amounts turned out intentionally incorrect, though they pack it, seal it, and often ship it off without a foreigner in the establishment ever having seen it. Sometimes a few inferior dollars may be returned, but the amounts are almost always correct. Money is received in untold sums ; it is counted or weighed, a deficiency in the quantity that should be received is rarely to be found, and if there is an error it is generally discovered to be a mistake on the part of the sender.

Silver plate is on the table before the servants nearly all day ; there may be a large party with numerous servants from other houses, as each guest brings his own valet ; yet it is rarely known that an article is lost. The servants are answerable to the compradore, and the compradore to the master. Sometimes, but rarely, there is an actual robbery : but then the robber decamps. When I first went to Shanghai, I had a young rascal that made a clean sweep of all the silver, and took even the watches and valuables out of my bedroom. He got clear away, and was never heard of afterwards : he had been made the instrument of a greater rogue than himself. None of the others in the house were to blame for the theft. I took the lad on the recommendation of a foreigner, and not of our own compradore; good servants were then very difficult to be had, and he had none to recommend.

It has lately become a custom in Shanghai and Foochow, and to a small degree in Canton also, to intrust very large sums of money to Chinese for the purchase of tea and silk in the interior. The money is lost sight of for months in a country where a foreigner could not follow; yet, such is the honesty of the Chinese that the instances are rare in which the man intrusted with it has made off. He may have been robbed by others, and instances are known where the money has been deposited in safe hands *en route* for fear of robbers known to infest the locality, till safe transit could be insured. I know an instance where a large sum had been sent to the tea districts near Foochow in different sort of coin. It was found that part of it would not pass current except at a heavy discount; the bulk was left up the country, and a man sent back with $8000 to get them changed, and return with the coin that suited the tea-men. Opium is even sent up the country for sale; it often goes to Soochow on foreign account. Here is a great opportunity for fraud, for the article passes through the hands of men we should call smugglers; it has to be sold not openly, and in a market which we cannot reach. There must be great honesty, and the plan must answer, for it has continued for years, I believe, without the property being lost, or the prices tampered with. Many manufactured goods are sent there; indeed one house established a sort of agency at Soochow for the sale of Manchester goods. And so little is the risk of dishonesty

thought of, that in money sent to the silk districts on
constituents' account, the charge has sometimes been
made of only 2½ per cent. for guarantee. There is a
certain degree of security in the known respectability of
the Chinese, through whom the business is conducted;
but it cannot be expected that he is in all cases answerable for robbery. There is doubtless immense risk when
the money gets into districts where the rebels are,—
anarchy is let loose, and the vagabonds of the place take
every advantage of the overthrow of the local authorities.
In one of the insurgent proclamations we find this complained of. Large sums on foreign account were in the
Ho-IIow tea district when the rebels were there, but the
losses were few, if any.

Out of a "chop" of some five or six hundred packages
of tea bought in Canton, seldom more than one per cent.
used to be examined throughout. The tea goes to England, the few chests opened being taken as a criterion of
the whole, and excepting from accidents on the way, or
indifferent care in storage, damaging the tea, the whole
proves to have been faithfully packed. Now and then
a chest has been plundered and filled with rubbish, but
considering the quantity of tea that is shipped from
China, such cases are very rare when the tea is bought
from the regular Canton merchant. There are few
articles where systematic fraud could be better concealed
than in tea—scented teas especially, where the number
of packages is great in one purchase, and the mani-
pulation and scenting of the tea is the most expensive
part. Certainly the tea-taster has the whole "chop" to
choose from, and he picks out any package he likes.
The tea is "laid down," i.e., every package is flat on
the floor, our friend the "Chaa-sze," as the tea-taster
is called, walks into the warehouse, jumps on the top

of a package, and walks across the whole chop, making
a mysterious halt now and then, shouting out "tarer,"
and a rush is made to the chest he stands on by a half-
naked Chinaman, who writes some chalk-marks on the
package and off it is taken. Some few chests are hurried
away as "tarers," and others pounced on to weigh
whole, these being marked differently by the fussy naked
individual with the chalk; down jumps Mr. Chaa-sze
from the chests, and takes note of the weighing. His
short-cut walk over the packages is an understood thing,
and something may be gained by it, especially from the
"tarers." When he steps upon a firm, hard, solid sort of
chest, off it goes to be emptied and stand for tare ; when
a fragile, thin-wooded, light package gives under his
weight, away it is sent to the scales, to act as a representative for the chop. The tea is weighed, off to the
office goes the Chaa-sze, the chests are coopered, and he
sends marks down for them. The Chinese do this in
first-rate style; put the tea in the boats, take it some
twelve miles to the ship, are generally out all night with
it ; it is taken on board and goes off to England or elsewhere, arrives generally without a suspicion of fraud,
neither the tea-taster, merchant, nor any one belonging
to the establishment, having ever seen anything more of
it from the time it was weighed. Valuable silk piece-
goods are sent off in the same way. In Shanghai there
is this difference, that the tea and silk are shipped from
the foreigner's warehouse; there are often a hundred
dirty vagabonds packing perhaps £10,000 or £20,000
worth of silk, every pound weight being worth about a
month's wages to the scurvy-looking coolies that are
handling it; yet there is rarely false packing or theft.
Some silk was once going overland to Southampton
via Hong-Kong ; a bale on arrival proved to have been

plundered, and the space filled up. A claim was made for loss in weight, but it appeared so curious that a theft had been managed when such an occurrence was so rare, that the claim was refused until the articles used to replace the silk were mentioned. The answer came that the space had been filled up with stones and jute ! In Shanghai you can hardly find a stone to throw at a dog, and certainly no jute to make a rope to hang him with.

In all places in China you may see a string of coolies rushing through the streets carrying loads of money ; there is not a policeman to be seen, except occasionally at the gates, or in time of trouble.

You may see a shroff [1] with a lot of dollars in a flat tray, examining them intently as they pass click, click, over his thumb, sometimes a posse of idlers, consisting of chair-bearers, coolies, cooks, and servants, all looking on. There does not seem to be even the suspicion that any one might attempt to kick the tray over, and bolt with what he can get in the scramble. Why, even in that nest of iniquity, Hong-Kong, you may see at the door of that most comfortable of buildings, the Oriental Bank, a lot of Chinamen counting and examining, perhaps, thousands of dollars that are being paid to them,[2] and some of the greatest scoundrels unhanged passing constantly: perhaps they think that the men in the street would most likely be honest enough to catch them, but it is rather doubtful if they dare. Money and valuables are exposed in a way that would never be dreamed of in England ; and the similarity of dress, the narrowness and crowded state of the streets in China, all would aid in the escape of a robber. In Canton there are a great

---

[1] "Shroff," one who examines money.

[2] It is only lately that iron-guard railings have been put up between the open place of examination and the street.

many pickpockets; I never heard of them elsewhere. One afternoon, while passing through the back streets, I lost a pocket-handkerchief. I knew the exact spot, but could not make out the thief. I returned to the factories and got another, fastened it in my pocket, and passed the place again in hopes of getting "a nibble;" the fellow was on the look-out, and did it beautifully, —"filched the fogle" with the finest hand, but, feeling it was fastened, let go and made off. I never felt his touch, but saw the 'kerchief hanging down to my heels, then just caught the fellow's eye as he looked round to see if he was detected; he knew his position at a glance, and being about twenty yards from me, and about as many people between us, he ducked and dived into a recess in front of a banker's shop. I wondered at his going into such a respectable place, and when I got there could not see him; at last he was discovered, and to the astonishment of the banker I hauled him out, and having provided myself with a good vine-stick, made him feel the weight of it smartly, and helped him out, *en reverse*. The wretch tried to get up a row outside, and to advise the crowd to mob me, but on making a dash at him he bolted, having had enough of the vine.

Pawnbroking is carried on to a larger extent in China than in any other country. This may show how greatly the Chinese trust each other. There are very extensive banking establishments in most large cities; interest being allowed on deposits. The interest on loans varies much. Men in business get it at moderate rates; the range is generally one-half to three-quarters per cent. per month, in ordinary times! but during the rebellion in the Canton province, the wealthy men withdrew their funds from the banks, put their money into gold, and secreted it. Much money must have been lost in this way as the owners frequently suffered either from the rabble or the soldiers. A number of the chief places of trade were partly destroyed by fire ; the burnt houses were laid bare by plunderers. They had a clever way of finding out where money was stored under the floors : most of the lower rooms are paved with tiles or bricks ; the rubbish was cleared away, and quantities of water poured over the ground, and where it sunk fastest, the floor was opened, and the ingenuity of the searcher often rewarded.

The Chinese have no silver or gold coin of their own. Silver in "shoes" of various sizes, generally about fifty taels (£16 worth), and gold in bars or leaf, are used where foreign money is not current. The banker puts his stamp upon it, and the "touch" is thereby sufficiently guaranteed. Any tampering with the quality is rare, but, of course, roguery is sometimes attempted. As a general rule, however, perfect trust may be placed on the value ; a slight examination satisfies the shroffs. The reliance placed by the Chinese upon the stamp or chop of the bankers may be gathered from the fact, that in Canton, foreign dollars are so marked by the guaranteeing stamps of those who pay them away, that the original character of the coin is often obliterated. And in the north, where Carolus dollars *unstamped* are preferred, it used to be the custom to mark them with the banker's seal in ink.

In sales to the Chinese, it is rare that any written document passes between the Chinaman and foreigner. The transaction is entered in the foreigner's book, and considered closed. The goods may not be delivered or paid for till some time after, but I don't remember an instance of the price being disputed, even when the market had fallen. It is the same with purchases, though sometimes the petty traders in Shanghai are called upon to produce a chop, showing that they are empowered to sell the produce.

No cognizance is taken in the consular courts of opium transactions. Millions of dollars' worth are sold in a year; and though it is contrary to the general rule to deliver the opium before the cash is paid, there are many instances, especially among the Indian native merchants, where credit is allowed; and the sums are nearly always duly paid, though there could have been no claim against the Chinese by law.

This subject could be indefinitely extended, but the above will show, that as far as honesty is concerned, the Chinese do not deserve the bad character generally laid to their charge. I question much if the worthy colonists in Melbourne, or the citizens of San Francisco, could bear comparison with the Chinese for uprightness in their dealings, and yet they try to expel them from their neighbourhood, as if their presence were contamination.

Of the enormous amounts of gold sent to India every year, the greater part is guaranteed by a certain touch; and though fraud in this article could readily be carried on without much fear of discovery, if the quality were only slightly tampered with, it is rare indeed that any such act is attempted. There were many palpable attempts at such fraud in the first lots of gold dust sent from California.

The Chinese are models of propriety and quietness in their towns and daily avocations of life; disturbances rarely occur, a drunkard is seldom seen, and one uproariously drunk, never. There is seldom such a thing as a policeman to be seen in a Chinese town. What a contrast to Hong-Kong! where there are daily fights among drunken sailors, and uproar at night—in spite of police fully armed—enough to awaken the dead.

Their Coolies and Boatman.

There is one point in the appearance of the Chinese at variance with the usual European ideas of them : they are generally depicted with slanting eyes pointing downwards to the nose. This may be a characteristic of the race, but the majority of Chinese that have come under my observation (and I have sketched hundreds) show no such peculiarity. The inner part of the upper eyelid turns down a little, but the eye, though small, is oftener horizontal than otherwise. The fishermen on the coast have the eye frequently drooping downwards at the *outer* angle. This arises no doubt from the manner of half-shutting the eye to avoid the glare at sea. There is another point on which persons who have not been in China form an erroneous notion. The tail of a Chinaman is not a little tuft on the crown of the head, but is formed of hair suffered to grow luxuriantly in a mass, at least four inches in diameter. The hair is smoothed down, and the tail, plaited from it, begins at the nape of the neck, and hangs below the waist, often to the ankles. Labouring men, while at work, generally have it wrapped round the head. There are so many styles of dress in China, that a great variety of sketches might be made of them. Among the valets there are several styles ; among the dealers many different tastes ; and as for the soldiers in general, " motley is the only wear." The dress of all classes is always loose and comfortable, well adapted to the climate, and remarkably cheap, except in winter, when some indulge in very expensive furs, which are well preserved. The Chinese, even rich persons, frequently pawn their winter clothes during summer, and summer clothes during winter, being assured that they will be well taken care of.

There is one point I would draw attention to. Notwithstanding the large import of English and American cotton goods (and the majority of Chinese are clothed in cotton), it is seldom we see a man dressed in foreign cotton manufacture.   Our goods are not so lasting, nor are they so warm as the native hand-woven nankeens. The Chinese surpass us in making good cheap cottons, strong and durable.   This is the more strange, as the " staple" of the native cotton is remarkably short.   Their cloth is very narrow, only about eighteen inches wide. This may admit of the shuttle being thrown with more telling power, and partly account for the strength and durability of the material.

Of all dresses well adapted for a warm climate there is none more comfortable than that of the Chinese coolie. The neck left bare to the collar bone ; a free, loose jacket reaching to the thighs ; and wide trousers, double at the waist, and folded double across the stomach, thus securing warmth there ; leather or grass-straw sandals, complete the costume.   The head-dress in summer is the

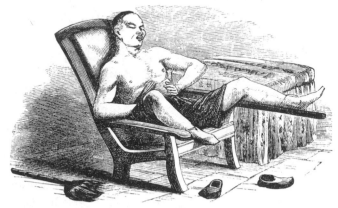

Caught Napping.

broad-brim peaked rush hat.   Often in hot weather the jacket is discarded, and the nether covering reduced to the smallest limits.   The fellows look like savages, and some of the lowest class have a debased, almost a brutish expression—mere beasts of burden. Upon the coast the poorer classes are still more savage-looking. The fishing-boats are manned by men often perfectly naked. I have seen them, even in cold weather, out at sea in an open boat without a rag of clothing to protect them. These men are quite brown from exposure. It is a fine sight to see a fishing fleet off Namoa, beating out to sea ; as many as five hundred boats in sight at once, all the same rig, and well matched in sailing. Their crews, poor devils! must have a hard life. I have heard of one place losing 150 boats, its whole fleet, in a typhoon ; not one ever heard of. They are wonderfully good judges of the weather, however, and generally know when a gale is coming on, but are very superstitious.

A fine new boat was picked up at sea, upset, with some men inside. They were cut out, and the boat taken in to Namoa by one of the coasting schooners ; but the men would have nothing more to do with her, nor would any one buy her, though she was exactly similar to the other boats.

Their boats vary in rig and build, nearly every fifty miles up the coast. The coasting captains can generally tell where they are in fogs or thick weather, if they fall in with a Chinese fishing-boat. And so well adapted are the various boats for the water and kind of seas in which they are used, that the boat of each district can outsail those from an outside place. At Amoy, the boats are peculiarly ugly, but have extraordinary sailing powers. They are shaped just like a spoon. Ningpo boats were got up to Shanghai at one time by foreigners, as they appeared to be the fastest and most comfortable ; but it was found that Shanghai boats of equal size could out-sail them there.

The Chinese have been jogging on so quietly for ages, without alteration in their institutions, that they have brought all the material appliances of life to perfection ; that is, they obtain their ends with the least possible waste of power and materials, at the cheapest cost. Their dress is the most comfortable and the cheapest ; their vessels suit all their wants, and have had water-tight partitions for ages—a discovery we are only beginning to appreciate. They make the most beautiful silks with a loom that is simplicity itself. Take the tools they work with : their saw requires far less iron than ours ; their bellows gives a *constant* draft of air, and is merely an oblong or cylindrical box, with a piston worked in it. But I never saw a windmill in China, not even a picture of one. In their water-mills for grinding flour, there is no trouble or expense in keeping the machinery in order while at work. To each pivot or axle a small bamboo pipe constantly supplies a dropping of water, which pre-

vents all heating from friction. In propelling their boats the powerful scull admits of a child doing as much work as a man could do with our stupid methods. Take the keelmen on the Tyne, or the bargemen on the Thames ; if their boats were fitted with a long, bent, well-balanced Chinese scull, hung only on a small iron pivot, and with a rope on board to give extra purchase, one man would do the work of at least two, without half the exertion.

Watch how the Chinese cook their food; they will cook a dinner for a dozen with a mere handful of fuel. Their boiler is cone-shaped and large; say two feet in diameter by one foot deep; it covers the whole of the fire merely with a small portion of the lower part of the cone, but the heat and flames enfold the rest. Water and rice are put at the bottom, with an open frame over them about half the depth of the pan; on this are placed dishes of fish, fowl, or vegetables to boil; the whole is covered with a wooden cover, in the centre of which is a round hole about four inches in diameter, and in this another bowl is often placed, the contents of which are cooked by the steam.

In the erection of their houses the Chinese get quite sufficient strength and solidity by building the walls hollow. It would be an easy though a tedious task to show how they have, by long experience, brought almost everything to a certain degree of perfection; and this has made them self-sufficient and averse to all innovations: but while the intellect and science of the nation may have suffered, the character of the people as a hardworking, industrious race, has thus been carefully maintained.

As a people they are generally a healthy race; epidemics are not frequent, and severe diseases are not common. This may be accounted for by their usual moderate diet, but 1 am inclined to believe that the health of their large cities, where filth unbounded is collected together, arises much from the purifying effects of charcoal, the chief fuel of the Chinese. The abstinence from cold drinks, and the use of tea, has probably a beneficial effect; and I cannot but think that the free

exposure of the neck prevents attacks of catarrh and
sore throat, so common among Europeans. The thick
felt soles to their shoes must also be conducive to the
health of the Chinese, and are admirably adapted to
their houses and the climate.

If we knew more of their medical science we might
find many useful remedies : the Chinese have long administered arsenic as a cure for fever and ague, and
European doctors now find that it is almost the only
certain remedy. Their system of acupuncture and
counter-irritation is doubtless worthy of study. In
Europe it is becoming the practice not to bleed in cases
of fever. The Chinese have always opposed it ; they
say, " The body is on fire, why take away the liquid required to cool it ? " They have a slight knowledge of
electricity, but they do not understand it. I once saw
an itinerant doctor in Canton at work curing a man of
a pain in his arm ; he put on two or three lumps f
warm tar or pitch, then holding the arm straight out,
dragged his hand down it, pressing strongly with his
thumb on the inner part of the arm, as if trying to
work all the blood down towards the hand ; the fingers
did assume a sort of gouty pink appearance, and the
doctor called a bystander to put his finger in front of
those of the patients, and certainly there was an appearance as if electric sparks were being drawn from the
man. In skin diseases the Chinese doctors are very
successful, probably from their having large practice, as
such cases are very prevalent ; and in a kind of itch
they apply an ointment to the part affected, which
causes a small worm to come out of each pustule. They
have a method of extracting teeth without drawing
them, and many external applications as remedies for
various diseases, which it might be useful to know.

They drench their patients with ridiculous decoctions, and whole piles of physic, but probably the really beneficial medicine in each could be discovered. The late intelligent Dr. Harland, of Hong-Kong, told me of a strange cure they adopt for that sickness in infants where the child wastes away almost to a skeleton and dies. The Chinese put faith in a monkey, which they bring for the child to play with, and after they have got friendly together, in a few days the unfortunate monkey is *boiled down into soup*, which is given to the rickety infant, and in two instances that are known to have been tried, a cure has been effected !

CHAPTER XII.

Chinese character — Chinese witness — Value of knowing the language —
  Great want of interpreters — Chinese employed by Europeans — Their
  satisfactory conduct — Chinese "Sepoys" — Growing rapidity of communication with Europe.

I WAS present at the trial of a civil case in the Hong-
Kong supreme court, which brought to light curious
phases of Chinese character. It was a dispute about the
purchase and delivery of some tea. By a Hong-Kong
ordinance it is not necessary to *swear* Chinese witnesses,
they placed so little value on the oaths that used to be
administered; they are now merely reminded of the
penalties for perjury, and are subject to them if they
make a false declaration in court. One witness appeared
to be greatly puzzled by a long cross-examination by the
Attorney-General; the interpreting seemed unsatisfactory; a *Portuguese* translating English questions into
Chinese, and again translating the answers, according to
his own notions. The jury, of which I was one, thought
the witness had made a very clear story; we could
quite understand the nature of the transaction. The
Attorney-General was of a different opinion; he called
upon the judge to commit the man for perjury, and the
man becoming confused, the judge committed him on
the spot, and he was taken out of court to go to jail
for six months, with hard labour. The case was a very
long one, and the plaintiff having thus lost his best

Chinese Boys   North Part of Kwangtung

witness, was likely to lose a large sum of money. The defendant, to make his case stronger, brought forward a witness, who, after giving rather adverse than favourable evidence, was seized in court upon information that he had in his possession a paper showing that he had been bribed by the plaintiff. The evidence on this point was not very satisfactory, and we were of opinion that there was a conspiracy against the plaintiff, and, much to the astonishment of the Court, gave a verdict in his favour. I then asked the Court's permission to put a question to the interpreter: What do you call "defendant" in Chinese ? He told me. But I said, "That is not the name you used when interpreting." He replied, "No ; I called him by his nick-name, 'Sam-Kwei-Choo.'" "But you called the other, interpreter, about whom the whole confusion of evidence was, by his nick-name too." "Yes, his nick-name is Sam-Kwei." "Well, then, the perjured witness may have mistaken between Sam-Kwei and Sam-Kwei-Choo, which was the real point of the perjury." "Yes, sir, I think that it is very probable !" This happened on the day subsequent to the poor man's committal. The whole jury gave it as their opinion that the man was innocent, and the good judge at once ordered him to be released.

It turned out that the plaintiff would have been ruined had the jury not acted as they did. I was astonished some days afterwards, by several children coming into my office, and falling on their knees before me, the plaintiff with them, to return thanks in gratitude for the part I had taken in the matter. I felt very thankful that my slight knowledge of the language had been so useful, and that it had saved an honest man from six months' imprisonment among the rascals that burden Hong-Kong jail. Several respectable Chinese spoke to me about the case afterwards, being delighted that the defendant had been defeated.

The difficulty, above all others greatest in China, is to get good interpreters. Government should offer every inducement to young men, especially military officers, to study the language; even if they only learn a little, it would often prove of incalculable benefit. In fact, it is scarcely fair to enter into any great military operation against China, while we have such a small staff of interpreters. There is no saying what the result of active warlike operations may be. Even when we took Canton, it was thought imprudent to attempt to govern it, and by putting the Chinese officers again in power, the chief moral effect of taking the city was lost. The attempt should have been made, even if all the Chinese had to be driven out. As it was, Chinese plunderers ravaged the city in all directions, and no one could tell who were the rightful owners of property that was allowed to be taken away. Of course the foreigners are blamed for all that was lost. No time should be lost in having officers, and even some of the men, taught at least a little Chinese. With steady application, enough to make a man very useful can be learned in six months. Even a few sentences may be of great benefit. Certain classes might be formed for the Canton dialect, others for the mandarin, and high prizes or staff appointments be given to all who made satisfactory progress. No man-of-war should be without an interpreter. In many expeditions against pirates, I have no doubt, numbers of innocent people have been killed, because we are always ready to fight though often not prepared to speak. To prevent difficulties, it has too often been the custom to burn, kill, and destroy, taking care not to bring back any prisoners. Hong-Kong is notoriously badly off for interpreters, and the local government has apparently made no effort to effect any improvement in this respect. Pirate vessels are fitted out in the harbour, plunder sold in the streets; a proper class of interpreters would have prevented this mighty disgrace long ago.

It is most interesting to watch the development of the Chinese character when associated with European affairs. For several years many Chinese have been employed in steamboats as deputy engineers and stokers, and have given great satisfaction; their sobriety and carefulness being quite exemplary. As pilots of steamboats and foreign-rigged vessels they are excellent; quickly learn sea-terms; and many can "handle a vessel" in first-rate style. Those employed in yachts about the Canton river understand their business so well that full charge is given over to them in regattas. As oarsmen they are second to none, after a little practice; and the style with which some practised crews pull is well worth seeing. In Canton there are several boys who pull sculls in tiny wager boats through a crowded river steadily, and with perfect confidence. As boat-builders, few can equal the Chinese. They will build a racing cutter, or a wager boat, as light and true as Biffin or Searle; the amateurs in Canton getting "the lines" from England, or improving upon them. The boat-house in Canton, before the war with Yeh, had as fine a show of racing-boats as any single establishment in the world.

As ship-carpenters, when under foreign superintendence, it would be difficult to find better workmen; and lately, some who have been employed in setting up iron steamers, speedily learnt to perfection the art of riveting, under the guidance of a clever engineer, sent out by Messrs. R. Stephenson and Co.

A ship-captain, who took home some Fokien boatmen as sailors, said, on his return, that they were the best men in his ship. It would be well worth the consideration of Her Majesty's Government to employ Chinese as firemen and supernumeraries in steamboats while cruising within the tropics on the east side of the Cape of Good Hope. With proper training they would make excellent sailors, and there would be little difficulty in making good soldiers of them.[1] The day may come when China, or a part of it, may undergo the fate of India, and be under the rule of the Anglo-Saxon race, governed by a second East India Company. The opportunity at any rate will not be wanting. Chinese "Sepoys" would astonish the world if well led ; and from what we have seen of the bravery of the celestials under plucky leaders, Asia may congratulate herself on the peace-policy of China, for with its teeming millions there would be armies sufficient to rival the conquests of the most ambitious monarchs, especially if science had fair play in China.

As assistants to medical men in hospitals, as warehouse keepers or shopmen, as mechanics, wood-engravers, stewards, and cooks, with proper teaching, they become exceedingly useful. With a little looking after they make capital grooms, and will keep a horse in first-rate condition. It would be difficult to find better gardeners, when they have been well trained, and it would be well worth the attention of the colonists in Australia and New Zealand to get labourers of this kind from China.

[1] Since writing the above we have had experience of the " Bamboo rifles," as the Chinese coolies in the military train were called. Lord Elgin brings this subject under the notice of the Government in his despatches from China.

Some of the Protestant missionaries in China have lately been distributing works in Chinese upon the steam-engine, and other scientific subjects ; and if the country were not cursed with a laggard good-for-nothing Government, we might see the glorious rivers of the empire made doubly valuable by the impetus steam would give to commerce in all its branches. The Chinese, who have bought steamers and foreign ships, have, however, been particularly unfortunate, paying extravagantly high prices for indifferent craft ; it is a pity that their enterprise should have met with such ill luck at the outset. They have not yet learned the value of *despatch*, and the time lost in making up their minds, and haggling about price, makes sad havoc with profits. Some years ago it was the custom not to send away new teas until the month of October, when the monsoon changes ; but year by year the teas have been hurried down from the country, and at present we see new teas shipped in the month of June ; and so much has the style of ships improved, that more rapid voyages are now made against the monsoon than were formerly made with it. Each year there is a gigantic race of magnificent ships all the way from China to England. The finest specimens of naval architecture are engaged, and the most experienced captains employed. The *douceurs* now given to captains in the event of success, exceed the former annual wages, and the result is watched with intense anxiety.

The Chinese begin to appreciate this feature of foreign character, and the energy with which some set to work when despatch is necessary, is quite cheering to witness. They only require example, and to see the benefit to be derived from it ; then they are capable of almost any

I

demand made upon their energy.   What a vast field has
yet to be opened here to European enterprise !   When
will the millions of China be roused from their trance
and take their place in the march of progress, and their
share in the toils and anxieties which surround the rest-
less couch of modern civilisation ?

CHAPTER XIII.

THE MANDARINS.

Emperor's description of his officers—Wickedness and baseness of the man-
darins—Ho-Kwan's prodigious gains—Other degraded mandarins—The
Foochow bank failure—Wholesale execution of angry creditors—Murder
of Englishmen—Attack on missionaries—Resolute conduct of the British
Consul—Supported by a British naval captain—The offenders delivered up
—Accounts of mandarins punished—The conduct of soldiery at Shanghai
—A Chinese admiral pockets pay and avoids fighting—A Chinese battle
a farce—Missionary hospitals.

WE shall first take the Emperor's account of his officers
Pih-che-le, in which province Pekin is situated, and
therefore the one we may expect to find under best
command. When the rebel army entered it, and before
the cold weather had destroyed their hopes of capturing
Pekin, city after city rapidly fell into the hands of
the then victorious insurgents. The imperial officers
behaved with such cowardice that the Emperor issued
orders that if such conduct continued the commander-
in-chief should " behead the offender with one hand, and
write the report of it with the other !" So indignant was
the sovereign at the conduct of his head-officers, that he
addressed to them a special edict. First exhorting them
earnestly, he concludes,—" After all, the influence of
reasoning may have little or no force with you, and you
officers, great and small, may deem it too much trouble
to acknowledge right principle, thinking that to deceive

us at the head of the State is àn easy matter ; but lift up
your heads higher, and think of high heaven intelligently
inspecting all below, and see if there be not something to
be dreaded *there !"* Deception, exaggeration, and false-
hood, characterize the acts of those mandarins who have
played a prominent part within the last few years. I
would say nothing against the Emperor, nor do the
people ever venture to whisper a reproach against him
further than that he is young. A few say he is dissi-
pated—in a regal way ; but deep, deep, are the anathemas
against the mandarins. Very few do we find as their
apologists ; in fact, there is only one Chinese of my
acquaintance who has persuaded himself that they have
acted correctly : he gloried in the executions at Canton !

No wonder insurrections occur when the people have to
endure the wholesale extortions of the mandarins. When
Ho-Kwan was degraded, he had, besides his horses,
lands, and immovable property, as one account, probably
not without exaggeration, says, 80,000,000 taels, or
£27,000,000 in bullion or gems in his treasury. We
must remember, too, that there are parts of China where
the government has little or no control. About twenty
years before the present revolution assumed its vast
proportions, Le, the Governor-General of Kwang-Tung
and Kwang-se, was transported for life because his
miserable army was defeated by the clans from the
mountains that separate these provinces from Hoo-nan.
He-gan was sent to retrieve the losses ; he did not go
with soldiers, but money ; paid 900,000 taels, or £300,000
to buy a peace, when the high officers, &c., were allowed
to withdraw unmolested. These men have never been
conquered, and their hills and valleys form a rallying
point for the Canton rebels. Here the forces of more
than one rebel army have been recruited, ready again to

march against the imbecile troops of the rotten government of China, and wrest their ill-gotten gains from the mandarins who so basely serve it.[1]

Were there a redeeming point in their character there would be more pleasure in writing about them. The character of the mandarins is generally so well known, that it seems almost superfluous to seek proofs of their arrogance, their injustice, and their cruelty. However, to satisfy those who may read these assertions with doubt, I shall give the opinion of those who have had dealings with them. Lord Napier says, in a letter to Lord Grey in 1834, that " the Tartar government being in the extreme degree of mental imbecility and moral degradation, deeming themselves to be the only people on the earth, being entirely ignorant of the theory and practice of international law, that government is not in a position to be dealt with or treated by civilized nations according to the same rules as are acknowledged and practised among themselves." Sir John Davis, Sir George Bonham, and Lord Elgin, have had ample proof what faith is to be put in promises, even when signed and sealed by solemn treaty. The official organ, called by foreigners the *Pekin Gazette*, is a tissue of exaggerations and falsehoods, issued for the purpose generally of deceiving the people. Poor Keying was about the best of the mandarins that foreigners ever came in contact with. The Emperor and his advisers, while acknowledging the decay of the government and the demoralization of the people, degraded him as a wretch without shame, guilty of cowardice and incapacity to the last degree. He was appointed one of the Imperial High Commissioners, deserted his post at Tientsin, to make explanations to the

[1] For more information regarding Chinese officials, the reader is referred to the works of Staunton, Davis, Meadows, and Huc.

Emperor, and was sentenced to death while Lord Elgin was in China.

There was Seu, the Viceroy of Canton; to him may be attributed nearly all the trouble of the empire; he reported the rebellion quelled, and prevented steps being taken to stop it, just as it was getting to its height. He reported victory upon victory, instead of defeat after defeat. It was this mandarin who prevented the entrance of foreigners into the city of Canton, when, by treaty, the English had right of access; for this he was held in honour by those who are inimical to foreigners, and five splendid triumphal arches to commemorate the event were, by Imperial permission, erected around Canton. Some of these were destroyed after Canton was captured. It was under his administration that Governor Amaral, of Macao, was basely murdered, and the proofs of Seu's participation are circumstantial.

At Foochow, bank notes are current, and there, as elsewhere, it sometimes happens that the bankers are unable to meet their engagements. In 1855, several banks were in this position, and as the people were heavy losers, they clamoured vociferously at the offices, and even commenced pulling down the houses; the mob was too strong for the mandarins. On the first day, the soldiers, who should have been ready, could not be mustered, but enough were assembled next day to clear the streets, which they did effectually by beheading those who were the largest holders of notes, and taking the others prisoners! The beheading was openly performed in the public streets, without trial, and caused great consternation. A petition was got up and presented to the viceroy, demanding the release of the other prisoners, but no attention was paid to the request.

Monsieur Callery, who should know a good deal of the

mandarins, having had intercourse with them when attached to the French Legation in China, and has had ample opportunities of learning from numerous Roman Catholic missionaries who have resided in the country, says, "An ordinary Chinese lies often: a mandarin always lies."

Of the cruelties of the mandarins we shall have samples enough when we treat of the insurrection; and some of their unmitigated falsehoods will then be clearly exposed. A case that created a considerable sensation at the time will serve to illustrate their character, and at the same time show the broad contrast between the English and Chinese officials. At the latter part of 1847, at a time when the mandarins had been instigating the people against us, six Englishmen were basely murdered near Canton. This caused great excitement among all foreigners in China; and at Shanghai, where the people had been very peaceable, we were congratulating ourselves that we did not run such risks as those that beset our fellow-countrymen in the southern part of China. The congratulatory feeling had scarcely passed away when we were disturbed by some vagabonds belonging to the Grand Canal grain junks, which had been thrown out of work by some damage to the canal, owing to which the grain tribute had that year, contrary to custom, to go to Pekin by sea. The Rev. Dr. Medhurst, accompanied by Dr. Lockhart, and some other missionaries, were at Tsingpoo, a city near the hills, about twenty-four miles from Shanghai; a band of these grain-junk vagabonds were in the neighbourhood, and had been plundering the poor people. They attacked the worthy missionaries, and very nearly killed Dr. Medhurst. All were considerably, but not dangerously hurt. They got back to Shanghai, however, and complained

to the British consulate. The consul, Mr. Alcock, an
officer possessing a thorough knowledge of the Chinese
character, demanded that the ringleaders should be seized,
identified, and punished. The mandarins pleaded inability and weakness, stating that the rioters were a powerful body of men, and could not be loosely treated with ;

Bridge near Tsing-poo.

but Mr. Alcock insisted on the men being taken, and, in
conjunction with Captain Pitman of H.M.S. " Childers,"
arranged that the port should be blockaded until the
culprits were brought forward. The Taou-tai was told
that not one of the four hundred junks, with grain for
the Imperial tribute, should leave the port. Mr. Interpreter Parkes, who has since greatly distinguished himself at Canton, boldly delivered a notice to the above
effect on board of each of the junks. It must be borne
in mind, that at this crisis there were only the "Childers"
and a merchant vessel in port, and the foreign community did not then number 100 souls. The crews of the

Government grain junks must have numbered 15,000 men. After the blockade continued some days, the mandarins produced ten men, but none could be recognised. Another batch was afterwards brought forward with like results : the prisoners were probably old jail-birds. Mr. Alcock desired the captains of the opium-receiving ships at Woosung to be in readiness to move up to Shanghai, to protect foreign property in case of need. The junks attempted to move, but the first were boarded and sent back. Other vessels, not containing grain, were allowed to depart. The mandarins at length hit on the expedient of despatching some of the junks empty down the river, and sending grain to them in boats. This was discovered, and many a hard chase had the " Childers'" boats after them, firing blank charges to bring them to. H.M.S. " Espiègle" luckily arrived, and relieved us of a good deal of anxiety by adding to our force ; but as no satisfaction could be got from the local authorities, Mr. Alcock boldly decided on despatching her to Nankin (that city had not then been taken by Tai-ping-wang), with the vice-consul and Mr. Parkes on board, to communicate to the Governor-General his desire that the offenders should be produced, and that the Imperial Government would be *minus* the grain until they were forthcoming.

No sooner had the " Espiègle" sailed, and her destination become known, then the Taou-tai found that his deceit was discovered, and that he must be on his mettle to get the right men in their right places. There was great excitement ; some of the junks made an attempt to force the blockade; but Captain Pitman, who had displayed exemplary patience for nearly a fortnight and who, with his men, had worked hard in the boats night and day, at length thought the time had arrived for serious action and round-shot. Down came coolly one or two of the junks to pass the " Childers," as if there had been no blockade, when bang went a shot across the bows, splashing the water over her bluff entrance; round she came, and over went her anchor; a boat boarded the next, and down went her anchor too. It was rare fun to see the jolly-boat, with two boys and a middy, dash up to a huge junk, and to see it come round instanter. One or two of the junks were placed in-shore of the brig, and kept close prisoners.

The Taou-tai had managed by force or bribery to get hold of nine of the delinquents. They were identified, tried, and sentenced to a month in the *cangue*, had to parade the foreign ground daily, and then to go to the " cold countrie." Fine-looking fellows they were, standing nearly six feet, with more of the Tartar look than of the Chinese. An officer, high in rank, came down to Shanghai after the " Espiègle" visited Nankin. He was a jolly-looking fellow, but appeared to be *incog.*, as he was not in the mandarin dress when he made his complimentary visit. The blockade was taken off, and the junks got under weigh. Mr. Alcock and Captain Pitman received the thanks of the community, and both deserved much credit for their able management of an unpleasant affair. There was no further trouble about this matter; we moved about the country in all directions without the slightest difficulty. Had the same bold and dignified attitude been taken at Canton, our relations with the Chinese officials there might have been on a very different footing, and another war possibly averted.

The list of high officials who misconducted themselves during and since the first war with the English might be multiplied *ad infinitum*. Davis says—" The mandarins were by no means loth to be the disbursers of the vast sums raised to protect the country, as they contrived to embezzle thousands themselves."

Eleepoo, one of the commissioners at Nankin for the English treaty, was a Tartar. The Chinese charged him with cruelty. Sir John Davis gives him credit for being honest to a certain degree. He called for his own punishment for being forced to submit to the English ; and was banished as a common convict.

Yeu-Puh-Yuen, another of the commissioners (a Chinese), was executed.

Keshen, at one time acting at the head of the army on the north bank of the Yangtze-Kiang, has had his share of good and bad fortune. He had been an imperial commissioner, and amassed immense wealth by extortion, &c. He was degraded ; his fortune, estimated at ten millions sterling, was confiscated ; he lost all his family ; his whole seraglio was put up to auction— wives, concubines—and all ! After this he got a post of honour at Thibet, where we had news of him through M. Huc. He has been degraded since the Rebellion began.

Yeu-Keen, another Tartar, during the English war, Davis calls " the most savage and remorseless brute that among several others disgraced his name and nation." He flayed one of his English prisoners alive. This wretch poisoned himself.

Yeh-Shan, a Tartar, commissioner at Canton, was sent as a criminal to Pekin, and banished.

Lin[1] filled the same office ; and during that time several thousands died in prison.

---

[1] Gutzlaff, in his *Life of the Emperor Taou-Kwang*, tells us of Lin's doings in an insurrection in the west : " He marched against the people, who, according to his own confession, had been excited to insurrection by

Since the Revolution began there is not a single mandarin of any note, who has been opposed to the rebels, that has not been degraded.

Seu-Kwan-Tsin, after holding the highest posts, was sentenced to be beheaded.

Sai-Shang-ah, the next Tartar general, met the same fate ; but in both cases, I believe, the sentence was remitted.

Heang-Yung, the Chinese general at Nankin, was several times deprived of his rank.

The reports these generals and others sent to Pekin are most ridiculous, if we may judge of them by the samples published in the *Gazette*. The Viceroy of Pih-che-le, and the redoubted Shing-Pou, who were chiefly employed in the north, exterminated all the rebels *several* times ; and when they were sent to retake Ching-Kiang-foo were, *of course*, successful, but " on account of the narrowness of the streets, the general thought it *more prudent* to encamp outside of the barrier ! That happened in July 1853. The rebels held it for four years afterwards.

At Yang-Chow, Keshen once reported a great victory. The rebels, he said, made an attack with 1000 men, out of which he killed upwards of 1000, and took 400 prisoners ! Heang-Yung had only 17,800 men; Keshen, and the Viceroy of Pih-che-le, had only 17,000, and Hwuy-Ching had only 11,000. The moving army of

rapacious functionaries. His whole course from first to last was marked by blood-thirsty treachery. He inveigled the people into his power by false promises, and then butchered them, or burned them alive. Thus he expected to quell the insurrections, but the aborigines fought with desperation, and he was obliged to return several times to finish the work of extermination. It was a costly war ; the Chinese soldiers were cut off by hundreds, and the victory would have been doubtful, if the never-failing panacea, silver, had not been properly applied."—Page 242.

Tartars, &c., to check the rebels as they went north, numbered only 24,000. In June 1853 the besiegers of Nankin, Yang-Chow, &c., report the slaughter of 15,850 rebels in one month, while the rebels in fact at that time were nearly always victorious !

Le-Suy, who commanded Tchang-Chow, the city nearest to Shanghai, was called a cowardly and incapable general, because he reported that the walls were in a dilapidated condition and useless for defence. He was degraded to the rank of captain.

Yeh-Kee, a cousin of the Emperor, was degraded to the condition of a common soldier for cowardice when the rebels were near Tien-tsin. The Lieutenant-Governor of Hoopeh was beheaded because the rebels took Woo-Chang, its capital, a second time.

The general commanding near the Poyang Lake, early in 1855, was ordered to be executed for reporting a victory when he had actually been defeated. We can put little faith in what the generals report, but credit may be given to the following proclamation, as most surely it would not have been issued without cause ; it represents the troops to have been as bad as the generals, and was posted for the instruction of the soldiers near Ching-Kiang-foo.

" Besides the scamps who follow the army, and, in the name of the troops, perpetrate gross outrages, there are many in the army whose conduct is perfectly detestable. Every day I hear complaints of robbery and rape by the regular soldiers. Robbers even, who have nothing to eat, and have no wives, are thought unfit to live when detected in committing crimes ; but you, soldiers, who eat the people's taxes, who have money and wives, how can you, so much less excusable than robbers, expect to escape death if you persist in such flagitious misdemean-

ours ?   Are your hearts at ease ?   Dare you look up to
heaven ?   If your property were carried off and your
wives ravished, would you not be incensed ?   I exhort
you to repentance.   If you do not give heed to what I
say, but continue your evil practices, you certainly will
be put to death !" [1]

The soldiers around Shanghai were equally bad.   The
country was almost desolated in their neighbourhood ;
the Chinese flocked to the foreigners' quarters for protection.   The poor people who could not afford to leave
their little farm-steadings endeavoured to make known
that they were under foreign protection, by pasting on
their doors, paper with foreign writing on it ; no matter
what it was, such as marks from tea-chests, pages out
of an old *Illustrated News*, and other scraps of paper.
The French Consul allowed the tricolor to be hoisted
over villages occupied by Roman Catholics.   One Sunday we met two men struggling with each other on the
foreign ground ; on going up to see what was the matter,
one of them said he was going to take the other to the
camp, as he had stolen his hat.   I asked him rather to
take the man to the British Consulate, but the fellow
insisted, and unbuttoning his coat, showed a soldier's
dress.   I persuaded him to go to the militia guard-house
close by ; he promised to settle the matter there, and we
went on.   When we returned we found a man lying
close to the spot where we had left the two in dispute ;
he was not recognisable, for, unfortunately, his head was
off !   I have no doubt a military act of summary juris-
diction had been executed, and the soldier got his reward
for bringing in the head of a " traitor."

A Chinese battle is as good as a farce.   Some of the
little fights at Shanghai were very amusing.   One day,

[1] Dr. Macgowan's Notes, published in *North China Herald.*

when a great many soldiers were out, I saw more of the combat than was pleasant. Having got into the line of fire, I was forced to take shelter behind a grave, the bullets striking the grave from each side every second. Why they came my way it was difficult to discover, for they *ought* to have passed on the other side of a creek, about twenty yards distant, to the people they were intended for ; but to see the dodging of the soldiers, then of the rebels, each trying to evade the other, was almost amusing. One fellow, ready primed and loaded, would rush up the side of a grave-hillock, drop his matchlock over the top, and without taking aim, blaze away. There is no ramrod required for the shot they use, the bullet or bar of iron is merely dropped in loose upon the powder. There was a fine scene on an occasion when the Shanghai rebels made a sortie : one of the men was cut off by an Imperial skirmisher, who had his piece loaded. The rebel had no time to charge his, so he ran round and round a grave, which was high enough to keep his enemy from shooting him when on the opposite side. Hare-hunting is nothing to it: Red-cap described hosts of circles, and the Royalist was fast getting blown, when the gods took pity on his wind, for, by some unlucky chance, the rebel tripped and fell ! The soldier was at him in a moment, and, to make sure of his prize, put the muzzle of his matchlock to Red-cap's head, fired, and took to his heels as fast as he could go ! It is difficult to say who was most astonished, when Mr. Red-cap did exactly the same ! The bullet that dropped down readily on the powder, fell out as easily when the barrel was depressed. The rebel got off with a good singeing of his long hair.

There were frequently, however, some very ugly wounds ; and where surgery is at such a discount, the poor wounded must suffer severely.   The Chinese rarely, if ever, amputate.   They use strong drawing plaster to extract the ball.   The missionary hospitals at Canton and Shanghai, under the able charge of their indefatigable managers, Drs. Hobson and Lockhart, as also that under the good care of Dr. Parker, late plenipotentiary for the United States to China, did great good.   Indeed it is impossible to tell what grand results may follow the labours of these gentlemen ; their hospitals were often crowded with wounded, soldiers chiefly being benefited by their skill.   There were frequently fights close to Dr. Lockhart's hospital, and men of both parties have been carried thither.   Dr. Hobson relieved upwards of 1000 Canton soldiers, and his reputation is far spread.   Even the mandarins have deigned to notice his aid.   True to their usual policy towards foreigners, they give the barbarian no credit ; but his services were so great that they could not be passed over ; so they selected a Chinese lad, who was a sort of medical pupil, and paid assistant at the hospital, and dubbed him mandarin of the sixth rank.   A grant of land for an hospital would have done more good.

CHAPTER XIV.

PRISONS AND PUNISHMENT.

Horrors of a Chinese prison—Prisoners nailed together—Prisoner in a cage—Starving to death—An address to the throne—Salutary interference of Lord Elgin—Instances of fatal effects of ill-usage—Various kinds of torture—Imitation of official cruelty—A poor wretch saved—Curious customs regarding wives—Deliberate act of vengeance—Other instances of the like kind—Flogging big boys—A servant flogging his master— More cruelties—Life for life—Gods in the rain.

JUSTICE is depicted blind, but in China, the bandage that darkens the eyes should cover the ears also. The horrors of a Chinese prison are so great that prisoners, deeming death an escape, go with apparent contentment to the place of execution. In Shanghai, I have seen them crammed like wild beasts in a cage, rolling about in the midst of filth and disease, begging for food. In the depth of winter, prisoners are chained to each other in strings, one of them not unfrequently hanging dead to his comrades! Once a party of pirates were seized and landed near the foreign houses; there had been a deficiency of chains, so the poor wretches were joined together with a large nail clenched through the hand of each! At Foochow, I met a prisoner whom they were carrying into the city, in a cage barely large enough to contain his body, cramped up in a sitting posture; two of the bars at the top had been cut to allow his head to pass through, every jostle or stop in the movement of his

K

bearers causing his neck or face to be dashed against the broken bars. It is in the recollection of Canton residents, when four men were placed in the *cangue* with a guard around them, and publicly starved to death in the open streets!

No matter how good the laws may be; let us see how they are carried out, and not judge of the country by its maxims or its rules. I will not even grant that these are always correct. Sir George Staunton gives us the following translation of an address to the throne from the Foo-Yuen of Canton regarding the prisoners in that city :—" Among the prisoners, many had been brought up from the country under charges of theft, murder, and the like, accompanied by the *witnesses and accusers* respectively concerned,—the cognizance of their offences having been referred to the magistrate of the provincial capital ; but whether the parties were more or less implicated, the charges serious or trifling, it was usual to expose them for many months, or even a year, to the hardship of a tedious and indiscriminate confinement, in authorized places of detention. These were employed to enforce by oppression and arbitrary confinement, nothing less than a system of fraud and extortion. I hastened to remedy this grievance, but already many persons had perished under confinement, and the inhuman nefarious practice has been so long established, that it is difficult to ascertain the year in which it originated, or conjecture how many lives have been lost by its contrivance. To two women curators, all the female prisoners who had not yet received sentence or been discharged were committed ; and the younger part of them were not unfrequently let out for prostitution, and the wages thereof received by the curators as a part of their regular profits." The character of the present holders of similar appointments leads us to suppose that the practice referred to still exists in many places.   It even existed for some time after the British flag waved over Canton, until Lord Elgin insisted upon the Chinese governor putting a stop to it.[1]

Out of 500 banditti some years ago in the prisons of Nanshaou (Kwang-Tung), 300 sickened.   Hundreds of prisoners are reported to die annually from ill-usage in the jails.   In 1829, the Governor of Canton reported that one of the prisons had been burnt through carelessness, along with twenty-one of the prisoners confined in it.   The Emperor suspected " that illegal torture had been applied to the prisoners, or that something had been done by the governmental officers, the traces of which they wished to obliterate by consigning all to the flames."   He must have had a fine opinion of his officers !   During the famine, when I was in Shanghai, in the winter of 1849, the prisoners were put upon such short allowance that they actually threatened to *break out* if more food was not given to them.   Poor wretches, how were they to break off their chains !

The tortures for confession are too revolting to enumerate, and many of the punishments are worse,—dismembering, emasculation, flogging in all its horrible varieties, kneeling on hot chains, &c. &c., form but a mild portion ; the most frequent is bambooing on the inside of the thighs, and exposure in the *cangue.*

The people sometimes ape the cruelties of their rulers. I remember an instance of the creditors of a man hanging him up by his great toe to extract payment ; and I once cut down a poor wretch I discovered with his hands tied behind his back, and hung up by his thumbs.   He

[1] Mr. Wingrove Cooke's " China, 1857-1858," gives most interesting particulars of the Canton prisons.

had been in this state for six hours, could hardly get his arms back to their usual position, and his hands were purple, the fingers as thick as wrists: he had only been *suspected* of going to steal!

There are some curious customs existing in China regarding punishments to unfaithful wives, and concerning marriage generally. Men, on leaving home for a long period, sometimes sell their wives, or lend them during their absence; this, however, is only among the poorer classes. I know a man that killed his wife. She was young and handsome, but he doubted her faithfulness. The gay Lothario suspected was the son of one of his most intimate friends. He pretended he was called away on business, made all the preparations for a long journey, and invited his friends, including some relations of the suspected party, and him also, to a feast at an adjacent tea-house. Supper being over, he started for his boat, bidding the guests good-bye. Late at night he returned home, armed, and with two trustworthy servants, he had arranged for his entrance into the seraglio; his other wife was sister of the young lover, and connived at the connexion. His worst fears were confirmed. He stabbed to the heart the son of his friend, and dreading to slay his faithless wife with his own hand, made his servants destroy her, and then having cut off the heads of the guilty couple, marched off with them to the magistrate to report the occurrence. An extraordinary trial then took place, by order of the mandarin, to prove the truth of the man's testimony. A large tub was procured; in this was placed a quantity of water and some lime. The two heads were then put into the tub, and the water quickly stirred round. The result was satisfactory. The guilty heads spun round in the centre, with their faces lovingly towards each other, and the unfortunate husband returned tranquilly to his deserted home, the mandarins rewarding him with 20,000 cash for doing an act of justice. He is now a wealthy merchant in Canton, a native of Chin-Chew, and rather a fine-looking Chinaman.

Many of the oldest residents in Shanghai will remember the man who dragged his wife into the water at the Soochow Creek, and held her there till she was drowned, the Chinese not interfering. Husbands have a certain power of life and death over their wives, and fathers over their children. The children, however, seem to behave very well, and it is rare to see them punished. I once saw a very old man give his great lout of a son, a full grown man, a good sound thrashing. The fellow offered no resistance, nor did he attempt to run away, stood quietly, but blubbering like a child while his father laid on with a stick. It was ridiculous to see the great booby crying; but the northern men are very much given to it. When there has been a fight in the street, you generally find the combatants in tears; and if there is a coolie doing something particularly vexatious, and an angry foreigner gives him a good " punch in the ribs," the Chinaman will drop down and have his cry. The southern people are different, and will even resist a blow. There is a story told of a gentleman in Canton, with a stronger mind than body, who attempted to chastise his servant, but the celestial valet locked the door, and gave the master more than he bargained for. The cruelties perpetrated by high government officers, under the head of punishment, are startling. It is sufficient to allude to the shocking case of Captain Stead, whom that wretch Yeh-Shun skinned alive. Some of the rebels at Shanghai, when captured, were tatooed to death. The people are almost as bad when their evil passions are let loose, though they are generally peaceable. The six young Englishmen who were killed by them at Hwang-Chu-Kee, in 1847, were barbarously murdered; but at that time the authorities had been instigating the people against foreigners. In mentioning this last case, we cannot too strongly press on the public notice the dangerous precedent that was then allowed to be established. Our authorities acknowledged or acted upon the Chinese principle of life for life. Six Englishmen were killed: the Chinese said they had killed two natives, and made up the balance of six by four prisoners out of the jails, as it is supposed. Now, it should not have been "life for life" that we should have exacted, for hundreds must have been guilty, and scarcely one suffered. The village should have been razed to the ground at the time—a blot of desolation left as a monument, over the ground once occupied by Hwang-Chu-Kee.

But enough of this dismal subject. Before closing, however, we must not forget to tell that the gods themselves sometimes come under man's displeasure, and suffer punishment. The Chinese are a most practical people, and have their own way of doing things. While distress existed in the neighbourhood of Ningpo, in 1849, on account of inundations and continued rain, the magistrates went frequently to a temple to implore the gods to be more sparing of their watery bounties. At last, when the weather looked as if it were about to clear, the priests recommended an unfailing remedy; they told the magistrates to put the gods *out in the rain*, and see how they liked it! This was accordingly done, and fair weather followed!

CHAPTER XV.

THE INSURRECTION.

Frequency of former revolutions—Peculiar character of the actual insurrection—New kind of Christianity—Scepticism of foreigners regarding the religious character of the movement—Same feeling on the part of officials exposed and condemned—Difficulty of arriving at truth—Two distinct rebellions—The Triads—The Dagger-men—Mode of recognition—Secret societies dreaded by the mandarins—The English war and the internal troubles—Forces on paper—Volunteers—Amour not love—Origin of insurrection—The first converts—Effect of a missionary's tract—Preaching of Hung-siu-tsuen — Fung-yun-san's first congregation — Religious belief—Yang, the eastern king—Obligation on Christians to consider the religious movement in China—Unjust interference of foreigners.

THOUGH the empire of China has existed for so many ages, and its line of emperors can be traced back almost to the days of Peleg and the " confusion of tongues," it, too, has had its share of troubles, caused by the ambition or the wickedness of man. No country has undergone so many revolutions. It has spread gradually like circles in water disturbed by the throwing of a pebble; and, like these circles, as its extent increased, the line of its boundary became less distinct. There are tributary princes and tribes, then chiefs, who merely occasionally own the sway of the Chinese emperor, and on the outer borders are those who dispute it. From contentions among themselves, then from the Mongols, and at last from the Mantchoos, the Chinese may be said never to have enjoyed peace. With an elasticity of character peculiar to themselves, and without being fatalists, they take little heed of any distant commotion, and seem to think that " sufficient unto the day is the evil thereof."

Blessed with the forms of a government which, in theory, is considered perfect, the Chinese have seen their conquerors adopt the same groundwork, and no leader of an insurrection has ever dared to dispute the theoretical correctness of the constitution, but has based his reasons for the overthrow of the throne he would usurp, on the plea that it was held by a tyrant, a debauchee, or a foreigner. All despots run equal risks. When we consider that the majority of the first rulers of China endeavoured to improve the condition of the people, and the brightest periods of Chinese history have been cotemporaneous with the rule of native princes, we need not wonder at their pertinacious adherence to ancient forms. A country that chronicles the institution of government works which were undertaken before the Greek or Roman empires existed, and can even point to large public undertakings for the common good, begun so early as the days of Abraham, may well be expected to look with reverence on bygone days.

But within the last few years, a poor scholar has struck a blow against the reigning dynasty that has made it totter on its throne ; not only does he revolt against the government, but he has preached a crusade against idolatry—his followers carrying out his iconoclastic measures with the utmost rigour. Strangest of all, a species of Christianity was preached by them, as consistent in its form as that of some sects known in England. This phase of the revolution is so strange, that we find, especially in China, more foreigners disposed to question the possibility of the Chinese becoming Christians, than to rejoice in happy appearances justifying a contrary anticipation.

Would that I had power to write more strongly than I do against those who hold up the Chinese to such scorn, that they believe none are good enough to become even "almost Christians."

Some there are, too, who look on the Chinese as mere parcels of humanity to make money out of, and while charging them with dishonesty, yet trust them more than they would their own brothers. We cannot be surprised at mercantile men railing against the revolution, as, doubtless, it interferes with their trade, and would especially do so, if the rebel prohibitions of opium-smoking were carried out. The earnest zeal of those really good men who remain as missionaries in China, striving to do good while surrounded with difficulties, is partly encouraged by the flickering sparks of good that emanate from some of the rebel publications. The backwardness of some of our government officials has prevented these sparks being fanned into a blaze of light. They have most aided in attempting to prove that error was blasphemy ; and instead of fostering the flame, have endeavoured to hide the light, and let China remain almost in pagan darkness. Their ideas of their own power and opinions seem to cast Providence into the shade, and the extraordinary proceedings of the rebels in publishing God's Word, in a country where it was all but a sealed book, is looked upon by them more as a crafty device on the part of the leaders, than as an act that is likely to be of everlasting importance to the Chinese race.

What will be the feelings of the people whose countries they represented, should the result of the insurrection prove that it was the beginning of a real Christian crusade, scoffed at and doubted, while we waited for tangible proof of its success ? Who will have to answer

for the tardiness of the aid which might have saved so
much bloodshed ?   And in after years, when this revolution is commented upon by historians, what answer will
they find to the inquiry, " Why Christian nations did
not rather encourage, in some way, a people who proclaimed Christianity and the Decalogue, than render
assistance to their opponents, in more ways than one ? "
The blight of expediency grows like a parasite about
our politicians, pressing down that power of doing right
with might, which was once the Briton's boast.   We
have seen the rebellion struggle on in spite of all difficulties, and if it be eventually smothered, when shall we
again see such an opportunity for doing good in China ?

Uncertain and meagre are the accounts of the commencement or progress of the insurrection; the theoretical
conclusions of MM. Callery and Yvan do not aid us.
The superficial notice of the foreign plenipotentiaries
has given some assistance to our researches, but what
can we expect from the hasty visits of Sir George
Bonham and Mr. Maclean to Nankin, or even from
Lord Elgin's expedition up the Yangtze-Kiang, which
I refer to elsewhere.

To constant communications with many intelligent
Chinese, merchants, tradesmen, and literary men, both
in the north and at Canton ; to the copious translations
that have from time to time been made by intelligent
Sinologues, and to many other sources on which depend-
ence could be placed, I have had recourse before forming
the following opinions on the rise of the Rebellion.

In the first place, it must be distinctly understood
that there are, or were, at one time *two* Rebellions, the
chief of which is that headed by Tai-ping-wang.   This
has a moral as well as political reformation as its basis.
The other is formed by a host of leaders of secret so-

cieties, which have long been established to subvert the Tartar dynasty, and for the mutual assistance and protection of its members.

Glancing first at the last-named of these, it is sufficient to state that the societies bear the various denominations—San-ho-hwui, or Triads; Seou-taou-hwui, or Dagger Society; Pih-leen-keaou, or White Lily Society, now almost extinct; and the Hung-kea, or Hung-clan. They have secret terms and slang words, which can be used by the members; signs, too, made by the hand, such as prominently using three fingers to lift cups, &c., and leading questions, by which they can distinguish members who reply.[1] These societies have long been a terror to the mandarins; but the secrecy with which their proceedings are conducted, has led to a want of unity between the different lodges, thus causing great disorder when they took up arms against the Government. Each lodge had its proper officers, but there was no real head. It was arranged that whichever chief first took Canton should be the leader of all the bands.

The first success of the Rebellion may be mainly attributed to the system of corruption and deceit practised by the mandarins. They pocketed the pay of an army that was supposed to exist, but which consisted only of mock muster-rolls on paper. There was no force sufficient to withstand the increasing forces of Tai-ping-wang. He marched through the heart of the empire, from Kwang-si to Nankin, in a few months.

During the progress of the Rebellion, we have seen that the Government soldiers have been of little use, and that the chief checks sustained by the rebels have been from bands of *volunteers*, induced, by the high pay of wealthy men, to engage themselves against the enemies

[1] From Triad book of instructions, found on a prisoner.

of the Emperor. At Tien-tsin it was the volunteers who saved Pekin, when it was almost in the grasp of the insurgents. It was these "braves" who routed the Canton rebels, and inflicted their chief disasters ; and even the much-vaunted Tartar troops brought from the Amour,[1] were defeated the first time they met Tai-ping's followers.

The province of Kwang-si, where the insurrection originated, is naturally difficult to govern. The country is intersected by chains of high mountains ; the inhabitants, like nearly all Highlanders elsewhere, have an independent spirit, and will not submit to exactions or oppression, as the defiles of their native hills form secure places of retreat, from which they can defy the powers that be. Not only were the independent tribes under no restraint, but the people of different districts were scarcely under subjection. Local disturbances and clannish feuds were only increased by the disorderly military forces which were sent to quell them. Bribery served the purpose of the mandarins when affairs looked serious, and ill-judged oppression kept the sore from entirely healing. In seasons of scarcity, immediately anterior to the outburst of the revolution, one village robbed its neighbour, and the troops helped to rob both. In the country places, anarchy was let loose ; but it was not till the early part of 1850 that any of the unsettled people had force to take towns. The southern portion of the province was then in a state of complete disorganization. Numbers of different factions were in existence, but without any general leader. Kwang-Tung predatory bands infested some parts of the province, and villages formed by settlers from other districts, were looked upon with distrust by the people of Kwang-si.

In a small hamlet in Kwang-si were a few families,

---

[1] In a recent work on China, innocently translated " Love."

who, led by the teaching of two Canton men, had embraced the worship of the true God, discarded idols, and encouraged by the teaching and precepts of these two young men, humbled themselves before Shang-te, the Supreme Ruler, taking portions of the Scriptures, the Ten Commandments, and some fanatical ideas of their teachers, as their guide. Hung-siu-tsuen, the elder of these two men, had accidentally received a missionary's tract, which awakened the wild ideas of his excitable imagination. The good seed had fallen on fruitful ground. It only wanted careful culture to bring it to perfection; but this was wanting. Earnestly striving to gather information upon the all-engrossing topic of his mind, Hung-siu-tsuen procured further publications that had reference to it, and it is said even sought instruction from one of the foreign missionaries.

The result was, that Hung-siu-tsuen converted many people to his doctrines, and established congregations in the mountains of Kwang-si; bringing them to his way of thinking partly by the merit of the doctrines themselves, and partly by working upon the superstitious fears of the people. His assistant teachers were Fung-yun-san, a young man, native of the same district which gave birth to the leader,—to him the credit appears due of having first formed a congregation; Yang-siu-tsing, the Machiavelli of the future insurrection, married to a sister of the chief; and Seaou-Chaou-Kwei, a Kwang-si man, who married another sister. Their doctrine spread, and soon included among its adherents some leading men, who had both rank and influence; one was a literary graduate of high class, and another brought a number of his clan to join the worshippers of Shang-te. We find at one time ten of this clan (Wei) in high command.

It may naturally be supposed that in the disturbed state of Kwang-si this new sect would soon become implicated with some of the contending parties. Many who were in danger elsewhere took refuge among the followers of the new religion, willingly giving up the worship of their idols, and conforming to the rules established in their asylum. Such a change might readily be made by any Chinese except an actual priest, for there is so little real religion in the hearts of the people of this country, that conformity with the maxims laid down by the ancient sages is more thought of than the power of any idols. Long experience has proved to me that the Chinese, as a nation, are not idolaters in the strict meaning of the word. This may be a bold assertion, but when we find that all the blessings and calamities of the Chinese are traced by them to be rewards and punishments emanating from Heaven, that they implore the universal Creator to relieve them from their misfortunes, and beseech Him to endow them with plenty; when we consider that they have from time immemorial acknowledged a Supreme Power, and that their chief tribute is paid to Shang-te, the invisible God, there is good reason to place the graven images that some bow down to, merely in the same category as the saints and relics which meet with adoration as auxiliaries in even Christian religions. There is no real religion of the State, nor is there any religion of the heart among the people beyond the sway that is held over their minds by an all-searching Providence. Their temples and idols are propitiated by offerings; but when the hand is opened for charity, what other deity than Heaven is supposed to witness it; and there are few eastern nations more charitable than the Chinese.

By some strange infatuation, foreign missionaries,

jealous of the doctrines they wished to propagate, have tended greatly to confuse the minds of the Chinese by the complication of the terms used for the Almighty in the native language. The Roman Catholics ignored the Supreme Ruler (*Shang-te* of the Chinese), and preached their doctrines, using the title Lord of Heaven (*Teen-choo*). Then came the Protestants, who—strange as it may appear—evidently wished the Chinese to believe that they did not worship the same God as the Roman Catholics, and therefore chose a different term, but could not agree which term to use; the one party contending for the word *Shang-te*, while this was repudiated by the others, who upheld *Teen-choo*. One party wished the word *Shin* to be used, as it was more significant of a spiritual existence; but again it was argued that this word *Shin* meant evil spirits as well as good. A distinguished linguist, after a very short residence in China, and merely a slight knowledge of the language, came to the rescue, and proposed introducing a new word, and, to make the matter still more difficult, voted for the capital letter of the Greek Θεος being introduced for that purpose. The Chinese use something very like this character already, when they wish to obliterate writing, or end a sentence! *Shang-te* seemed, however, to be the term most in use, and was freely used in missionary tracts, &c.[1] The God-worshippers adopted *Shang-te* as their sole God, adding and employing the words, "Heavenly Father."

This digression brings us to a point at which the Insurrection became deeply interesting. The mandarins, being suspicious of the growing influence of the new sect,

---

[1] The Protestant missionaries in Shanghai, in their address to Lord Elgin, suggested that the term "Yay-Soo-Keaou," or the religion of Jesus, should be employed to describe the Protestant religion, as distinguished from the "Teen-Choo-Keaou" (religion of the Lord of Heaven), the designation of the Roman Catholics.

seized one of the members ; a remonstrance was made, but
without avail, and eventually an expedition was sent to
seize the leaders. This resulted in open defiance of the
Government. The different congregations were called
upon to assist. Rebel or robber bands joined the fast increasing forces ; a city was taken, and eventually a stand
was made at Yung-ngan, and the revolution began in
earnest,—the empire was the prize; Nankin was the goal.

The haughty ambition of Hung-siu-tsuen, or his conviction of his Divine mission, is the groundwork from
which we may yet see rise a glorious structure of heavenly
light. God grant that so it may be; but the wild growth
of insidious error seems to check in the bud the ripening
of the fruit so strangely planted. To Yang, afterwards
Eastern King, may be traced all the bad points of the
insurgent's creed, and to him are the impositions ascribed.
He acted the part of the hidden priest in their Delphic
Oracle, speaking as if he had the gift of prophecy, even
personating the Heavenly Father, and for a time assum-
ing, probably in ignorance of its meaning, the sacred
title of the Holy Ghost! He was at one time the most
prominent character in the whole rebellion, and evidently
had great power over the other chiefs, who, when fortune
did not follow so fast as it did in the early part of their
career, seem to have lost much of their original enthusiasm and simple-hearted goodness ; or perhaps like Yang,
as they grew in power, learned to be presumptuous.

> " Of all that breathes or grovelling creeps on earth,
> Most man is vain ! calamitous by birth :
> To-day, with power elate, in strength he blooms ;
> The haughty creature on that power presumes :
> Anon from Heaven a sad reverse he feels ;
> Untaught to bear, 'gainst Heaven the wretch rebels ;
> For man is changeful, as his bliss or woe :
> Too high when prosperous ; when distrest, too low."—
> POPE, *The Odyssey.*

Time will show whether the strange mixture of good maxims and dangerous error introduced by the self-taught propagators of a religion they scarcely understand, will be the commencement of a new era in China. Will God's Word, which has been rudely opened and disseminated by this wonderful faction, lie fallow and uncultivated, till it be properly taught to those who as yet only ignorantly believe? The time is most propitious; the Chinese are well prepared for some eventful change occurring to relieve them from the troubles in which their country is enthralled. It is only now that their language is becoming properly understood by an intelligent staff of Protestant missionaries; and it remains for the English Government to lead the way, by insisting on the withdrawal of restrictions, to let foreign enterprise open up China both to our commerce and our religion.

CHAPTER XVI.

TAI-PING-WANG AND THE INSURRECTION.

Tai-ping-wang and the progress of the insurrection—Who was the first rebel chief?—Teen-teh's execution—Connexion of the Tai-ping movement with secret societies—The different leaders—Dead alive—Repression of vice in the rebel camp—Christian doctrines—Blasphemous assumptions of titles by rebel chiefs, and other anomalies, explained—Exaggerated accusations—Expected results of the movement.

WHETHER the first name publicly mentioned as that of the rebel chief really represented more than a myth, or whether Teen-teh was the leader of a separate revolution, which may at one time have joined with Hung-siu-tsuen, is of little importance now. That character, if he ever existed, has passed into oblivion, and the celestial kingdom of Tai-ping, " universal peace," has taken the place of that which was to have borne the title of " heavenly virtue."[1]

Let us now trace the progress of the new faith, and watch the extraordinary delusions that arose from the ignorance of the teachers.

At Yung-ngan, Hung-siu-tsuen formed his court; the leader took upon himself the title of emperor, or Tai-ping-wang; and, according to Callery's version of Teen-teh's confession, the latter held a short-lived second position in the affairs of state; but Yang-siu-tsing, who was dubbed the eastern king, was the chief that had

[1] For further information regarding the commencement of the insurrection, see Appendix A.

taken second rank to the new emperor. Fung-yun-san, one of the original teachers, was made king of the south. He was a literary graduate of the rank of Siu-tsai. Seaou-chaou-kwei, the first western king, and Wei-ching the northern king, quite young men, were both natives of Kwang-si. The first-named is reported to have been killed accidentally by the explosion of a cannon at the siege of Chang-sha; but his name appeared in the rebel publications some time after the date of the above siege; and though his body was disinterred, and his remains scattered to the winds, according to the Imperial gazettes of March 1853, he was making proclamations in Nankin in May 1854! The assistant king, Shih-ta-khai, the Imperial edict says, ran away and was killed; and that the southern king was nowhere to be found. His Imperial Majesty is mistaken again. Fung-yun-san was in Nankin in February 1855; and Shih-ta-kai has been for several years one of the most active generals in the rebel army.

After the court was formed and the army embodied, there was a regular appointment of officers. We can scarcely expect that a hastily collected body of men should at once become converts to the religion of the leaders, and conform to the strictness of the rules inculcated; but nothing seems impossible to Chinamen; and when the fear of punishment hangs over them, they will perform extraordinary actions. There appears to have been no punishment in the rebel camp but *death;* and, with determined men to execute it, an army of bold men will soon be formed when they know what awaits them if they run away. Plunder, rape, opium-smoking, and even the use of tobacco and wine, were prohibited under the same penalty. The Ten Commandments were similarly enforced.

A belief in the heavenly Father, and Jesus Christ as the Saviour, was enjoined; and there is nothing whatever in the rebel publications or proclamations that can be cavilled at by any liberal-minded Christian, *so far as the doctrine taught is concerned*, and if it were not for the titles the chiefs have adopted, we might hail with gladness the promulgation of the religion preached and taught by the insurgents. The chief Tai-ping-wang taking the rank in the universe next to the Saviour, and pretending a direct descent from heaven, may not have appeared strange to the Chinese mind, considering the titles the Chinese emperors have always assumed. That he even pretended to such a relationship when he called himself the second son of God, was, doubtless, only done to assist his power, for knowing that he had real relations and connexions in the camp, and a host of original followers, who knew him as a poor teacher, how could he suppose his title would have been admitted, except as a title of rank; and further, when the other kings have the titles conferred upon them, of the third, fourth, fifth, and sixth sons of the Most High, not one being related to the other, why should we charge the men with blasphemy, when it is only their mode of showing their superiority to others in the world, who are daily taught to call upon the Almighty as " *Our* Father who is in heaven."

Why should we scout the cause on account of an ignorant assumption of titles, which, perhaps, drew respect to men who were fighting a hard fight to proclaim the worship of the one true God ?

" The heavenly Father is the Holy Father in heaven; the heavenly Elder Brother is the Holy Lord, the Saviour of the world. Only the heavenly Father and the heavenly Elder Brother are holy. From this time forth let the

troops address Us as Lord[1] simply; they must not
entitle Us holy, thereby offending against the heavenly
Father and heavenly Elder Brother."[2] We know that
they published and spread broadcast the Holy Scriptures
as given to the Chinese by Protestant missionaries—
distributed tracts that are almost exact counterparts of
those issued from the mission-press; did this not only
among their own followers, but even floated numbers of
their publications in tiny barks down the stream among
the fleets of their enemies; when we know that they
destroyed idols wherever they were found, can we doubt
that they were trying to pave the way for a change
which the most sanguine Christian never expected would
be accomplished for ages ? but which may yet happen
in our day.   They used new words for " soul," for the
" Spirit Father," and also coined a new word as a title
for Yang.   As they used a term for the Spirit Father
different to that by which they called Yang, the Holy
Spirit and Comforter, it shows that the meaning given
to the apparently blasphemous title of Yang, had not
the importance we attach to it.   Thus we see the difficulties they have had to encounter, having to create new
words to express their ideas, and it must be remembered,
too, that the books of Scripture which they possessed
were by no means perfect translations, for it can scarcely
be expected that the missionary translators have mas-
tered all the difficulties of the Chinese language; and
even in rendering translations of the rebel publications, the difficulties have again to be encountered.   I

---

[1] Choo in the original.   It means sovereign, when used of kings and
emperors.—Meadows' *Chinese and their Rebellions*, p. 424.

[2] Extract from edict of Tai-ping-wang.

The Chinese Emperor is self-styled king of the universe.   " Heaven rules
above, the emperor rules below."   As he does not appoint officers to rule
out of China, his kingdom, for which Tai-ping-wang aims, may naturally
be only considered to be in the " Celestial Empire."

do not hazard this opinion without good authority, for Mr. T. T. Meadows, who has studied Chinese as deeply as any one, states not only that the Scriptures are badly translated,[1] but shows, that by the use of the term heavenly kingdom to represent heaven, the Tai-pingites were led by it to infer that China was meant, and *Tai-ping* is used to render the " peace on earth " which the heavenly host sang at the birth of Jesus.[2]

Some cavil at Tai-ping-wang having a harem ; but do they consider that such is part of the supposed requisite state of a Chinese emperor ; do they expect that these men are to become pure Christians before they have had time almost to read through the Bible, even supposing that they possess the whole of it ?   As far as we know, they have not published further than to the book of Joshua, and of the New Testament, merely the Gospel of St. Matthew.   Were there no harems mentioned in the Old Testament as part of the household of even the most righteous kings ?

Are the foolish questions or ridiculous answers of some of their raw followers, to be taken as criterions to judge of the good that may ultimately result from the propagation of the gospel among a people to whom it is strange ?   We should get curious replies if we questioned some of our own soldiers or sailors on the subject of theology.

Let the religious creed of the insurgents stand on its own merits.   It is perhaps well that foreign nations have not interfered.   Should the movement prove successful, none can lay claim to any of the honour attending it, or rob Him of the glory to whom it will be due. We shall be contented if foreign nations abstain from aiding the enemies of the revolutionists.

---

[1] *Chinese and their Rebellions,* p. 79.   [2] *Ibid.* p. 462.

Some people have scouted the insurgents for their massacre of the Tartars in Nankin, and murdering the Bhuddist priests ; it has been proved that both of these acts were greatly exaggerated : but even supposing that the sanguinary deed was no fiction, we have no right to judge the rebels by our own standard of mercy to the vanquished. We have only to look back to the history of men who were not further advanced in civilisation than the Chinese are at present, and we shall find many parallel cases, or even more frightful massacres. Take the Bible history of the Israelitish victories ; it would be difficult to find a more detailed statement of wholesale massacre than is to be found in the 10th chapter of Joshua—a book the rebels are known to possess.

It is not a small matter with which we have to deal : it is the wonder of the age, and the destiny of millions is at stake.

" Experience shows," says Locke, " that the knowledge of morality by mere natural light (how agreeable soever it be to it) makes but a slow progress, and little advance in the world. The greater part of mankind want leisure or capacity for demonstration, nor can carry a train of proofs, which in that way they must always depend upon for conviction, and cannot be required to assent to till they see the demonstration. Whenever they stick, the teachers are always put upon truth, and must clear the doubt by a thread of coherent deductions from the first principle, how long or how intricate soever that be. And you may as soon hope to have all the day-labourers and tradesmen, the spinsters and dairy-maids, perfect mathematicians, and to have them perfect in ethics this way ; hearing plain commands is the only course to bring them to obedience and practice ; *the greater part cannot know, so they must believe."* I contend, therefore, that at the commencement of the revolution, it matters little what are the abstruse doctrines believed in by the leaders (these can be remedied hereafter), so long as their followers are not troubled with the difficulties of the religion, but are taught to practise and obey the simple and sacred parts of the faith which they profess to believe.

The fact that they have published, and are still publishing, many parts of the Scriptures, is a striking one, and is difficult to account for on any hypothesis, but that those who do so are sincere believers in the book. No political prophet could have foretold that a body of revolutionists in China would have spread their opinions by the printing and circulating Christian books. We never expect to hear of Hindus or Malays, when commencing a warlike movement, adopting such a method of propagandism. To show that the effect of these books, and of the religion they teach, has been something more than ordinary on the moral condition of these people, we shall detail an interview with a former follower of Tai-ping-wang, whom we met at Shanghai. His name was Wang-fung-tsing. He had come into the city to join the rebel force that then held it ; but we believe he soon left them, dissatisfied with the state of affairs prevailing among his new friends. We met him in one of the Protestant Chapels. He told us that he had been baptized by Dr. Gutzlaff seven years before. A convert in Hong-Kong had taken in hand to instruct him in Christianity, had supplied him with a little money, and recommended him to unite himself to Dr. Gutzlaff's Christian Union. He became a member of that body till the death of its founder. He then proceeded, by the advice of his old friend, the convert, in search of other members of the Christian Union, who had then joined Tai-ping-wang, and were engaged in organizing an armed opposition against the Government. He joined them in time to be with the Tai-ping army on its march through the interior provinces to the important city of Woochang-foo. Favoured by a shower of snow, they took possession of that city, with the two adjoining ones, Han-Yang and Han-Kow, and then descended the Yangtsze-Kiang to Nankin. From this point he returned to Hong-Kong, and afterwards found his way to Shanghai. He told us, in answer to inquiries, that there is the administration of baptism in the Tai-ping army to men and women, old and young, by sprinkling. They have the Lord's Supper every month, and not upon the Sabbath day. At this ceremony they use wine made with grapes—a curious circumstance, grape wine scarcely ever being seen in

China (except in some interior provinces), showing the anxiety of these Christians to maintain as exactly as they know how, the creed and practice of Christianity. They admit new applicants for baptism after not more than a day's instruction. Twenty-four elders or *chang-laou* have the office of preaching assigned to them. There are also priests who superintend the sacrifices. The practice of offering sacrifices, they have unquestionably adopted from reading the Old Testament without guidance as to what parts of it are, and what are not, intended for imitation by Christians. He told us he met several men who had been baptized by Dr. Gutzlaff, holding posts of influence in the Tai-ping official staff. He denied, when asked, that he smoked opium, saying that it was forbidden strictly in the regulations of Tai-ping-wang. When the question was repeated, he replied, " How could I tell a lie, who am a disciple of Jesus ?" The effect of this interview was to strengthen our impression of the extent to which the imitation of Christian preachers was carried by these people. —Rev. J. EDKINS, *Religious Condition of the Chinese.* Routledge, London, 1859.

CHAPTER XVII.

THE MARCH ON PEKIN.[1]

The march on Pekin—Scarcity of grain excites anxiety in the capital—
First success of the insurgents—Favourable disposition of the people—
Several towns captured—Jews of Kai-Fung—Panic in ʻPekin—Siege of
Hwui-king—A descendant of Confucius slain by the insurgents—This
event serves the Imperialists—Frequent defeats of the latter—Movements
of the insurgents—Curious exposure of the state of the empire by a
Chinese official—Anger of the Government—Difficulty of obtaining
contributions—Odd expedients to raise money—Poverty of the Government, and its possible results.

EARLY in 1853, the northern part of Kiang-Soo and
the province of Shang-Tung suffered severely from famine,
—many of the people died in consequence of the great
distress. A deficiency in the supplies of grain caused
much anxiety in Pekin, and the Gazette at this period
has many warnings to dilatory officers in Che-Kiang
and elsewhere to hurry on supplies. It was even recommended by one censor, that a guaranteed fixed price
should be given at Tientsin, the port of Pekin, for rice
from Kwang-Tung and Fokien, so as to induce exports
from these provinces.

Under these circumstances, the rebel army made a
bold dash across the Yangtsze-Kiang, opposite Nankin,
within two months from the capture of that city. There
appears to have been no resistance until a large portion
of the army of the north had passed ; but when addi-

[1] In place of giving a written account of the march to Nankin, I have
provided a chart of the Rebellion, in which will be found particulars of
the route. This will show how much more serious the insurrection has
been than is generally imagined.

tional men were being sent, a Tartar force of picked troops was sent against them ; these were utterly routed, and all their camp *matériel* fell into the hands of the insurgents. Shortly before the northern march was attempted, there had been some local disturbances in the districts between Fung-yang and Nankin, and it was through these districts the route was taken. Up to this time, the people there seem to have had a leaning towards the new *régime*, for small parties of rebels passed to and from Lew-chow to Nankin, apparently unmolested, until they reached the camps of the besiegers at the former city, which was long held for Tai-ping-wang.[1]

Town after town was taken ; a resistance was made at Kwei-teh, where three generals were slain. Kai-fung-foo, the capital of Honau, fell an easy conquest to the victorious rebels, though their forces were divided before arriving thus far, one division securing an advance over the Yellow River (Hoang-Ho), by seizing the fords or passage near Y-Fung, a position which it would appear they retained to protect their retreat, and keep up their line of communication with the chiefs at Nankin. A glance at the map will show what a wise choice was made ; reinforcements could be sent either by the western route, or by the canal, and it will be seen hereafter how admirably this was arranged.

The city of Kai-fung-foo, famous for its Jewish synagogue, was inhabited by a small remnant of Israelites, who possess the traditions and writings in Hebrew of ancient date. This city has rapidly fallen from its former grandeur. The inroad of the rebel army must have completed the ruin of its dilapidated walls.

It is many years since the synagogue existed in full

---

[1] The insurgents left Lew-chow at the end of 1855.

power. Persecutions and religious restrictions probably went far to thin the ranks of the followers of the Tabernacle. An interesting account of the Jews at Kai-fung has been published at the mission press of Shanghai. Though the sect has nearly died out as such, there are many Chinese of evidently Jewish origin ; in Canton, especially, I have noticed their peculiar physiognomy ; and it is stated that the rearing of silk-worms was formerly a trade confined almost entirely to Jews.

How strange it must have been to those in Kai-fung-foo, who had seen the decadence of the Jewish congregation, to find their city suddenly beleaguered by a powerful army, marching successfully towards the capital, proclaiming obedience to the same ten heavenly rules that were held sacred by the insignificant sect which the insurgent publications held up as the people of the Great God's especial care !

It was here that a limit was put to the successful advance of the northern army. The Yellow River was crossed in the middle of summer ; and the wondrous speed of the rebel marches bid fair to place Pekin in their power ere the autumn ended. There was panic, distrust, and almost despair in the capital. Thirty thousand *families* had left it. In Canton the city of Pekin was considered doomed.

For some unknown reason the rebel army made a long siege of the city of Hwui-king, and thus lost so much time that their campaign in the north was extended into the winter. Their men must have suffered far more from the severity of the weather than from the force that was brought against them. It appears very probable that the siege of Hwui-king was purposely prolonged to attract troops from Pekin, which it did, though not to the extent expected.

The piercing cold of a northern winter, equal in severity to that of St. Petersburg, must have been a bitter enemy to the southern rebels, and militated against an attack on the capital. The disorganized state of Pekin at this time, as shown by the paper given in the following chapter, would have gone far to aid the insurgents in their siege. But no attack was attempted.

Appropriating the translation which appeared in the Shanghai newspaper, of a remarkable memorial published in the Pekin Gazette, we find what appears to be the true position of affairs in the capital. The memorial was printed without permission, owing to some irregularity, and caused no little stir among the officials connected with the Gazette.

The boldness of some of the censors in exposing the real state of affairs, is not unusual, though they often suffer for their temerity. Some of the most interesting documents relating to the Chinese are to be found in the outspoken criticisms of the honest censors. They doubtless often speak the real feelings of the people, and deserve much credit for openly exposing abuses, and not secretly making a tool of them for their own benefit. We see the seeds of true patriotism sprouting forth from the cold soil of a discouraged heart. While the rebels were within seventy miles from Pekin, the censor, Fungpaou, inspector of the central district of that city, humbly sets forth " the want of discipline in the military preparations for the defence of the capital, and the distressed condition to which the inhabitants are reduced. These matters he begs leave, with the utmost earnestness, honestly to set forth for the Imperial inspection." The memorialist proceeds carefully to state the real circumstances of the present time. " Now the things which are most confided in, to relieve the mind from apprehension, are the civic guards and the trained bands. All that the trained bands are good for, is just to catch a few paltry thieves, and all the guards accomplish consists in the apprehension of a few rebels ; but should any unforeseen emergency arise, both would be insufficient for defence. The soldiers of the capital, whether belonging to the Chinese or Tartar regiments, exist chiefly in name ; and since the approach of the insurgents to the neighbourhood of the metropolis, the best of these troops have been ordered off to the seat of war. Those which remain are merely such as have been considered unserviceable, together with those men temporarily engaged to supply vacancies. When the memorialist was on a tour of inspection, he observed that the number was deficient at every guard-house. This was the case wherever he went. Sometimes the watchmen and guards were found to be weak and incapable men, and when the memorialist remonstrated, the officers paid no attention to his remarks. When he came to look at the soldiers on guard at the different gates, he found them standing daily, from morning to evening, shivering with cold and hunger, exposed to the wind and the snow in a most distressed and miserable condition. On examining the weapons piled up there, he found that the greater part of them were useless.

" At present, the rebel camp is only seventy miles from the capital. Shing-paou and Tsang are by no means agreed in their views, and they have not yet succeeded in any plan for exterminating the insurgents. Tuh Lew (the rebel encampment) is only an insignificant place, and it may be easily conceived that the rebels will not remain there long. According to the confession of the spies, who are being apprehended every day, it appears that very many have come to the capital, where they hire houses, and secretly try to enlist persons in their cause. . . .

"Ever since the spring (of 1853), the officers employed about the court have been inventing excuses to get away from the capital ; and the rich inhabitants have removed, with their houses, to the extent of 30,000 *families.* In every street, nine out of ten houses are empty, and the residents are daily diminishing. Even in the north quarter of the city, where the population was previously very dense, in 1852 it was rated at 18,000 families, and now, though scarcely a year has elapsed, the number of families in the quarter in question does not exceed 8000. From one quarter, we may form some idea of the rest.

"On the 24th December, the memorialist had to superintend the distribution of cotton-wadded garments to the poor, when he found that the applicants were much more numerous than in former years,—especially in the eastern and northern quarter, where they had increased. When he inquired into the cause of this, he found that it originated in the absence of the rich families from the capital, in consequence of which the poorer classes could find no employment ; and the means of subsistence being procured with difficulty, poverty was the consequence. In fact, those who could not afford to remove, were obliged to starve and die. Moreover, the Board of Revenue being straitened for means, had petitioned the throne to be allowed to take a percentage from all rentals. The memorialist having to collect this percentage, has frequently seen with his own eyes the distressed and impoverished inhabitants, who had been accustomed to depend on the rental of a few small houses, in consequence of having no money, actually tendering their tenements in payment, saying,

that they found it difficult to procure food and clothing,
and, therefore, had no power to pay the percentage.
This is the case in every quarter of the city. Recently,
he has seen poor old women, almost naked, bringing,
with tears in their eyes, the cotton-wadded garments
which they had received in charity, to offer as money in
payment of the demand. If at such a time as this,
when it is difficult to know whether to be severe or
lenient—if the heads of the wards would inquire into
the circumstances of each family, they might carry out
the system of percentage ; but when the regular taxes
sometimes run short, it is not very suitable to be urgent
in demanding these extraordinary payments. . . .
Taking the five quarters of the metropolis, the sum total
collected during the month of December, from both
large and small houses, barely amounted to 15,000
strings of cash" (not 10,000 dollars) ; " now, if it be
impolitic uselessly to harass the people, without much
benefiting the Government, how much more impolitic
must it be to harass the people, and weaken the Government at the same time ?   The memorialist having been
a personal witness of these distresses, has felt deeply
grieved, and has frequently remonstrated with his
brother officers in their meetings for consultation, on
the above topics, when they merely looked at each other,
and fetched an empty sigh.   Now, the memorialist con-
ceives that the capital is a most important position,
and should be most strictly guarded ; the soothing
of the miserable and distressed inhabitants is also a
matter of extreme importance : he thinks that if he
were to study his own ease, and maintain silence from
day to day, he should be placing himself beyond the
pale of the imperial protection : and if he were to dread
the animadversions of his superiors in rank, he should

be making a very ungrateful return for all his majesty's bountiful favours. He therefore ventures to intrude on the Emperor's attention, with an honest statement of his views, requesting his majesty carefully to receive the admonitions afforded by heaven, and condescend to inquire into the condition of the people, reflecting at the same time on the difficulty with which his royal ancestors established the fortunes of their families, and the extremely important interests of the country at the present crisis." The good Fung-paou then makes some suggestions, and concludes thus, " The imperial protection and benevolence will then be duly appreciated by the people, and the blessing of heaven will descend equally on the monarch and on his subjects, which will cause the rebellion to be speedily quelled. The memorialist, relying on the sage-like intelligence of his sovereign, does not heed the animadversions of his fellow-officers, but sends up a faithful report in all honesty and simplicity, while with the most trembling anxiety he implores that the imperial glance may be cast upon it."

This is an interesting peep behind the scenes, and gives a valuable addition to our information of the state of the empire.

The Gazette of the third day following the appearance of the above memorial, stated that it had been published without proper authority, and ordered a strict investigation into the affair, naturally leading people to believe that the printer had added to and altered the statement sent in by Fung-paou. All the printers were seized, and several other parties examined. It appears that another censor had given in the document by mistake to be printed. Fung-paou must have been a sort of Joseph Hume; when he found out an abuse, he stuck to

M

it. He was called up to give an explanation how the
memorial got into the Gazette, but leaving Government
to find this out through their own resources, he set to
work, and brought forward a host of evidence, of papers
that should have been published, not having appeared
at all; reports of battles; Imperial orders, &c., all
omitted. He did not deny a word of the memorial
that was printed under his name. A month later, the
Gazette reported provisions to be scarce, because the
soldiers made a practice of seizing the conveyances, and
not paying for them, whereupon the carriers would not
bring either their carts or camels to the capital.

Rice became scarce, money too was wanting, and
various methods were proposed to meet the difficulty.
Iron, lead, and paper, were all mentioned as good sub-
stitutes for the ordinary currency.

The taxes throughout the empire came in slowly, and
the principal reliance was on contributions.

The system of obtaining contributions in times of
difficulty is a curious one. I have had it all fully explained to me by men who were contributors, but I
never expected to see it openly set forth in the Pekin
Gazette. Tsang-Kwo-fan, an officer of Kiang-si, proposed it early in 1854, and his recommendation was
adopted. His plan was to give out 4000 blank receipts
to certain officers for distribution to contributors to the
wants of the empire. Half of these receipts should be
entitled to certain minor offices, and the other half promised nominal literary honours. There was a new
order of merit established, too, at a later date, to in-
veigle subscribers, but the Gazette does not explain the
working of these plans. In the Canton province, where
the exactions were probably higher than in any other

the mandarins held a series of blank receipts, that is,
receipts filled in for certain amounts, say 2000 to 10,000
taels, but the *name of the payer* left blank. Most of
the wealthy men of the province had already bought
honours to their hearts' content, so there was little inducement for them to contribute farther until the new
plan was adopted. The richest people were called upon
for money, and, to relieve themselves, they might point
out other men of means, who were also squeezed to a
certain extent ; and in proportion to their payments,
they got blank receipts, which entitled them to honours
or rank they already possessed, but the name being left
blank, they were enabled to sell these honours to others,
certainly not getting nearly so much as they paid for
them, but still receiving something, and preventing their
contribution being a total loss. For instance, a button
of mandarin rank, that cost at one time $10,000 is now
procurable for about $2500. The rich man who pays
this $2500, anxious to get part of his money back, sells
his blank receipts for from $400 to $1000, to a man
desirous of the rank, and just fills in his name ; he pays
his respects to the mandarins, receipt in hand, and is a
blue-buttoned dignitary without further trouble, so that
a rank which formerly cost $10,000, is now procurable
for a mere percentage of that sum. When Shanghai
was besieged, Keih-ur-hang-ah, general in command,
once asked the chief native merchants to a grand entertainment; the excuses were numerous, as it was known to
be a meeting for the sale of buttons, and likely to prove
a dear dinner.

After the breaking out of the insurrection in Kwang-
Tung, and its subsequent spreading to Kwang-si, the
tribute available for the imperial treasury must have

been small indeed out of the revenues collected by the
now celebrated Yih, then viceroy of the two Kwang.
It was stated, however, in Canton, that he spent nearly
the whole of his private fortune before appropriating
any of the funds properly intended for imperial tribute.   Many other provinces were also in arrears with
their taxes; the insurgents held many of the most important points in the empire ; and the drying up of the
Grand Canal must also have crippled the resources of
Hien-Fung.

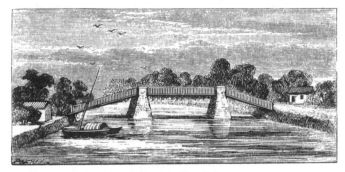

Bridge near Shanghai.

CHAPTER XVIII.

THE AMOY REBELS.

Movement not connected with Tai-ping-wang—Admiral Ma-gay ; his history—Cruelties of the Imperialists—Humane interference of English officers—A Chinese trial—An affecting incident—Battles arranged before-hand—Death of Ma-gay—The innocent and guilty punished alike—Rebels saved by a British ship.

THERE are so many conflicting accounts about the rising in Fokien, in 1853, that it is difficult to give any correct account of it. It had no direct connexion with Tai-ping-wang. At first the people were in favour of the overthrow of the Government, but when they had experience of the sort of rebels they had to deal with, and the cool appropriation of property for the common good, it was only the fear of punishment that kept them in arms. The insurrection died a natural death. The fighting chiefs were men of no standing. Their admiral at Amoy, one Ma-gay, had been a pot-boy in the service of a store-keeper on Koolang-soo, when the English troops held that island ; his military service consisted in serving the soldiers with grog and nuts. Afterwards he was under a renegade Neapolitan in a lorcha, and thus learned the naval tactics which brought him into supreme command of the rebel flotilla. When Amoy was attacked by the Imperial fleet, and the people and houses were suffering from the shot, he sent a message to the Chinese

admiral challenging him to an engagement of the two
fleets at a distance from the town, so that the poor inhabitants might not suffer. The Imperial admiral was
of a different opinion, and throughout the siege showed
strong symptoms of cowardice, lost many good chances,
and shirked fighting, " either from want of wind or inclination."

When the rebels first came to Amoy, nearly all the
people joined them : for this they afterwards suffered
severely. The mandarins showed no mercy. Women
had their breasts cut off, and as for heads and ears they
were as plentiful as buttons. One man was put into
a hole dug in the ground and packed up to his neck
with quick lime ; the lime was then slaked, and the
flesh burnt off his bones while he was alive. Supplies
fell short, and the rebels had to clear out ; many got
away in their fleet, but the people were seized, and a
wholesale massacre began. There was at first no trial :
every one was considered guilty. The Imperial fleet
was crowded with prisoners, whose heads began quickly
to be severed from their bodies, and the corpses thrown
overboard. Captain Fishbourne, of H.M.S. " Hermes,"
was there at the time : this was too much for him, and
he threatened to fire into any of the junks that continued the slaughter. The foreign residents, and a
party landed from the " Hermes" and " Bittern," endeavoured to stop the beheading that was going on in front
of the foreign houses. The men were being driven
down like sheep, their heads hacked, or partially cut off,
and a most horrible scene going on at the beach. One
smart little middy, of the name of Tweeddale, took a
couple of marines and charged the executioners and
soldiers, clearing the street of the bloodthirsty wretches.
Many of the semi-decapitated men were taken under the

care of the foreign doctors, and some wonderful recoveries effected : hundreds were saved, and the exertions in the cause of humanity have added much to the natives' respect for foreigners.

But the craving of the mandarins for blood was not appeased, though 2500 had been beheaded in one day. People were seized daily, and mock justice administered. From an eye-witness I have an account of one of these trials. The mandarin sat in state, surrounded by his staff of lictors, executioners, &c. The poor prisoner was dragged in and forced down on his knees before the judge. There was no prosecution, no witnesses ; the whole evidence was, that " the fellow had been caught, supposed to be a rebel." He was asked his name, and then made to give the name of his father and mother, their place of residence, and number of their family, a list which would only serve to add to the bloody sacrifice of ruthless revenge. He was then asked if he was a rebel. His defence was taken, but only answered by the charge being reiterated against him. The judge then ordered him to receive twenty-five blows of the thick bamboo upon the inner part of the leg and thigh. He still maintained his innocence. The order was given for twenty-five blows more ; and after receiving about a hundred blows, his flesh being beaten almost to a jelly, the poor fellow, helpless, and regardless longer of life, stammered out an extorted false or real confession, which doomed him to decapitation next day. Some died before the time for execution, and some would boldly declare their guilt at once, and suffer for their crimes with the stoicism of heroes. From the same authority I heard, that on one occasion, when a host of prisoners were sent down and executed, a poor woman rushed forward, and threw herself over the headless trunk of her husband.

No one attempted to seize or molest her as one attached by relationship to a rebel; she and her husband were well known. He, poor fellow, had just been incarcerated for debt, and in the confusion had been hurried out to death in the midst of the rebel prisoners. Inquiry was set on foot, her tale proved true, and the charitable contributions raised by foreigners for her future maintenance may have partly alleviated her cruel distress.

People at home little think of the sufferings we witnessed during the troubles in China, and the heavy claims upon foreign benevolence; otherwise the missionaries would less frequently have to pass by, disregarding the misfortunes their means are unable to relieve. The risks run by foreigners have sometimes been fearful, and have often been ill repaid. With many instances of earnest gratitude, I could mention numbers of cases of cold forgetfulness, enough to steel man's heart against aiding the Chinese in future.

There is one curious circumstance in Chinese warfare exhibited at Amoy as well as at Shanghai. The day and hour of most of the fights were coolly arranged beforehand. The fighting men on either side would often give notice when there was going to be a better skirmish than usual. They were certainly worth seeing as farces; but as military displays they were sadly deficient. Their whole system of military tactics is at variance with ours. There is rarely an account given in the Pekin Gazette of a victory gained, that the general does not say he *divided his forces*, and so accounts for success.

The end of the Amoy rebels who escaped can be traced in various directions. A good many of the junks got to Singapore; the leader wanted to sell them for his own benefit, but his plans were frustrated by the owners putting in their claims. Ma-gay was shot by accident off

Macao ; his fleet got divided during the night, each part mistaking the other, and a severe engagement ensued. Some of the rebels live unmolested in foreign employ. One lorcha was manned by them, the owner merely having to find them in food and clothing : he sailed her himself. Others became pirates off Formosa. It was lucky this rebellion, which seems to have been distinct from all the others, was so thoroughly broken up. With the Fokien rebels, as with many of those in Shanghai, the bettering of their own condition was their chief aim. Their real leader kept aloof ; he was a man of considerable influence, and is still at liberty.

The city and suburbs appear to have suffered but slightly, when we compare their state with the position the mandarin troops left the surrounding villages in. The power of the destroying angel could scarcely create more direful results : such cowardly acts of destruction vented against the innocent as well as the guilty, by the Chinese troops, causes us to forget the acts of the rebels, making them pass into insignificance before the unparalleled atrocities of their miserable foes. Captain Fishbourne, who was present when the rebels left the city, tells us that nearly all the fighting men got away, but that the mandarins set the pirates that were *in Government pay* to kill all the people they could, giving them six dollars a head, innocent or guilty. It fills one with indignation to find himself working hand in hand with officers of such a Government. Why, they actually begged assistance to prevent their own rascally hired pirates from attacking them after the rebels had gone !

One of H.M.'s steam-ships going on a cruise about this time, fell in with some thickly-manned junks that tried to evade her ; so she fired upon them, dismasted and took one, and found it was full of Amoy rebels.

The disabled state of the junk left her at the mercy of the winds and the mandarins, and she was towed into Amoy.   The Chinese officials applied for the men ; but no ; a mistake had been made.   They were taken away and set at liberty at what was considered a safe place.

F. Schenck Lith: Edinburgh 50 Geo. St.

Rebels at Shanghai.

CHAPTER XIX.

THE REBELS AT SHANGHAI.

Shanghai seized by a secret society—Docile character of the citizens—
Tai-ping-wang acknowledged—Foreign property respected—A heroine—
The siege operations—Singular details—A conchologist—Two marine
deserters—Curious contrivances—Conspiracies in the city—Picturesque
costumes—Rebels' penal code—Motley arms—Silk armour—Desire for
rank—Bribery—The leaders described.

THERE is very little doubt, that had no insurrection
troubled other parts of this celestial empire, Shanghai
would have remained in peaceful quietude. The rebellion was both the cause and the excuse for the capture
of the city. Many people deny the right of a political
status to the men that held Shanghai against the
government for eighteen months; as the narrative proceeds, we shall learn how far these people are correct.

It was taken on the 7th September 1853, by members
of a secret society, with wide ramifications, and who, it
was well known, aimed at the overthrow of the Tartar
dynasty. The local government had no power to resist;
indeed, the body-guard of the Taou-tai appears to have
been in league with the captors. The Che-heen[1] was
killed, an officer not likely to be favoured by the men
who aided in his assassination, as, doubtless, not a few
had felt the weight of his power. The people of Shanghai, a quiet peaceable race, had nothing whatever to do
with the outbreak, the whole being planned and carried

[1] Equivalent to a mayor, but appointed by the Government.

out by Canton and Fokien men, sailors from the junks belonging to the latter province forming the chief part of the force.   Property was at first strictly protected, a local government formed by the rebels, and Tai-ping-wang (unauthoritatively) acknowledged as Emperor. The Taou-tai being a Canton man, and probably once one of the brotherhood, was spared, and eventually permitted to escape.   The government offices were sacked, and the custom-house on the foreign ground was pillaged.   In this the people took part when they found there was nothing to fear from the mandarins.

Part of the rebel force was detached and sent to occupy some of the small towns in the neighbourhood.   At Tsing-poo there was a separate rising, but it was soon suppressed. The country people resisted at some places, but a temporary settlement was made at several points of mere local importance.   It will suffice for the present to state that the foreign officials proclaimed a species of neutrality, and took upon themselves to withhold payment of duties, but collected them in the shape of promissory notes from the foreign merchants—a highly creditable and honourable proceeding, but subsequently greatly abused and mismanaged by both the British and American plenipotentiaries.   However, the rebels did not get the duties, though they sent down a guard to protect the custom-house when they learned that it was in the hands of a mob.   They also guaranteed a guard for the protection of foreign property, gave up all goods belonging to foreigners and stored in the city.   Many of the native merchants took advantage of this to get their valuables placed in safety in the warehouses of their foreign friends, for the rebels laid an embargo on everything within the walls.   They eventually appropriated a good deal of property, and shipped it off in Fokien junks.

These junks being gone, the men that remained to stand the siege must have counted on assistance from other sources, if not from the insurgents at Nankin. They had opportunities of getting away with a goodly stock of plunder, had they so chosen, but there appeared to be a determination to fight the mandarins—a feeling which began to infect the natives. A woman, who had lost either father or husband by some unjust sentence of a mandarin, and who was said to have been wealthy, recruited a corps of northern men, paid and commanded them herself. Many Ningpo men attached themselves to the cause, and were good fighting men. A number of boys were trained to arms and afterwards did considerable service. In addition to the government stores, large supplies were collected from the country, and a goodly amount of provender was supplied by foreigners and Chinese in their employment; to these latter sources the rebels were indebted for most of their arms and munitions of war. They likewise got powerful assistance from deserters from the ships in harbour. If I am not much mistaken, the bad odour the rebels fell into from those acts of their foreign mercenaries went far to bring them at last to ruin.

The history of the siege as it progressed might prove tedious; but as much of the *character* of the Chinese was seen at this period, it may be interesting to relate some of the events that bear more strongly on that subject. Some of their appliances and resources are curious; we had many opportunities of observing them, as visits to the city and to the camp were frequent; some ladies even ventured to satisfy their curiosity thus far.

The Imperialists opened a battery within a hundred paces from the walls, on the north-west side, and wasted a good deal of powder against them. The walls are of

brick, and about thirty feet high, backed by a thick embankment of earth, rising two-thirds of the height. The
top of this earth-work forms a road round the city. At
intervals there are bastions that would throw a flanking
fire along the walls. Outside these is a broad moat, and
the whole surrounding country presents an endless plain
as far as the eye can reach; numerous hillocks, containing graves, relieving the monotony of the interminable
flat. The land rises but little above the level of the sea,
and water is found on digging a few feet under the sur-
face. Notwithstanding the difficulties to be contended
with, the Imperialists actually mined under the moat,
itself a water-course, and carried their sap beneath the
city walls, and effected a large breach by springing a
mine. Their object was effected thus : they dug deep
wells to drain the water from the mine, and pumped
them by means of chain-pumps working on an incline.
The workmen suffered greatly, and many died. They
had to work in the mine on all-fours, carrying forward
the drain they made by successively getting forward a
sort of cask, with the ends knocked out. A series of
these mines must have been made, because the rebels
discovered some of them, and took a curious way to
countermine ; they set chain-pumps to work, and carried
a stream of water *over* the wall, flooding the ground over
the mines, and readily destroyed them. There were no
less than six different breaches made by the springing of
mines—good practicable breaches ; they were gallantly
defended ; on one or two occasions the soldiers got within
the walls, but suffered severely for their temerity. At
one time a picked body of Cantonese troops formed the
forlorn hope ; they dashed onwards over the moat, and
up the breach, but the cowardly hounds that should
have followed, truly Chinese-like, did as no other people

on the earth would have done, hauled back the bridge
that was thrown over the moat, that their Canton comrades might be forced to fight. Poor fellows, the greater
part never returned ! At the south gate, portions of the
wall, many tons in weight, were hurled some distance
by explosions, and so extensively was that part of the
city mined, that the rebels built an inner wall, a sort of
breastwork, so that when a breach was made no rebels
were to be seen, but a rattling fire could be poured upon
their enemies. Batteries were built upon a level with
the city wall, and even *higher*, within fifty yards of the
walls; yet the rebels rebuilt the outer wall, *strongly*,
whenever a breach was made.

Their bullet-moulds were original : they polished two
bricks smooth on one side, cut two semi-globes on each,
accurately adjusted with a channel for the molten lead.
One man held the bricks firmly together, while another
poured in the lead ; two bullets were quickly made in
this way. Saltpetre was extracted from old bricks by
a process said to have been taught the rebels by a
deserter from Nankin. They made shells, but being
ignorant of the way to cast iron, they made them in brass
or zinc, welding the hemispheres together. A man that
was said to have been a marine managed to make the
fuses, and load the shells. He was one of the cold cal-
culating class, doing everything for dollars ; a quiet,
sanctimonious-looking fellow, and like anything but a
rebel ; always demanding more pay, and threatening to
join the Imperialists ; which he eventually did, but tired
of their service, and went back to his old quarters in the
city. He arrived there at a critical time, when few
that had served the rebels badly need expect good treatment. He was seized, put in chains, and cast into
prison. The half a dozen other foreigners in rebel em-

ployment remonstrated, but without avail. They found afterwards that his prison was changed, and could not tell where he had been put. After living on rice and water for three days, the " conchologist," as he was nicknamed, managed to work off his irons, got hold of some Chinese clothes, and escaped, not only out of prison, but over the city walls, where he was assisted by two rebels that were deserting.

It was reported by some of the naval officers that two marines, who deserted in one day, could not agree which of the contending forces they should join, and at last, with haphazard carelessness, parted company, to try their fortunes, one to join the rebels, the other to the Imperial camp. They met in a skirmish, and one shot his old comrade dead.

Round the city walls, and in front of other defences, there were pit-falls, some very large, and at the bottom a plentiful crop of sharp-pointed bamboo spikes. The ditches surrounding the Imperial camps were similarly provided, making an admirable defence, when the sandal-like shoes of the fighting men are taken into account, and promised a horrible death to any one that fell into them. The worst kind consisted of small holes, about a foot in diameter, in which the spikes were placed on the sides, with the points slanting inwards towards the bottom, so that any one who " put his foot in it" was regularly entrapped. But the most ingenious defence was made use of in the houses that formed the inner line of defence; they were loop-holed, and the exterior whitewashed: over each loop-hole there was a sheet of white paper pendant on the outside, so that a musket could be pushed through, and aim taken; but when it was withdrawn, the similarity of the paper to the colour of the wall prevented any loop-hole from being seen, so that no return shot from small fire-arms need be feared.

The Imperialists planned a grand scheme for taking the city. Large inclined planes were made in the camps, on a scaffolding as high as the walls; these were to be secretly conveyed to the ramparts, and the troops to charge up them, and "annihilate the stinking horde." It was an amusing sight to see these immense machines in the camp—the Trojan steeds of this Chinese Troy. "Practice makes perfect;" so the troops boldly charged up them day by day, but as there was no wall at the other end, the charges in camp ended in a vain flourish of arms in empty air, and the troops became equally accomplished in rushing down again—a portion of their exercise they did not forget.

Frequently the rebels made sorties against the camps, and sometimes were successful in destroying one or two. Rarely more than 200 or 300 insurgents were engaged. They retreated when a large force was collected against them, but generally kept up a good fight against some thousands, until the imperialists got pretty near the walls. These retreats were curiously managed, the whole fight being carried on in skirmishing order: the rebels had two young fellows, one entirely clothed in red, kept on the right, and another in blue, on the extreme left; it was the duty of these men to keep moving on each flank, so that they might be seen as much as possible, while the rest kept up a fire on the enemy from the centre, as much under cover as they could. The greater part of the imperialist shot was directed at the two men on the flanks, who daringly appeared at intervals in some prominent position, flourishing their flags. I have seen them do this within twenty yards of the foe, then quickly retreat.

N.

The uniform was most picturesque—fine gaudy colours, red turbans or red sashes. The people called the rebels *Hung-Tow*, or "red heads" (foreigners are called "red-hair men"); but the best way to explain the dresses, is to refer you to the sketches. The hair was long, and gathered up into a knot on the crown, in a similar way to the ancient style in China, before the Tartar conquerors forced the Chinese to adopt the tail. It is said that the Tartars took this extraordinary mode of showing their power over the Chinese from policy, that the Chinese might not be able to see how few Tartars were among them, and be led to attempt a revolt, both people being made to dress alike. The style of the Shanghai rebel dress was doubtless taken from the Nankin rebels, or the ancient dress of the Chinese, in some particulars, but the foreign dress gave several additional hints which were adopted, such as pockets, belts, &c. Chin-ah-Lin, one of the leading chiefs, wore English shoes and stockings. Some of the others had boots, and many wore foreign gloves, but the latter are getting into great vogue in the north, among the Chinese generally; the native glove being like a baby's mitten.

The arms of the rebels were of a most motley description,—muskets, matchlocks, horse-pistols, and revolvers (Colt's being preferred); some Minié rifles, with sword bayonets. Regarding rifle-balls, the rebels stated a curious circumstance. As a protection against them they wore dresses thickly padded with floss silk; they said that while the ball had a twist in it, revolving in its course, it caught up the silk and fastened itself in the garment. One man told me that he took out six so caught, in one day after a severe fight. The experiment might be worth trying; they said the dress was of more use within a hundred yards than at long range, when the ball had lost its revolving motion.

The laws in the city were those of the Triad society, a mixture of common sense added to a strong tincture of Lynch justice. The men were under considerable control, and property was respected. Papers with the Tai-ping seal on them were pasted over doors and windows; these served as guards, and were for a long time quite effectual. After the city was recovered, one of the missionaries found his house and furniture in exactly the same state it had been left. The churches were respected, though a good deal damaged by shot from the Imperialists and French.

At one time the Shanghai rebels renounced idolatry, and proclaimed the worship of the True God; but there may have been little sincerity in this; it was probably done to curry favour with foreigners.

The laws of the brotherhood consisted chiefly in terrific penalties for injury done to any of the members of the society, and were as horrible as those of other secret societies. They were sworn to on oath. Each chief had them drawn out on a large yellow sheet of parchment. One of the leaders pretended to read them to me one day; but as I knew he scarcely could tell a single character, it was rather a farce; however, he knew them by rote, and when he had gone through them, as there was nothing but penalties and no rewards, I observed that all their rules were intended to govern bad men, and that more people would be induced to join the rebel standard if the laws promised good rather than evil. This staggered him. I forgot at the time that our own code is entirely penal, and that with all our boasted enlightenment, we have no honours for probity or chastity.

When speaking of the class of men that are rebels, it must be taken into account that there is no class in China corresponding to our gentry ; all are either workmen, tradesmen, or in official employment. The *literati* rank rather as officials than as a distinct profession. They are all expectants. It will be seen, therefore, that it must be the lower classes who become rebels, the majority of whom have little to lose. The disaffected and dissolute of the Shanghai and Ningpo men joined the ranks, but the force was recruited chiefly by Canton and Fokien adventurers. Many of the wealthy Canton and Fokien men who remained outside, were anything but neutral, and aided the rebels in many ways. The chief who ultimately took command, was Lew, a Canton sugar-broker, who had started the Triad lodge many years before, at Shanghai. Another leader was a green-tea broker. The best fighting chief was a young groom who had served in the British Consulate stables at Amoy, Foochow, and Shanghai, and been in the employment of others in the latter place. There were several servants of foreigners among the rebels, and tradesmen that had formerly been accustomed to deal on the foreign ground, but there was no one of any standing. They were something like the Chartists of England, with this exception, that the class from which they sprung is relatively much larger in China than the Chartist class at home. One thing is to be remarked, the people made no active opposition to them.

CHAPTER XX.

THE FRENCH ATTACK ON SHANGHAI.

Proposals to the rebels by Admiral Stirling and Sir John Bowring—Their unfortunate failure—The French resolve on picking a quarrel with the rebels—Hostilities commence—Imperialists attack at the same time— The author ventures into the beleaguered city—Preliminary politeness under difficulties—State of affairs within—Resolution to resist the French—Interview with the chief—Harmless shells—Return with answers—Objections on points of form—Another visit to the city— Camp-bearers of the chiefs—Dresses worse for wear and warfare— Wadded armour—The chief's changed appearance—Diplomacy nearly baffled by a green-tea broker—Agreement at length signed—Foreigners in rebel pay—The French Admiral implacable—A skirmish—Another venture into the city, and offer of submission to the three Treaty powers brought back—French proclaim a strict blockade—Firing at an old woman—City bombarded—The great assault—The Imperialist assault — The Imperialists repulsed—French retreat—Boldness of the rebels— Attempt to starve the city—Fair treatment of prisoners by the rebels— Visit to the wounded Chinese—Further and more fortunate communications with the rebel chief—Agreement to surrender made nugatory by the perverseness of the French admiral—Last efforts of the rebels— Entry of the Imperialists, who set fire to the city—Horrible atrocities— The *finale*.

It was a sad day for the rebels when the French admiral Laguerre eventually found a *casus belli* against them.

Admiral Stirling and Sir John Bowring had at one time, with the best intentions, made proposals to get the city of Shanghai given up, and offered an asylum to the rebels. The negotiations, however, unfortunately were not carried out. As the men were under the impression that the leaders were arranging merely for their own safety, they were unwilling to trust to promises of an amnesty, granted at the solicitation of foreigners. Rank and rewards were several times offered to the chiefs by the Chinese officials if they would surrender, but the contending factions of the Canton and Fokien men were always distrustful of each other, and it is probable that the devotion and fidelity of the chiefs were often as much compulsory as sincere.

The ground allotted to the French at Shanghai for mercantile purposes is situated close to the city, on the north side, consequently the French were nearest of the three treaty powers to the rebels. They kept their ground intact. The British, owing to some official bungling, lost command over the portion allotted to them, and it came at last under a sort of municipal government formed by the foreign residents themselves. But these are merely local matters not worthy of being particularly detailed. The French consulate, and the residence and shop of a Parisian watchmaker, were the only foreign premises on the French ground ; but at the south side of the city, outside, was the Catholic cathedral, with its buildings attached. Whether it was from this unpleasant proximity to the city, or from some petty squabbles about the rights of Chinese Christians, or perhaps from accidents to the French ships of war, entailing a cost of $100,000 while at Shanghai, or because "the time was out of joint," the French admiral had long been desirous of picking a quarrel with the insurgents. At length, upon their forming a battery or breastwork to cover the retreat of small sorties from the city, opposition was shown by the admiral, as he stated that shots fired against the breastwork might reach the two French houses. The rebels were prevented taking out a field-piece, and a man with the gun was shot. Two

days after this (December 1854), Admiral Laguerre
sent an armed party to protect workmen in demolishing
the rebel battery, as the rebels would not take it down
when ordered.   A blank shot was fired over the workmen, to make them desist.   Upon this, the French
opened fire, the rebels returned it with effect, and the
foreign community were soon in an excited state.
Neither the British nor American commanders would
violate their neutrality, by assisting the admiral in his
hasty act of doubtful justice.   There were two rows of
houses between the battery and the French ground, so
that the danger to the French residences must have
been imaginary upon this side, though bad shots from
the Imperialist guns on the *opposite* side of the river
which passes Shanghai, sometimes struck the consulate.
At two P.M., the French steam-ship Colbert opened fire
upon the city with shot and shell.   The French lines
were alive with sharp-shooters, but the rebels kept remarkably quiet.   We expected they would surrender,
or attempt something desperate.   It was a horrid sight
to see the shot flying along, tearing down the roofs of
the houses, smashing in the walls, and at last setting
fire to two temples on the ramparts ; it was heart-rending
to see this done when the city contained probably some
twenty thousand poor innocent people whom the rebels
would not allow to come out, as the supplies brought
to the city depended much upon the Shanghai natives
having friends inside.   Knowing well what a quiet
unwarlike people the Shanghai folks were, it appeared
cruel to kill them in this way ; and while the French
kept up an active fire from the east and north sides, the
Imperialists attacked from the west.   Small chance of
escape would the poor people have if the soldiers once
effected an entrance.   The foreign ground was strictly

guarded, and the French cut off all communication. I went to a place where it was likely some of the poor people would fly to ; there were about fifty old women crying for assistance ; the bridge being cut down, they were unable to cross the stream. The sentry said he had no orders to prevent the people crossing, but that the French had cut away the bridge. Meeting with ready assistance from Chinese lads, I quickly got a raft floated over, and had the satisfaction of seeing the poor old creatures brought safely across.

There was no sign of surrender, and the crashing fire still poured into the devoted city. It appeared probable that a satisfactory arrangement might be made with the chiefs if they could be communicated with, or be induced to write to the foreign consuls. There was no time to be lost. I at once determined to go to the city, thinking I might have some influence with the chiefs. Informing one of the English officers of my intention and my motives, in case any accident befell me, I crossed the stream and made for a part of the walls just between the French and Imperialist attacks. I could soon see that the rebels were at their batteries in force, and, as I got nearer, saw them training a gun to bear on me, and lots of small arms pointed in the same direction. Walking unhesitatingly forward, raising my hat and motioning for them not to fire, I soon got to the moat. They hailed in Chinese to know if I was a Frenchman, and I quickly gave them a satisfactory answer, for the guns were raised from the unpleasant level in which they had been directed. None of the men at the bastion could speak English. I told them to send for one of the chiefs, from whom I could get a letter to the consuls, to see if some arrangement could not be entered into. They asked me to wait, said the French were very bad, but seemed to care little

for the Imperialists, who were getting alarmingly near,
almost cutting off my retreat. Sitting down behind a
tree, in case any stray shot came across me, I could
calmly examine the state of affairs. A large temple
was burning furiously about a quarter of a mile to my
left, and the sharp crack of the Minié rifles from the
French wall sounded very *telling*. The boom of the
Imperialist guns rung on my right, and I could see the
shells bursting in the air. After waiting about half-an-
hour an active young fellow was let down the wall by a
rope, and a stool thrown over to him. Taking a cautious
look around, he brought the seat, using it as a bridge to
cross the half-dry stagnant moat, and politely asked me
to sit down. This was an act of coolness and kindness
I scarcely expected, and made me feel more confident.
He said it would be far better if I would go into the
city, that the chiefs might see what I wanted. As my
object was to save life, thinking that the poor people
must be suffering from the continued bombardment, I
thought there could be no harm in running the risk,
and confidently trusted that I should get back in safety.
Crossing the moat, the rope was let down from the walls,
and, to show full confidence in the rascally-looking set
that were staring down at me, I unbuckled my revolver,
and, unsolicited, gave it to the young rebel, and was
pulled up. Jumping down among the fellows, I was at
once surrounded by an eager throng of hasty questioners.
The pistol was offered to me, but refused, and choosing
the young fellow as my guide and guard, I set off to find
one of the chiefs. The sight that met me as I went
along the walls surprised me not a little. Expecting to
see fear and disorder, the determined, cool look of the
men, all armed to the teeth, prepared for the worst,
quite astonished me. "When are the Frenchmen com-

ing ? " " Why don't they try to come into the city ? "
was often asked, and all seemed ready for a fight.   One
or two of the foreign mercenaries came up too with their
questions.   I told them they had better get out of the
mess as soon as they could, but they said they were
ready to die rather than give in to the Frenchmen.
Well protected by the embankment from shot, the insurgent force was not to be despised ; and I felt assured that
if the French did attempt to escalade, they would be
defeated.   Passing into the streets, the poor people were
all at their doors dressed in their best clothes, probably
thinking the time of their deliverance was at hand ;
they seemed to guess my mission, and thanks were
showered upon me as I passed.   On the way I could see
the temple that was burning, now nearly destroyed.
Two lads went by at a sharp trot, carrying between
them, suspended from a gaily-decked pole, a large French
shot as a present to Chin-ah-Lin.   In the tea-gardens
we crossed over the *débris* of a wall just rattled down
by a shot from the " Colbert."   We soon reached the
quarters of the chief.   I thought to have found him
among his men on the walls ; but no, there he was at
home as cool as possible, just returned from his station
quietly to take his dinner, which was laid out ready for
him.   English plates and spoons, and a hot dish of rice
and mince collops, with wine-glasses and wine on the
table.   He wanted to know why the French attacked
them ; but I told him there was no time for explanations,
that he must get a letter sent to the English and
American consuls to see if they could not settle affairs
with the French, and if need be arrange that the city
should be given up.   All I wanted was that the Imperial
soldiers should not run riot in the city while so many
of the Shanghai people were there.   He said they were

not afraid of the French, and would wait for them and fight if they came ; that they would not be the aggressors. However, a little reasoning got him to order the letters to be written. The French firing had now ceased, and this not only made me feel safer, but had some effect in making them think that my arrival was the cause of the cessation. While waiting for the letter to be written, I got some account of the fight. The rebels had only lost one boy, who was killed early in the day, and a horse : thirteen of the natives had been reported as killed. I certainly saw neither killed nor wounded. There was the broken part of a French shell upon the table. It was of curious construction, and had evidently been of a detonating nature ; the screw of the fuse was perfect, and it had two passages through it, both apparently filled with lime when it had struck. It is curious how few of the shells exploded : in the yard near the house there was quite a collection of shot and a good many howitzer shells that had not gone off. For each brought in the bearers got a small reward. Chin-ah-Lin said that when they first took the city the men ran away when a shot came near them, but now they almost fought with each other for who should get the shot !

Having got the letter duly wrapped up in a grand envelope, with " Tai-ping-wang" on it, I set off. Just as I was leaving, a man galloped up on horseback, and asked if I was the person who came to get letters from the chiefs, and on being answered in the affirmative, handed me a despatch from Lew, the principal chief, but who had then less real power than Chin-ah-Lin, as he had not so many followers. Taking the despatches, I hurried off to the walls, was let safely down, got back my pistol, and, wading through the moat, reaching the foreign settlement without a shot from the

French guard, sent off the letters to their destination. Negotiations being set on foot, I had the satisfaction to see that there was no renewal of hostilities the next day.

I was told semi-officially that the letters were written in too " bumptious" a strain, the chiefs writing as " generals in command of forces under Tai-ping-wang," and was told that if any good was to be effected, the letters should be written as if from chiefs of the brotherhood in possession of Shanghai, and that one should be addressed to the French consul. Having entered into the affair, it was only right to carry it out. Though I had made arrangements for having answers to the former letters sent into the city, I had no notice of any having been sent. However, as no very strict blockade was kept up, I got into the city over the walls, and found everything comparatively quiet, and with great difficulty persuaded Chin-ah-Lin to drop his assumed titles, and have the letters written in the names of the chiefs of the brotherhood. He offered to use Lew's name as he held his seal, but I insisted on visiting Lew accompanied by Ah-Lin, that I might see the communication was *bonâ fide* from the chiefs in council. Much time was lost by the presence of a party who, I feared, was a spy for the French ; and it was nearly dusk before the retinue started for Lew's Ya-mun. Ah-Lin walked by my side, though he had his horse with yellow saddle-cloth led in his rascally-looking train. War and ill-usage had brought the grand gala dresses of his followers into a beggarly condition, looking all the worse for the gaudiness of the colours. The long straggling hair, standing out from beneath the head-dresses, gave a wild look to the fellows ; and as it was known that Lew's men were not on the best of terms with Ah-Lin's braves, the visit was rather exciting. The people in the streets all stood still as we passed; those who had been seated rose. Men that came suddenly round a corner upon us, gave one of the Triad signs, some of which are similar to those of the brotherhood that is " veiled in allegory." Arrived at Lew's, we did not wait to be announced. There was a general flurry about the house as Ah-Lin marched in, hunting-whip in hand, and proceeded directly up stairs. What a different appearance the room now presented to that when I last was in it ! Then it was the hospitable residence of Mr. Consul Alcock.

I had seen Lew only once before ; he was then on horseback in great state ; patent-leather holsters, gold sword hung across his back, and lots of jewellery. Now he looked an emaciated little wretch, slovenly dressed, as if he had just turned out from an opium smoke. His quick eye was the only sign of energy about him. He listened quietly for about five minutes to what I had to say in the way of persuading them to put the city in the hands of the three treaty powers, and seemed inclined to comply, but a low, forbidding-looking fellow, not dressed as a rebel, and whom I had known as a green-tea broker, argued strongly against it. He said the French were only a small people ; and he worked up his enthusiasm to such a pitch, that Lew said he would sink the men-of-war at their anchors, and that we foreigners had better not interfere or we should suffer too. Fortunately I kept cool, and began quietly to explain what I thought the French *could* do; gave some statistics of their army and fleet at random ; said the English were their allies, and would perhaps assist them at Shanghai ; would certainly do so if the rebels committed any act of aggression ; and then wound up by a strong appeal against the arguments of the green-tea broker, and expressed my wonder that the rebels should follow the advice of a fellow who would not assume their dress, and who, while calling on them to fight to the last, would be the first himself to skulk away. I gradually brought matters round by taking a high hand in abusing this fellow, until Lew signed the letters for the three consuls, asking what could be done to settle affairs. The secretary at Ah-Lin's wanted to put the French name on a lower line than either the English or American, which would have been a direct insult; fortunately I noticed it, and got the letters all re-written.

It was quite dark when I left the city. Outside I met two of the foreigners in pay of the rebels, and tried to induce them to leave with me, but they flatly refused, and marched on in their dangerous patrol. There were six of these men in the rebel pay; one, however, was bedridden; the other five were magnified into nearly a hundred by most of the foreigners, the officials especially, few giving the Chinese credit for being able to fight, even after eighteen months' hard experience.

The letters seemed to have little effect with the hot-tempered admiral. He moved his frigate off the city; could not be persuaded by the consuls to listen to reason; kept quiet one day, but next morning, under cover of a fog, surprised the rebel battery at the little east gate. The boats went in cautiously, and were not perceived; it was well managed, and the attack was completely successful; the rebel guard were all killed. No prisoners were taken; and the rebels appearing in force, the French retreated orderly and coolly, keeping up a fire on the battery for some time to prevent its being manned. The guns were all spiked, and the flags taken away. The rebels lost fifteen men killed; one was a

Canton petty chief, whose loss was much deplored by his clansmen. In a day or two the spikes were out of the guns, some larger ones placed in the battery, and the flag of Tai-ping-wang hoisted again under a salute of three guns! Still I thought, as it was certain the city would be taken, this might be mere bravado, so determined on another visit to try and persuade the leaders to surrender without further bloodshed. The affair at the battery had evidently damped their ardour. Fortunately I found Ah-Lin alone, and proving to him by the lost battery that the French showed best generalship, I at last succeeded in persuading him to surrender to the three treaty powers on the same conditions as they had previously made to him ; but he would not surrender to the French alone, and said he would fight to the last rather than give in to the mandarins. He pledged his word that he had full power to bring all the others to his own views. He would not give his promise in writing, but offered, if the proposal came from the foreign officials, that it should be at once met. On leaving the city I told the British consul how affairs stood, but he seemed disinclined to interfere, and in the kindest manner recommended me to desist from interference also. Seeing no good could be done, I did not return any answer to the chiefs. Next day the French proclaimed a strict blockade, and shot down all that attempted to hold communication with the rebels. We saw one evening a poor old woman that had been attempting to take a basket of food for some poor person in the city, struck by a ball from the French lines ; her thigh was broken, and she lay helpless on the ground. How horrible did war appear when the sentry levelled his rifle again, and fired at the poor old creature, driving up a shower of earth close to her side ; another shot, and another, were fired; at last she was hit again in the back! It was a pitiable sight. She cried to us for help, but we could render no assistance, except by sending to report the circumstance at head-quarters. Shot after shot was fired. There were some rebels watching the butchery from the walls; they could see us distinctly. We were within rifle distance, and feeling that if I were in their position, I would shoot at every foreigner I saw while foreigners were committing such acts, I went away really for safety's sake, sick at heart to see such monstrous cruelty. The woman, it was afterwards reported, lay on the spot moaning till nearly midnight, when her cries ceased, and it was supposed some of the rebels had got her into the city out of the way of further immediate harm.

A short time after the blockade was notified, the "Colbert" and "St. Jean d'Arc" again bombarded the city, but there was still no surrender. The French then built a breaching battery close to the walls, certainly within a hundred yards. A constant relay of riflemen kept up a sharp fire at any rebel that appeared; but one place in the lines was kept open to admit the escape of any who could leave the city; a considerable number of women and old people got out.

The French battery being in readiness, the attack began in good earnest one morning at daylight. It was a fine frosty morning. The keen bracing air of the Shanghai winter, cold as it was on that day, did not deter most of the foreigners leaving their comfortable beds at daybreak, when the heavy booming of the guns from the two ships of war and the battery gave warning that the end of the Shanghai rebels was close at hand. A body of four hundred men was landed, and about half that number told off as the forlorn hope. The Imperialists came from their camps in great force, and were distin-

guished by blue sashes, to prevent the French taking
them for insurgents when they got into the city. A
party of fresh militiamen were to be the van of the Imperialist forces, and had the north gate appointed as their
place of attack.

The breach was close to the French ground, and was
soon considered practicable. The gallant Frenchmen
dashed out, and by the aid of scaling-ladders and scrambling, soon gained the top of the ramparts, but were met
by a sharp fire from the rebels under cover. About forty
men were detached to clear the way for the Imperialists
at the north gate. Seeing such a good example, in
flocked the soldiers by hundreds, their gay banners floating over the walls as they marched along. Crash went
the shot from the frigates into the unfortunate city ; the
sharp crack of the rifles was ceaseless, and soon the work
of the soldiers was seen by the blazing mass of houses
they were destroying. I got into the French lines to see
the fighting that was still going on at the breach. The
brave band of sailors held it firmly, though soon some
of their number were *hors de combat*. What a scene
must have been going on within the walls! A rascally-
looking soldier came up to the lines, bearing the severed
head of one of the rebels, or probably one of the poor
natives, as they too had to wear long hair. Holding up
the head by its gaunt locks, the wretch boasted of his
trophy to the French sailors. Wo worth the day that
they had such allies ! Craven cowards that could not
retain the advantage that was so bravely won for them !
The soldiers began to plunder, got disorganized, and
were beaten back to the walls.

Nearly every one thought that the fate of the city
was certain ; but I had seen before how the insurgents

were likely to behave, and still insisted that they would maintain their ground. Proceeding to the guard-house that overlooked the north gate, we could see the soldiers still pouring in, but their energy was damped by the number of wounded, some fearfully slashed, that were being brought back. After the battle had lasted four hours, and the rebels had beaten off the Imperialists at the west side, we saw their yellow flags upon the wall near the north gate : on they came, pouring in a telling fire upon the unlucky soldiers, who found that the place was too hot for them. Then followed a terrible scene. Panic seized upon the troops, and huddled together in a crush, they were driven over the walls. Down came men, arms, and banners, in wild confusion. Some made for the breach ; the French tried to encourage them, but they, void of all discipline, fired upon the French, who had already suffered severely. As no reliance could now be placed on their Chinese allies, the French made an orderly retreat from the place they had so gallantly held, but where they should never have been, had their admiral shown proper judgment and temper. Out of 250 who went into the breach, four officers and about sixty men were killed or wounded. Of the Imperialist force, it is said, 1200 were left dead in the city, and about 1000 wounded carried away. The rebels kept under cover nearly all the time where they were exposed to the French, and their loss was comparatively trifling. The daring of these fellows, when they saw their success, was wonderful ; they pulled the scaling-ladders into the city, and even in front of the French lines, succeeded in getting a ladder in over the breach. They collected the bodies of the Imperialists, it was reported, and placing them in a large temple, burned the edifice to the ground. That the temple was fired there is no doubt, and the final offering made within it may have been composed of the victims of the day.

After this display, on the part of the insurgents, of a bravery that was not expected, and in consequence of the loss sustained in attacking them, it was determined to starve them into submission. The Imperialist camps were drawn nearer to the city, batteries were erected, and a long line of circumvallation was extended completely round the city, to prevent any supplies of provisions entering. But there is no doubt that the soldiers themselves assisted the rebels. Under the pretence of taunting them with food, the Canton troops hung ducks, fowls, &c., at the end of their spears, and I daresay, took means to lose them when near the city at places where they could be found. One mandarin, who had been taken prisoner, was ransomed by his obtaining for the rebels a large quantity of powder, and being successful in this instance, the insurgents established a sort of system of kidnapping, which was carried on at one time by their foreign mercenaries, till at last it brought them into such bad odour, that the foreign community, officials especially, were against them. The Imperialists were allowed upon the "foreign ground" (from which, for their bad conduct, they had previously been expelled), and even erected a battery upon it.

Houses were pulled down, by order of the British Consul, on the pretence of making a road. But it was very humiliating to see this subterfuge placarded about the streets, side by side with the mandarins' proclamations ordering that the houses should be pulled down, and even saying that the British Consul ordered it, that the "rebels might be exterminated." Several hundred families were thus rendered houseless in the depth of winter, and it went much against the feeling of a true English heart to see the British Vice-consul officiously superintending the destruction of houses, the owners of some resorting to suicide to escape from their distress.

Great allowance is to be made for the difficult position in which the English and American Consuls were placed; but the very inconsiderate zeal which characterized the conduct of Mr. Lay, the then acting vice-consul, and Mr. Wade, at that time one of the officials in the Chinese custom-house service, and the open manner in which these gentlemen lent their aid to the mandarins, was strongly commented on by nearly all the foreign community.

Leave was granted by the French Admiral to two English gentlemen to enter the city for the purpose of finding out a missing servant among the kidnapped prisoners. Ah-Lin received them, and gave them permission to enter the prison. There were about twenty men in confinement; they complained of only getting rice and water, but had not been maltreated, further than by the loss of some of their clothes. The servant was not to be found, but the prisoners earnestly begged to be released. One man, a carpenter, who had been seized because he made gun-carriages for the late Taou-tai, was begged off on the plea that the rebels afterwards got the use of the guns. All the other prisoners were offered to be given up to the two foreigners, if they would give their word that they would do nothing against the rebels when they were let loose. The carpenter was released upon these conditions; his solemn promise being given to his foreign liberators. The fellow went and gave information against certain people as soon as he got out, and acted openly against his word.

The wretched Chinese soldiers could not be again induced to make an attack; the temples near Shanghai had been filled with their wounded, who were but poorly cared for.   I visited some a day or two after the great repulse, and found the poor fellows lying on the ground, closely packed ; their wounds had been stanched with cotton-wool, and some suffered severely ; one or two were in the height of fever, others were able to sit up and were writing to their friends for assistance; most of the worst cases were among the Ningpo militia.   They were most grateful for the little assistance afforded them to buy medicine, and the attendants were very assiduous in pointing out those who required it most.

Some of the poor people who got away from the city gave melancholy accounts of the distress within.   The rebels had put the natives upon short allowance, and some were reported as starving.   I was surprised one day to receive a letter, which proved to be from the chief Chin-ah-Lin ; he stated that they could get no supplies into the city, and were in great distress.   He entreated me again to interest myself on his behalf, and implored heaven to reward me for the trouble I had already taken. His messenger had had a narrow escape in bringing out the letter, I was told, but a reply could be sent in at night.

In hopes that some good might arise from opening up communication, I replied that evening, using all the arguments I could to induce him to surrender, in order that the people might be spared, and told him that he could not expect any one to befriend the rebels while they kept the poor people in the city running the risk of a massacre, if the Imperialists got inside.   Judge of my satisfaction at the result !   After my note was received, free exit was granted to nearly all the women and children who wished to leave, and next morning, they poured into the foreign ground in hundreds, some looking hale and hearty enough, throwing discredit on the want which had been reported ! I was so pleased with the result of my note, that I vowed to do all I could to save more lives, letting my motives stand bail for the risk. Several notes passed, and at last it was arranged that a certain signal should be made on the city walls when the chiefs found themselves compelled to surrender, and that, then, I should communicate with Admiral Laguerre, informing him that the surrender of the city would be guaranteed to him if I were permitted to tell the chiefs that he would accept it.

The communications had been carried on with the greatest care—the letters written on slips of paper that could be concealed in the bearer's nostril ; but I was rather taken aback one evening, when walking through the Imperialist camp, to see the bearer of my message coolly walking among the soldiers : of course I took no notice of him, but for prudence' sake, went away. No doubt the rebels were in regular communication with the soldiers who blockaded them. This circumstance put me on my guard, and luckily the whole arrangements about the signal were settled by verbal message, but the messenger mistook the exact position for the signal. Certainly, the flag agreed upon was there, only it was exhibited at the wrong place. To be assured no error occurred in a matter of such importance, I let a whole day pass, so that notice might be given at night to have the signal at the proper position. In the morning, the fate of the city seemed sealed, the red flag was on the wall in the appointed place ! No time was lost, and accompanied by Mr. Wade, I waited upon the Admiral.

The whole story of my communications was explained, and the crowning point made known by pointing to the red banner in front of the French lines. Admiral La-guerre would accept an unconditional surrender, and would even consider the prisoners as his; his ire was particularly directed against one, and I felt, that when I went into the city, it would be to save all but the very one who had arranged so well for the rest. However, I was told the risk was too great ; and in spite of all entreaties, could not persuade his Excellency to permit me to trust myself among the rebels in their present position.

I was allowed to write, informing the chiefs that their surrender as prisoners to the French was accepted, but was not permitted to take my letter to the walls. I subsequently learnt that the letter never reached. Had I been allowed to take it, what misery might have been prevented !

The flag had been up two days, and the chiefs could restrain their men no longer. It was New Year's day ; [1] the greatest festival of the Chinese year. At midnight, fires were seen at various places round the city walls, and shortly after, the whole city, from east to west, was a mass of flame, throwing out a long, heavy curtain of dense smoke far away into the eastern horizon. There appeared to be no hope, and with a heavy heart, I thought the rebels had all met a fearful end, but it was no small consolation to remember that there were scarcely any of the poor people left to suffer by the heartless butchering of the soldiers. In the morning the truth came out. The bulk of the rebels had cut their way through the Imperialist camp ; some 200 or 300 had surrendered to the French Admiral (who after-wards gave them over to the Chinese !) ; a few escaped into the foreign ground—about fifty of them getting

[1] 17th February 1855.

into the American guard-house, where they were most kindly treated. One of these was a wounded chief; he made his exit from the city on horseback, his followers lost him, but finding that he had not reached a place of safety, they returned from the guard-house, notwithstanding the danger, and brought him in in spite of the risk.

The Chinese behaved admirably, and did all they could to assist in saving some who would have been speedily executed if the slightest information had been given. I had opportunities of seeing most extraordinary instances of devotion, as I did all I could to save life.

The scene in the city was a disgrace to the Chinese soldiers; they plundered everything that was left; and a quiet-looking, respectable man, entreating some of us to make the soldiers desist, said, "The rebels were bad but these soldiers are worse."

When the rebels began their move in the early part of the previous night, the soldiers feared to enter before their enemies had evacuated the city. The Imperialists fired the town, so as to drive the rebels from their hiding-places.

It would be needless and painful to recount the scenes witnessed in the city. Even the coffins were opened and corpses decapitated. Most of the rebels were hunted down in the country. In the course of three days about 1500 men were beheaded, many being first mutilated in the most horrible manner. Lew was beheaded five times, or five men were beheaded for him, for he escaped. Chin-ah-Lin was reported taken, but a subsequent reward of $15,000 for his head, gave the lie to this; besides, it is pretty well known that he passed through the Imperial camp with six of his body-guard in disguise, and reached the foreign ground, eventually get-

ting safe away to Singapore. Some of the men had
narrow escapes. One lay hid in the city for three
days after it was taken. A schooner, going from Woo-
sung to Hong-Kong, was suspected of being about to
take Chin-ah-Lin and several other of the city people;
a force, consisting of Chinese troops and some English
marines, accompanied by the acting vice-consul (who
seemed to be imbued with some extraordinary motives),
went down to search the vessel. This was discovered;
but those desirous of preventing further bloodshed
quietly continued, notwithstanding, in the work they
were determined upon, getting the unfortunate men
away from danger, following the force to Woo-sung,
passing it in the night, and sending away the vessel with
her refugees before the Chinese soldiers had a chance of
making any seizures. The foreign mercenaries nearly
all came to the end they deserved. I rejoiced that some
of the rebels escaped. The extreme devotion some of
them showed to their chiefs and their cause, braving
dangers most imminent, making sacrifices beyond belief, and manifesting, in spite of all that their previous
career might indicate, a goodness of heart and sincerity
of gratitude that would bear comparison with like
qualities among the most civilized people.

It was very gratifying, too, to see the anxiety of some
of the Chinese, who were quite unconnected with the
rebels, to try and screen such as they could see attempts
were being made to save. Shanghai, Ningpo, Fokien,
and Canton men, who had opportunities of bringing
some of the rebels to grief, and thereby being well rewarded, were as true in the cause of humanity and
charity to the wretched fellows as if they had been
rebels themselves.

There was no good leader of standing to guide them.

Their foreign friends often sought more after their own gain than the rebels' good ; but I doubt much if men of a similar stamp, acting in armed defiance of legal authority, in any other country, would have behaved as well, and maintained order in a manner equal to the Shanghai rebels, who throughout the siege exhibited traits which showed that they only wanted good leaders to become first-rate soldiers.

That they wished to join the insurgents at Nankin there can be no doubt. I have seen two letters that were received by them from that place; and when the city was evacuated, it was the intention of the rebels to fight their way to Ching-Kiang-Foo. Chin-ah-Lin took especial charge of the son of the southern king, and had him by the hand when the Imperialist outworks were passed, but the lad was lost when the confusion began. Lew's strength failed him in the retreat, and though his fellow-chief gave him his own shoes to assist him in walking, he had at last to be carried. I have heard that Lew was saved by a Buddhist nun giving him a disguise. Seaou-Kin-Tsze, one of the fighting chiefs, got away ; he was a Shanghai man, so his knowledge of the dialect would aid him. One or two more of the leaders escaped. Ignorant of the fate of their fellows, and without being aware of what their colleagues had said, their respective narratives of the evacuation of the city confirmed each other, and have assisted me in the above relation.

After the dispute with Yeh, Chin-ah-Lin came to Hong-Kong, and offered to assist in any way against the above imperturbable mandarin, but his overtures were of course rejected.

He was apparently leagued with some powerful party in the island connected with the rebel or piratical fleets.

He came one day and told me that Ma-chow-wang, or some mandarin agent, was kidnapping sailors, or people were doing it to get money from the mandarins for their heads. He explained that the men were engaged to go to Macao in lorchas, and when out at sea were seized and taken to Namtow, a place between Hong-Kong and Canton, where they were beheaded. I at once went and informed the police, urging that a warning notice should be put out to caution sailors, but no notice was published. Shortly afterwards, however, Commodore the Hon. C. B. Elliot attacked Namtow, and seized the Chinese admiral's junk with some valuable papers. Translations of some of these were printed in the *Hong-Kong Gazette,* and by them it appeared that a number of heads of foreigners had been procured and sent up to Canton for the reward. When the rebels that were taken by the " Niger" near Hong-Kong were given up to the Chinese by the police, the Shanghai ex-leader went away, dreading a similar fate. We heard of him as a compradore at Siam, doing a good business, giving two horses to one of the kings. It was said he took to piracy ; but he seemed to have a charmed life, for there he is still, though probably his end will be in prison, for his taste of independent life has doubtless made him unfit for any settled employment or honest occupation. He is a curious specimen of a Chinaman, and as such has taken up more space in these pages than either his doings or his cause would otherwise have warranted.

CHAPTER XXII.

SIEGE OF CANTON BY THE TRIADS.

Heads and ears—A walk round Canton—Miserable appearance of the place
—The braves—Author visits head-quarters—The commander and his
crew—Appearance of the rebel army—The combat—Imperialists retreat
—Lies of the Pekin Gazette—Extraordinary cowardice—A charge with
an umbrella—Mandarins' fear of the people retaliating the iniquities
of their rulers—Closeness of the blockade—Ingeniously-conveyed despatches from the rebels—Executions—Attempts at visiting the rebels'
camp—Odd artillery practice—The soldiers destroy what the rebels
spare—Popularity of the rebel cause—Partial proceedings of the English
in support of the governing powers—No means of opening communication
with the rebels—Wide spread of the insurrection—The "Avenger of
Sorrow"—Fearful scenes—Rising *en masse*—Defeat and reaction—A
million perish in the province of Canton within a year.

I RESIDED at Canton when the city was besieged by
the Triad rebels. There were horrible tales current of
the slaughter committed on rebels by the Imperial troops
at the north side of the city. Thousands killed, and so
many executed, that the baskets sent for the heads were
not sufficient to carry the whole, so that the mandarins
determined on sending to the Governor-General boxes
containing only the right ears !

Every one agreed in their terrific accounts ; but I was
sufficiently interested in the subject to venture on an
expedition to verify for my own satisfaction the actual
state of the case. It was a fine hot afternoon in July ;
I was accompanied by two good friends, and relied on
their superior knowledge of the language to get us out of
any difficulties that might arise : one of my companions

was a first-rate Chinese scholar, and was accompanied by his servant ; this made the excursion less dangerous.

We set off, and as we walked briskly through the long narrow streets, how deserted they looked ! Beggars seemed to be in the majority, generally poor *wo-begone* looking women, with the haggardness of care deep-rooted in their melancholy faces ; how brimful has been the cup of misery in this unhappy province ! At intervals we had to crush through the barricades formed in the streets.   At each was a guard of picked men in the pay of the householders in the neighbourhood. They were by far the best-looking of all the soldiers. The village braves were the next best ; long lanky fellows they were, poorly armed, and badly dressed,— the leg naked to the thigh, but dashing-looking men. And how different from the ragamuffin vagabonds that were ranked as *soldiers,* hang-dog, cut-throat, cowardly wretches, better fitted for a massacre than a fight. There was no redeeming feature in their appearance ; they were dirty, and evidently earned their livelihood in their present occupation, being unfit for anything else, and not adepts even at that.

The city walls had been repaired, and the creepers that had grown upon them were removed, taking away the picturesque appearance the ramparts formerly had at the west side of the city.   We stopped at a large guard-house, from which we had a distant glimpse of the troops moving about among the barren hills near the north road ; there was some firing, and an extensive display of flags.   The forts surrounded by tents presented a martial look ; they were strongly guarded ; the face of the hills had been scarped, and thickly studded with sharp-pointed bamboo spikes to prevent a sudden attack.   We were not satisfied with our position ; and as the soldiers were civil we pushed onwards, until we arrived at the pretty Mahometan mosque, about a mile from the city. This appeared to be the head-quarters of some of the *leading* mandarins, *their* post being where least danger might be expected. Another body of officials was stationed on a hill to our right, but the governor-general and principal officers were in the five-storied pagoda, making out all they could by the aid of their "thousand-mile inspector" in the shape of English telescopes. There was a queer medley of people about the mosque, ragged-looking soldiers from all parts of the province, rascally Chaou-chaou men, and a host of dirty coolies, with a batch of sedan chairs for the mandarins, and mountain chairs for the wounded. There

War Charger.

were some Tartar steeds that would have astonished Mazeppa, and from their size would have had hard work to carry him ; there was little of the Ukraine breed about them. The pompous mandarins stalked about in all the glory of badger-tailed white-button caps, their long robes inelegantly tucked up behind, and their tails braced in by their yellow girdles. The variety of arms was a wonder—matchlocks, gingals, swords single and double, sabres, pistols of the most ancient construction, one or two old flint muskets without ramrod or bayonet. The mosque within looked quiet and peaceful. There were boards and ornaments with Chinese and Arabic inscriptions hanging round the walls. A welcome supply of cold tea was politely offered us by perhaps the attendant priest. It is strange that this sect should still exist in China. There is a tradition that an uncle of the great prophet is buried near this mosque. These matters did not trouble us much during this visit: the firing was pretty close to us, but we could not make out the rebels, so we pushed onwards among some soldiers, and passed different groups, all apparently anxious for anything but fighting, in fact, looking perfectly indifferent, being at a safe distance. Bang went a heavy shot from the forts, whistling with a peculiar sort of hum over our heads at the rebels on a hill about a mile off. Before the year was out I got pretty well used to standing under fire. We at last got well forward, and had a good look at the rebels. Their main body was on a small hill among a cluster of flags ; another force was behind a wood to their left, near the village of San-yuen-le, and in front they had a cloud of skirmishers who were getting forward under cover of their shields. The Imperialists had many men in like order to meet them, but there was no firing in volleys or charging in companies,—the whole affair was a large skirmish with strong supports in the rear. If the rebels had run, the large straggling forces of the Imperialists would have followed them, but as they were rather advancing, the brave soldiers of the empire began to waver.

I placed a telescope on a soldier's head that I might have a view of the advancing rebel skirmishers, who were cautiously creeping through a field of young paddy, when a gradually increasing hum of many voices passed through the ranks ; there was an evident inclination for a run, and no attempt to stop it. Chinese troops are guided by flags carried by the mandarins' standard-bearers, and by the sound of the drum or gong. They may have tried a rally, but when we learned that the confusion among the troops was caused by a cry from the Governor-General's men calling for powder, we thought it better to move off. We had not got far when the rebels shouted and moved nearer ; there were screams of Tah ! Tah ! on all sides. The troops poured back towards the city in a long stream along the north road.

We shuffled up to the mosque, and in the general retreat missed one of our party among the crowd of soldiers. Leaving the one who remained with me at the city side of the mosque, I forced my way through the retreating men, and found our lost friend among some mandarins, who were entreating him to stop, as they made out the soldiers were *following us*, and if we stopped, his men would "do battle!" We had seen supplies of powder and buckets of tea going out to re-plenish and refresh the troops ; the coolies had gathered together with their burdens, and the men on getting their powder seemed less inclined to retreat. They began to extend their line on the flanks, and peppered away, we could not see at what, as the rebels did not push their advantage. The soldiers began to return, and as evening came on the rebels re-entered their camps, and thus the Governor-General had gained another *victory !* an account of which appeared in the *Pekin Gazette,* this trustworthy authority stating that 11,000 rebels had been killed in the victories around Canton that week.

I tried to ascertain if any shots told, but never saw a

Carrying on the Wounded. — Canton.

man drop on either side; one or two were carried past on chairs, about half a dozen soldiers taking advantage to get off the field by acting as guards to each chair. There was one man badly hit in the head, and a smart looking young lad had a shot in his chest, and bled profusely; we found him dead as we returned. I don't believe the loss on both sides rose to fifty men *hors de combat.* I never saw such a pack of cowards in my life, and would not believe that men with arms in their hands could be such fools if I had not seen it ; a score or two of school-boys armed with stones would run a fair chance of gaining a victory over the same number of Chinese soldiers. The rebels, too, showed little pluck, but some days before, had made a dashing attack on the forts during a storm ; they are said to have gone into action naked, and counted upon the rain preventing the fort guns being fired.

The rebels were dressed like labouring men. Some had red sashes, but I did not see red turbans. Some days after the fight that I had witnessed, three or four Canton foreigners and myself went out to see the ground in the hope of getting a glimpse of the rebel camp. We voted that none should carry revolvers or arms of any kind, as in case of a mishap, our small party could do little against thousands. It was fortunate we came to this conclusion as the sequel will show. What a different scene did the mosque now present : utter solitude, not a living thing visible ; the tent-clad hills crowned with forts looked down in quietness, and the space between the city and the rebel camp lay there as dull and silent as the graves which strewed the ground. The fields were trodden down, and the crops destroyed by those whose watchwords were order, obedience, and justice !

After passing the mosque we heard shouts in our rear ;

P

a mandarin with a hundred men had been sent out to stop us. He besought us to return, told us we were in great danger, and that the rebel devils rose out of the ground. We assured him we could not see any; he then gave a wave of his arm and said, "They are everywhere." He grew so earnest that we thought if we moved on we might get into a scrape with him when we came back, so out of apparent deference to his wishes we returned, greatly disappointed, for we were within half a mile of the rebel outposts. Our guardian mandarin marched us off in the midst of his soldiers as if we were prisoners; but as the men he commanded were a rascally-looking set, we told him to keep them back whilst we marched on in front. They gathered about the sides of the road and were not over civil, till, getting worse and worse, we were at last surprised by a great shout beside us; the vagabonds drew their swords and rushed at us with their infernal cry of Tah! Tah! Perhaps they did it to frighten us, but if they had had the pluck they might easily have given us the *coup-de-grâce*. None, however, drew blood; for, without a moment's hesitation, when I heard the Tah! I levelled my umbrella to the charge, and went right through them until I reached the frightened mandarin; we surrounded and seized him, and compelled him to send his followers forward, whilst we kept the worthy gentleman within easy distance of a knock-down blow.

We went through the camp, the Fokien and Chaouchaou men looking perfect demons in the dim light of the lanterns hung about their tents; gambling was going on to a great extent, and we observed, that as there was no fight that day, these respectable guardians of the public peace were not permitted to have fire-arms of any kind.

The mandarins of Canton have much to answer for.

The soldiers, that year by year they had taxed the people for, where were they when the danger really came ? They must now disburse their ill-gotten gains, and gather men from all the surrounding towns to fight their battles, leaving other cities unprotected! What misery have these cities not endured ! Capture and re-capture, fire, rapine, and destruction. The blood of thousands may be laid to their account, and a day of woful retribution is at hand. Anxiety, poverty, and disgrace are small matters compared to the heavy reckoning that will follow. They may gain a temporary triumph, and trumpet forth successive victories ; but were they ten times more fortunate, their acts will stand a lasting monument of execration, deeply graven in the hearts of an injured people.

The people of Canton were governed by terror. Jus-tice was left out of the question. Lies were not only spoken, but *acted*. If prisoners could not be taken in battle, innocent people were brought in for execution ; the citizens must be made to believe in the power of the mandarins, and most successfully were they deluded. The mandarins feared *them*, more than *they* feared the mandarins. For months the gates were closed, and only opened at certain places, with vast precautions. The people were made to wear badges, bearing their name, age, and residence ; all entering the city from the suburbs were at one time examined, and, doubtless, with reason, for had not the strictest caution been ob-served, Canton would have been taken by its own citi-zens. The panic was very great,—shops closed, trade suspended ; there was scarcely any communication with places in the neighbourhood. The streets were barri-caded, and besides this, in the suburbs, platforms were raised over the streets, so that, in case of fire or an attack, the people could move from one place to the other over the houses. Look-out stations were thickly scattered high above the streets in commanding places, and careful watchmen placed therein. So close was the blockade, that provisions became enormously dear; and so strict was the examination of people passing the gates, that they even stripped females. One case was reported of a rebel-despatch being found under a plaster over a pretended sore on a woman's leg! The trunks of a certain high mandarin were examined as they passed the gate, and papers were discovered, showing he was in league with the rebels, or had been in correspondence with them. He was taken prisoner, examined at first by one *Ya-mun* or court, and then by another; at last was taken to the Tartar general's, and there assassinated.

I went one day before the rebels laid siege to Canton, to see an execution of one of the rebel chiefs with some threescore men; the former was to be flayed alive. Though the streets were filled with soldiers, the chief, for the third time, was taken back to the cell, after being led part of the way to the ground; so great was the fear of a rescue. The rest suffered without any attempt at interference.

These were curious times to live in, and we saw extraordinary sights. There was little business doing, and a good deal of leisure. At first few foreigners ventured outside the factory-wall, but when some did so with impunity, others followed the example, and even long excursions, never dreamt of in time of peace, were now undertaken.

All the soldiers were not such a bad set; some were even fine-featured, sharp-looking fellows. Many of them had never seen a foreigner before, and doubtless were a good deal astonished to behold a couple of barbarian devils walking up to them, examining their arms, and trying to get up a conversation with the few sen-

tences at their command of the Canton dialect. I went
two or three times out to the camp at the east side of
the city; the rebels were in large force some three or
four miles off, and were visible from my bedroom
windows; we endeavoured to get out to them, especially
after a fight, for we could see them fighting from the
factories. We heard of thousands slain; but I walked
over the ground several times, and all that was visible of
the remains of a combat was some few drops of blood
on the road by which the wounded had been carried
back, some bullets, and one piece of bloody rag. The
ground was very rough, and had many points where
wounded men might have been concealed, or dead
passed over, but none were to be seen, even an hour
after the fight. The Imperial outposts on the hills at
the east of Canton were occupied by a few fine young
fellows from *Sin-whui*, a city attacked by the rebels.
There was one man, the *beau-idéal* of a light infantry
soldier. They were well armed, and had very high pay,
$7 or $10 per month; soldiers of the main body were in
receipt of but half this amount. Their post was one of
great danger and importance; but no mandarin risked
his valuable person there. They let us pass their lines,
and watched with interest our movements towards the
rebels; but we never could get to the " patriots." Their
scouts retreated as we advanced, until they got into a
bamboo plantation, into which we did not care to follow
them, lest the rebels should not like our appearance or
our approach, as they might easily have seen us when
speaking to the soldiers.

After the rebels were driven away from Canton, we
visited their encampments; the village had been utterly
destroyed on all sides. To the eastward they had held
an old Tartar camp, the intrenchments of which, and a
a long mound, formed their advanced defence: the chief

camp was on the side of a steep hill, with a plain in front.

I cannot understand how the rebels lost this position; it was strong, and there were two streams which might have been made available between them and the city.

On the north side they had a far worse position, but had strong supports to fall back upon at some twenty miles in their rear. I don't think they were actually driven away, but retreated from both places, the mandarins burning all the villages they had occupied. It was a heart-rending sight to see these deserted desolate ruins. Some of the villages were as large as many small towns in England. Some foreigners went over to see them after the rebels were driven out; the poor people were in a sad plight, and bitterly railed against the soldiers. Old men, and even little children, came up to show the foreigners the brutal dealings of the ruffianly troops. Some had both ears cut off. One poor old man had two pretty flower-jars lying in the wreck of his house; they now adorn the porch of a friend of mine in Hong-Kong, who was anxious to get them, and offered a high price for them. " Take them, take them," said the old man ; " they are yours; I can die, I do not want your money ; of what use is it to me now ?" Of such a scene, it is only right to speak with reverence.

Pity for the country that is so cursed, so rotten at the core; and yet, the people contain all the elements to make the Chinese one of the finest nations on the earth. Their institutions are good, their maxims and moral code unobjectionable ; but the whole is neutralized by the deceit, the cupidity, and cowardice of their rulers. The great historian, Gibbon, in writing of the Emperors Arcadius and Honorius, says, " Their laws, with few exceptions, breathe often the most admirable sentiments, and the wisest political principles; but this proves no

more than that there were some men of abilities who
were employed in framing them ; it was another thing
to enforce their observance, and while this was neglected,
the words were but empty sounds, to which the public administration of government was a daily contradiction."

How applicable similar remarks would be to Chinese
laws, may be gathered from many passages in these
pages, and from the Chinese Emperor's instructions to
his ambassador to the Tourgouths, which contained,
according to Staunton's translations, the following
words :—" In our empire, fidelity, filial piety, charity,
justice, and sincerity, are our ruling principles, the
objects of our veneration, and the constant guides of our
conduct !" It excites the indignation of every right-
thinking foreigner in China, to see the representatives
of Christian countries pandering to officials whom they
know to be corrupt, making no attempt to advance the
cause of true civilisation, except by breaking treaties
themselves, and passively bearing insults from a power
that is tottering to ruin by the uprising of its people
to avenge their wrongs,—wrongs to which our officials
appear to be most callous, while proclaiming themselves
" the bulwarks of freedom," and the " rescuers of the
oppressed." The very weakness of the revolutionists
might have been an additional inducement for us to
assist them, if we acknowledge that they had good
grounds for desiring and endeavouring to overthrow the
tyranny that weighed upon them. Willing though the
wealthy may be to see a bad government changed, they
will not risk their wealth until the new power is strong
enough to protect it ; consequently, a revolution must be
commenced by those who have little to lose, and their
force kept up by contributions and exactions, while
their progress from one place to another must often
leave the people of the city they have left subject to the

avenging laws of the existing power. Land, meanwhile, remains uncultivated, famine follows, trade is
disarranged, and eventually the rebels are driven to
plunder for an existence, and the last state of the people
is worse than the first.

We have witnessed such scenes in the Canton province,
and other fair portions of the Chinese empire : provinces
each as large as our own happy England have suffered
unbounded calamities from the vengeance of bloodthirsty mandarins.   Let us not be told that the rebels
were mere bands of plundering villains ; would that they
had ! we should not then have to mourn that humanity
had been disgraced by the indiscriminate slaughter of
thousands of innocent people.   The very numbers that
have been executed in cold blood proclaim not only that
the revolution was wide-spread and popular, but that the
government that destroyed them no longer deserved to
exist !

It is sad to stain paper with the records of cruelties committed in the Canton province, and still worse
to record them to our own disgrace, when it is patent to
all that we might have prevented them.   We pretended
neutrality, but carried on communications with one side
only, and took for granted statements that were made,
though we knew that our informants had often previously deceived us.

The large and populous town of Fuh-shan, equal
to Canton as a place of trade, was taken by the rebels.
After it had been held some time, it was reported that
they had burned the whole place, with all its wealth,
and had been driven by the Imperial troops to a village
in the neighbourhood.   As such an event was of great
importance to foreign trade, inquiry was made at the
British Consulate to see if the report were true, and
it was *confirmed*.   Doubting this, or being desirous

of more certain information, a party was formed, and we set off to endeavour to reach the place, as it was only about twelve miles' distant from Canton. We could not get up to the town that day, but went sufficiently far to learn that the Imperialists had burned a small suburb, and that the rebels were still in possession! Next day the United States' acting-consul went up with two armed boats from the United States' ship Vandalia, and found that the Imperial flotilla was some distance from the town. After communicating with one of the mandarins, the boats approached the rebel outworks, the consul wishing to have some communication with the rebels; but unfortunately using a white flag, and waving it as a flag of truce, the rebels took this as a defiance, a white flag being the signal for war, and the waving of it a challenge; the boats were fired on, and returned the fire before retreating. Being anxious to discover the real state of affairs, and if possible to communicate with the rebels to get information, a friend and myself arranged to go to Fuh-shan in a fast six-oared gig. Just as we were starting, the United States' consul returned and advised us not to go by a particular route, as the Chinese admiral had told him the people there were all disaffected; the gentleman who accompanied him as interpreter, told my friend that they had to use fire-arms; but, as I asked if they had seen any fighting, and was told " a little, but only one man was killed," considered that the fighting was between the contending parties, and that my friend, who was a foreigner, might have been mistaken as to the American boat having been engaged. We therefore started to discover, if we could get to Fuhshan by another route, and took the main branch of the river, passed some places where the rebels had been, and found the whole river deserted, though in ordinary times it is the highway of numerous boats of all sizes. We saw several dead bodies, but scarcely a living creature until we came to the fleet blockading Fuh-shan. Before proceeding farther, we thought it best to inquire about the American boats, and found that they had really had a skirmish with the rebels, and that two of the latter had been shot. Under these circumstances it would not have been prudent to go farther, but we found that the rebels were still in full possession, and they held the place for a long time after, even driving off the Imperial fleet. On our return we met a large reinforcement going to join the government forces; they let us pass without question, and we safely reached Canton by the route the Chinese admiral had stated to be so dangerous. The British consul, with right good feeling, requested that we would not again venture on such an expedition. You will see, therefore, that there was almost no opportunity for communication with the rebels. Admiral Sir James Stirling subsequently had interviews with the rebel chiefs at Whampoa, and was so far satisfied with their intentions, that he promised perfect neutrality;—a neutrality which Sir John Bowring did not countenance,[1] as he would not agree to a blockade of Canton, so far as Chinese boats were concerned, though the rebels intimated that no hindrance would be offered to our vessels passing; but they objected to our towing or convoying Chinese craft containing cargo or provisions. There may be little said in favour of the men the rebels had as leaders of their forces; but that they were as good, if not superior, to the soldiers of the Government there can be no doubt.

Many of the wealthy men of Canton, and indeed most of the people of that city, as it was the head-quarters of the mandarin power, professed to disown all connexion with the movement, and contributed large sums towards the

---

[1] Yeh applied to Sir J. Bowring for assistance to protect Canton. See p. 278.

Government troops ; but there was scarcely one who did not condemn the practices of the Imperial officers, and dreaded, perhaps not without reason, the advent of the rebels, for it was from Canton that nearly the whole power of the mandarins proceeded.

It would be easier to state the names of places which were not under rebel rule, than to number the cities in their possession. At one time, in the Canton province, there was scarcely a city they did not hold ; but as the province is intersected with numerous large branches of rivers, and the Imperialists were more powerful on water than the insurgents, the greater part of the best portions of the country were subject to invasions from the Imperial forces. The villagers could not cultivate their lands from fear of seizure, thousands being carried off, and after the revolution had run its disastrous course for more than a year, the rebel forces were gradually compelled to retreat ; ill success militating against them more by its influence with the people, than the reported successes of the troops. The chiefs still have numerous followers with them, and bid defiance to the mandarins from the borders of the province ; and as the exactions and cruelties of the latter still exist, we may again see a revolution through Kwang-Tung, to avenge with tenfold severity the atrocities that have been committed. When it does come, God grant that it may be done quickly ! and that it be not brought about by men like the Canton revolutionists, but that a moral, as well as a political change, may be effected in this part of China. There is but little fear of trade becoming worse ; it has lain fallow so long, that the natural wants of the country must soon cause it to shoot forth, and its previous dormant state will only make it rise with greater vigour.

The first outbreak occurred at Shih-lung, a large trad-

ing place, second only to Fuh-shan ; and situated in the
Tung-kwan district on the Tung-kiang river, about thirty
miles from Canton, is a small village called Sze-ma. The
people here had a dispute with the local authorities,
who collected a large force, and surrounded the village,
but those who had been in arms escaping, the women
and children were put to the sword, root and branch,—
all exterminated. The fields for a mile around the village were laid waste, and the houses razed to the ground.
It is said that Ho-Aluk, one of the Canton chiefs, and a
leading member of the Triad Society, lost a brother in
this massacre ; probably only a " brother" of the Triad
Society. He himself was in the service of the mandarins,
having charge of about a dozen large heavily-armed vessels that were used by the worthy official at Shih-lung
to carry on a smuggling trade with the outer waters,—a
trade that is quite respectable among the mandarins, if
we may judge by the number engaged in it. The triumph
of the Government was short-lived. Ho-Aluk raised
the rebel standard : taking upon himself the title of the
Avenger of Sorrow, he collected a considerable band,
raised chiefly in the Tung-kwan district. The towns of
Shih-lung and Tung-kwan were soon in their possession;
but their first efforts were by no means successful. It
wanted some additional atrocity on the part of the mandarins themselves to give the crowning point to the success of the rebels. A large force was sent against Tung-
kwan from Canton, and closely besieged it. The rebels
were few in number, and as yet but indifferently organized. The people of Tung-kwan felt they had but little
chance, single-handed, against the forces of the mandarins ; so they petitioned that Wa, a former governor
of the city, and a man much respected, should be re-
stored to the government ; and on this condition they
agreed that the city should be given up. Ho-Aluk and

Yang, the other leader, made their escape, and got away most of their guns, but lost nearly all their boats.

While the mandarins' fleet was proceeding to Tung-kwan, and before it dared attack the rebels, day by day vast numbers of prisoners were sent in for decapitation. I saw sixty-three beheaded in less than four minutes!— poor people picked up on the river or in country villages, all slaughtered indiscriminately. But when Tung-kwan was taken possession of, so numerous were the victims, that in one day three boxes of *right* ears were sent up to the Governor-General in lieu of heads. These fearful scenes served only to add fuel to the flame. The Triads rose *en masse*. In one short month, city after city was taken, and before the end of the year Canton was about the only place from which the mandarins had not been expelled. Then difficulties began.

The first great defeat was near Whampoa: the rebels had divided their forces, and when a large detachment was absent, the village braves, collected by some of the wealthy people in Canton, were sent against the body of insurgents in Blenheim Reach. When the attack began the detachment was returning ; but, unfortunately, H.M.S.S. "Styx" got up steam, and the river steamer "Sir Charles Forbes," turned from the course to give the passengers a good view of the fight. These circumstances caused some apprehension in the rebel fleet ; the forces never joined ; a hurried retreat was made, the Canton boats keeping up a brisk running fire, and capturing a fort and some of the rebel craft. Ho-Aluk got clear away, boldly fighting to the last, and keeping in a position that enabled him to protect the rear-guard of the insurgent flotilla. I have this fact from an eye-witness. Now commenced the downfall of the prestige of the insurgents in the province of Canton, and with it the most bloodthirsty acts of the mandarins—acts at which humanity shudders. I shall not detail them. Suffice it to say, that in the city of Canton alone, during six months, 70,000 men were executed ! In Shaou-hing, that number was exceeded. At other places thousands were put to the sword, hundreds cast into the river, tied together in batches of a dozen. I have seen their putrid corpses floating in masses down the stream,—women, too, among the number. Many were cut to pieces alive. I have seen the horrid sight, and the limbless, headless corpse, merely a mass of flayed flesh among headless trunks, that lay in scores covering the whole execution-ground.

It is estimated that more than a million perished in the province within a year after the revolution began ; upwards of 100,000 must have been beheaded in the Canton field of blood, which, strange to say, is a " potter's field."

I have ventured past the place where the sufferers were buried ; it is beyond the leper village on the east side of the city. At first each corpse had a separate grave, and a paltry new coffin, but the number became so great that at last they were merely cast into pits, the executioner making the same coffin serve for many burials, thus gaining no small sum from the allowance for interment. There could not be a more revolting sight than to see the long string of coolies carrying out their ghastly burdens on the otherwise deserted road ; the bodies plainly visible through the broken planks that were loosely huddled around them ; the blood drops marking their course to the grave. It tried one's patience to see the coolies going laughing along with the blood-sodden coffins, joking with their fellows whom they met returning with the empty boxes that had conveyed the first batch of corpses. Truly they " had no feeling of their business." And yet the greater part of

those who had been in arms escaped, and many of them
bear them still. The victims executed were chiefly men
who had submitted to the rule of the insurgents. This
is no rash assertion ; the information is confirmed from
many sources, and among others from mandarins themselves.[1] The Government went so far as to erect pavilions to encourage suicide among the people who
were in favour of the rebellion, and supplied these
places with different means of causing death, proclaiming
that those who thus sacrificed themselves, and escaped
the disgrace of decapitation, would save their families
from participating in the punishment of their guilt.
Several men quite unconnected with the rebels, or at all
events safe from the mandarins, are known to have
arranged for their sale as insurgents, that their friends
might get the reward offered for the capture of a victim !
A gentleman thoroughly acquainted with the southern
Chinese, goes so far as to state that a man gave himself
up as a chief when he knew he would be cut to pieces
alive, though he was perfectly innocent, choosing to represent that character, as the reward was considerable.
This is hard for us to believe, but it is well known that
in China a substitute can be bought for a small sum to
undergo capital punishment.

It must be acknowledged that the remissness of the
mandarins, as well as the bad conduct of their subordi-
nates, did much to bring about a revolution in Canton
province : for not only were the people allowed to arm
too freely under pretext of protecting their country from
the English barbarians (see Lin's proclamation published relative to the opium trade)—but the government
officials, relying on the prowess of the village braves, to
save their own pockets, neglected the regular troops,
thus leaving cities unprepared for any attack ; and actu-

[1] See Memorial of Tsang-wang-yen at the end of Cooke's *China*.

ally strove to hide numerous petty disturbances (precursors of rebellion) from the Imperial eye, going so far as to forgive the perpetrators of the tumult, on condition that the people where it arose should sign a paper stating that it never occurred !

Seu-kwang-tsin, the governor-general, having a pretty accurate idea of what was going to happen, petitioned for leave to visit Pekin, but was denied. His successor Yeh had communicated to the throne such a mass of falsehoods regarding the state of the province, that when he was appointed governor of Hoo-kwang, he petitioned that he might remain in his present berth, as he understood more about the state of the people, and how to manage them in the difficult times that existed, than could any man appointed to succeed him. His lies increased his difficulties, and he had to wipe them out in blood. In July 1854, he reported the rebellion quelled when it was only commencing, and that thousands were killed in victories that were never fought ; and either from his not reporting the occurrences, or from the *Gazette* suppressing them, there is scarcely an allusion to the capture of a single city in Kwang-Tung, until it was retaken, and even then it was not reported till the whole of the disturbances were nearly ended ! So far as we can learn, Yeh has kept from the ears of the Emperor any account of the execution of the tens of thousands in Canton, though he certainly reports the massacre of 30,000 people at Shaou-hing *after* the rebels had left it ! For his success in restoring reported tranquillity, he has been honoured with the high appointment of assistant-minister of the cabinet, but all his honours were taken from him when he suffered himself to be taken prisoner, and carried off by the " barbarians." The wretch died in Calcutta.

CHAPTER XXII.

EVENTS ON THE COAST OF CHINA.

Glance at the Chinese naval history—Marauding bands stop supplies to
Canton, and cause deep distress—The Chinese admiral ordered to break
the blockade—His imbecility—Rebels' blockade extended—Rebel fleet
never molested foreign vessels—Proof to the contrary never shown—
Vessels unjustly declared piratical—Instances of foreign vessels set free
after seizure—British ships chartered to protect junks—Questionable
attack by British ships—Destruction of rebel ships—An awkward error—
Homicide by misadventure—Curious artifice—Heads and cocoa-nuts—
Instances of unfair treatment of Chinese vessels—Question of the right
of a Foreign Government to destroy the fleets of the Insurgents—Defence set up examined—A claim for British law against British might—
Great strength of the Insurgents—Author's motives for urging inquiry
—Supported by instances of inconsiderate condemnation.

BEFORE the Kwang-Tung rebellion reached the coast,
there were many bands of lawless men assembled at
various sea-ports, and instances are known of attacks
upon foreign vessels. These fellows went to the assistance of the rebels, and did much harm, penetrating the
country as far as Shun-tih.[1] The rebels, though glad of
their assistance when the mandarin forces drew near,
were anxious to get rid of them, as it was difficult to
restrain them from plundering. A wealthy Chinaman,
who sent to Hong-Kong for a steamer to remove his
family and valuables from a place in the Shun-tih district, gave a lamentable account of them. The people,
adverse to the mandarins, and yet doubtful of the power

[1] A district city, south-east of Canton.

Q

of the rebels, suffered severely when the men from the coast moved off; it was they who got most of the plunder that was sold at Macao and Hong-Kong.

It is disgraceful to the Government of Hong-Kong and Macao that these places were allowed to be the marts for stolen articles. There is this to be said in favour of Hong-Kong, Macao received the most; and we must not give the pirates the blame of bringing the whole, for lorchas, and even British and American steamers, went up to places held by the rebels and loaded cargoes of produce, the ownership of which was very doubtful.

When the mandarins began to regain their sway, many of the rebels retreated to the coast, and took refuge with the pirate fleets. They formed powerful squadrons, and by no very difficult process transformed the fleets into rebel craft, with which they blockaded the coast and rivers, and stopped all supplies to Canton, thus producing a famine in the surrounding country. The price of rice rose so high in the provincial city that the attention of the foreign merchants was devoted to the importation of grain. Vast quantities were brought from Manilla, India, and the Straits; also from the provinces of Kiang-Soo, Che-Kiang, and Fokien, notwithstanding the prohibition against the export—a prohibition that the mandarins winked at, knowing the distress at Canton; but the foreign inspectors of customs at Shanghai, acting up to the letter of the law, seized a British ship that was loading rice, and confiscated the cargo, their minds not being sufficiently expansive to allow grain to be smuggled at a place where they permitted opium to be imported!

Some of the foreign steamers got high pay to break the rebels' blockade, and bring in a convoy of rice junks.

There was no doubt then about the fleets being rebels. An Imperial force was sent against them, but Macao harbour was more to the taste of the admiral than fighting on the high seas. His fleet went forth,—gongs beating, guns firing, giving ample notice to the rebels, who were waiting outside,—each junk heavily armed, and bearing a large white flag with two official sceptres crossed upon it. No doubt a flaming despatch was sent to Pekin of a grand victory, but the fleet returned next day without having accomplished anything.

Several squadrons of vessels, containing men who had been driven from Kwang-Tung, found a better field for raising funds and molesting the Government, by taking up their station in the intricate channels of the Chusan archipelago, and even as far north as the Gulf of Pih-che-le, and Leoau-Tung as far north as Pekin. They carried on a strict blockade upon the Government grain junks, as well as upon the native traders; but agreeing with the latter to convoy or pass them harmless upon certain dues or black mail being paid. The junks of the north were not fitted to cope with the heavily armed craft that blockaded them; the latter carried very heavy metal and powerful crews. In fact, both Captain Fellowes and Captain Vansittart, who had actions with them, affirm that they could easily take any foreign merchant vessel that sailed in the China sea; and this fact I wish to bring as prominently forward as possible, because the *fleets* in question have never been *proved* to have taken any foreign merchant ships, nor have they ever attacked one unless she was engaged in convoying or protecting native craft attempting to violate the blockade. I am aware that the testimonial epistle to Captain Vansittart, presented by some of the foreign merchants at Shanghai, stated that there was good evidence to prove that these fleets had destroyed several British and American vessels, and murdered their crews ; but I have been unable to find this *proved in any way,* and having asked several who signed the paper to state what evidence they knew, was answered that they had signed the document without being cognisant of such an assertion being made in it ! The public press of China names no ship that had ever been taken by these so-called piratical *fleets,* though instances are given of vessels having been attacked by them when they were accompanied by convoys breaking blockade. Cases too are noticed where foreign vessels have been threatened, and even taken, by piratical junks in the neighbourhood of Hong-Kong ; but these were mere local pirates, our colony being infested with such characters : they are not stated to have belonged to the large squadrons to which I allude.

The southern fleet, chiefly composed of men who were dispersed after the defeat sustained by the insurgents at Whampoa, &c., early in 1855, formed a blockade so strict that it was fully expected that the people of Canton would either have to join in the revolt or perish from want. Foreigners, however, brought plentiful supplies, broke the blockade, and the insurgent fleet were unable to prevent them. The rebellion died away in our immediate vicinity; and His Excellency Sir John Bowring and many others voted that the fleet should be considered as piratical, *because* it took some Chinese vessels from the convoy of an English merchant steam-ship that was breaking the blockade of a port she had no legal right to visit ; besides, she was violating the law as laid down in the neutrality ordinance published by the Hong-Kong government.

The squadron in the neighbourhood of Chusan drove off some English vessels that took convoys from Foochow to Ningpo. Sometimes native boats, and even foreign-built vessels, fell into their hands ; but the crews were let off with the loss of guns, &c., upon promising not to convoy again.

The rebel squadron once took two missionaries, who, upon stating their calling, were forwarded on their journey, though their boat had broken the blockade. A lorcha from Swatow was taken, but set free untouched, upon the captain mentioning the name of the foreigner to whom the cargo belonged. It would allow no native vessel to pass without paying for protection, and one pass was sufficient to free the craft from further detention.

The squadron in the far north, beyond the promontory of Shan-tung, prevented grain tribute reaching Pekin, and blockaded the ports of the Gulf of Pih-che-le and Leoau-tung. Trade from the latter place to Ningpo, in junks, was very considerable, and the cargoes were valuable. The guild in Ningpo, interested in that trade, offered $1000 per junk if the squadron would allow them to sail, and would convoy them to Ningpo ; but the fleet required double that sum for the service.[1] It then became a matter of calculation with the guild whether it would be cheaper to pay the $2000, or buy a foreign steamer to clear the way and protect the junks upon their voyage. The guild decided upon the latter course. It bought the British steam-ship *Paou-Shun* for the mild sum of £23,000, and the vessel was still to remain under the British flag, and be manned by a foreign crew at the guild's expense.

In 1848-49, a Ningpo guild chartered the British schooner "Spec" to look after pirates and protect a

---

[1] This information is from the best authority,—one interested in the affair.

fishery. Her Majesty's ship " Childers" saw the " Spec "
take a vessel said to be a pirate. She seized the schooner,
and the captain and crew were tried for their lives as
pirates, and further convoying was then prohibited.

These were comparatively peaceful times, but now,
when a civil war is raging, and neutrality proclaimed,
convoying is not only permitted, but the British Admiral
Stirling advertised ships to run at stated intervals to
convoy and protect the native coasting trade, thus most
powerfully aiding the reigning dynasty, if not actually
opposing those who wish to overthrow it. A regulation
existed previous to Lord Elgin's treaty that no British
merchant vessel shall proceed further up the coast than
latitude 32° N., that is, not further than the mouth
of Yang-tsze-Kiang. There was a penalty of $10,000,
the seizure of the vessel, and two years' incarceration of
the owner, if any British ship infringed this rule. However, though no British ship could be in danger from
pirates north of the above limit, it was arranged that the
" Paou-shun," under English colours, should be accompanied by Her Majesty's ship " Bittern," to release the
blockaded fleet, and destroy the so-called piratical squadron. These two vessels proceeded on their way, picking
up information from Chinese government officials as
they advanced. They found the junks in an unexplored
inlet in a gulf north of Pekin. No boat was sent to
communicate with them, but it was at once taken for
granted that they were pirates. The squadron was
hemmed in, and, not liking the neighbourhood of such
strange visitors (evidently there for the purpose of destroying it), endeavoured to escape next day in a drizzling
mist, but finding the vessels prepared to dispute the passage, fired at the blockaders, who returned the fire with
interest, and eventually succeeded in sinking nearly the

whole fleet : not a life did they attempt to save, and the whole of the prisoners from one junk, who surrendered, were handed over to the tender mercies of the mandarins on the coast. There was no trial, nor anything told us of the statements made by the prisoners. The two vessels returned to Shanghai after all this slaughter, without a single man having been wounded during the whole cruise !

The few junks that escaped joined the squadron near Chusan, and within a week after, these " bloodthirsty villains" quietly allowed the missionaries above alluded to, to proceed on their way, saying, " those were good men who preached the gospel of Jesus."

H.M.S. " Bittern" found a squadron at anchor in Shih-poo harbour prepared to resist any attacks of Her Majesty's ships, well knowing what these cruisers intended when they discovered armed native vessels. The Chinese, aware of the fate of their comrades in the north, determined to sell their lives dearly. They met the British vessels with a well-directed fire, which, however, was soon silenced ; the junks were destroyed, and their crews shot, drowned, or hunted down, until at last the whole number, about 1000 souls, were sent to their last account,—the " Bittern's " men aiding the Chinese soldiers on shore to complete the wholesale massacre ! The cowardly troops without foreign aid dared not even attack ; the *whole* were not killed ; *one man* who had volunteered information was remanded, and kept over for examination ! The evidence against the fleet, as pirates, was to be collected after the *execution* of the victims ! [1]

Certain junks belonging to the squadron, but unattached at the time of its destruction, finding all was

[1] *Hong-Kong Gazette,* 12th October 1855.

lost, and their power as a body destroyed, began to commit piracy in earnest, and the islands for a time were at their mercy ; boat after boat, however, was rooted out, and it was held by some to be a capital recreation to go out with the "Bittern" or "Paou-shun" "to shoot pirates."

It may be fortunate that these fleets were destroyed, but, as in nearly every case where prisoners have been taken, there has been evidence in proof of innocent people being on board of the captured vessels, the indiscriminate slaughter of all cannot be too severely condemned. In the last-mentioned attack the "Bittern" suffered considerable loss. This vessel did good service under her gallant commander in destroying many junks pointed out as pirates ; but one fleet which she sank near Namoa was, doubtless, composed of rebels, in fact, the notice in the Pekin Gazette *acknowledged* this. I maintain, as a general rule, that there is too great a readiness to fire into Chinese vessels. One example will illustrate this : Her Majesty's ships " Hornet " and " Bittern " were on the look-out for piratical craft between Macao and Hong-Kong. The night was stormy ; the " Hornet " saw five small junks, and wishing to examine them, fired a gun to make them heave to. The " Bittern " hearing the gun, at once fancied that her consort had discovered the pirates, and seeing the boats, immediately fired a charge of grape. Several persons were killed, and many wounded ; but the boats turned out to be innocent passenger-carriers. There was an inquest, and the verdict was " Homicide by misadventure." [1]

When Her Majesty's ship " Rattler," in conjunction with part of the crew of the United States' ship " Powhattan," went to Kulan to destroy the southern squadron

[1] *China Mail,* 5th April 1855.

above-mentioned, the number killed was estimated at 600 (the Americans said 2000). Captain Fellowes' despatch to Sir John Bowring states, however, that the "junks offered no further resistance after the boats got near enough to throw grape." The chief portion of the junks were destroyed, and, notwithstanding the number killed, only six prisoners were taken. The Chinese used a curious artifice for their defence ; they threw overboard a lot of *cocoa-nuts*, and then jumped into the sea among them ; it was difficult to tell which were heads, and which were nuts. The foreign force sustained some trifling loss quite disproportionate to the numbers of Chinese that were killed.

The six prisoners were brought to Hong-Kong ; upon being examined, three proved to be perfectly innocent men, who were held by the junks for ransom. Their evidence has been kept back ; perhaps they told of many more innocent people among the fleet, and it becomes a curious matter of speculation to discover, if out of six taken, three were harmless, how many were innocent among the hundreds that were killed ?

There seems to be very little doubt that some portions of this fleet were connected with the rebels, for some insurgent flags were secured as trophies. The Government in Hong-Kong appeared to be determined to make the men out pirates. The three remaining prisoners were tried, and found guilty of murder ; but as, by the evidence, it was shown that they were actually prisoners at the time, and away from the junk which blew up, the men for whose murder they were tried being killed by the explosion, the judge deferred passing sentence. The following extraordinary course was pursued by the Colonial Government :—

The executive council set aside the verdict of the

jury. The judge was sick : a new trial was, however, at once determined upon, and a judicial commission formed. The members of this commission were,—President, the acting Attorney-General, who had previously been *prosecutor*, assisted by two members of the executive council, who had set aside the verdict of the Chief-Justice ! The verdict was again " guilty," and the men were sentenced to death, but, I believe, were not hanged. I could relate many other stories,—some which are of recent occurrence, but enough has been written to show that the Chinese do not receive the treatment they ought from our ships of war. Our neutrality is a mere sham while such proceedings are allowed to take place ; if we must do police duty on the coast of China, we should, at least, investigate thoroughly the character and aims of the people against whom we act. In former years, when the trade of China was not open to the world, armed bodies of men in fleets upon the coast acting in direct hostility to the Government, and levying a species of black-mail or tax upon the people, but trading with them as Cochinga did, could not be classed under the category of pirates ; they had, doubtless, a political status. When we consider that only five ports are open to foreign trade, and that no foreign vessel was allowed to appear north of Shanghai, there are strong objections against our concluding that all armed Chinese vessels are pirates that are found in these waters during a period of civil strife. There is little doubt that the rebel forces on land made far worse havoc and interfered more with our trade than the fleets at sea, whether rebels or pirates.

In justification of the attacks made by H. M. ships, it has been said, that, in nearly every case, the Chinese have fired the first shot ; but when it is considered that on all the above occasions, H. M. ships have gone for the avowed purpose of destroying the squadrons, is it to be wondered at that they should resist when searched out and driven to desperation ? These events on the coast of China have attracted much of my attention, nor have I spared either time or labour in order to gain correct information regarding them ; and having enjoyed the best opportunities for collecting the opinions of those most competent to judge, it now appears beyond doubt that the two or three vessels that have been " missing " while on voyages along the coast while these fleets existed, have been lost in Tai-foongs, which they are known to have encountered. The fleets that were said to have taken them have been destroyed, and no evidence has been gathered from any of the few prisoners to prove that the " missing " vessels had been captured. It must be allowed, then, that we had no proper cause of quarrel against the squadrons that we went to destroy. Her Majesty's naval officers cannot be expected to be *au fait* of Chinese politics, nor can they, while unprovided with proper interpreters, act with common justice in doubtful cases,—the Will-o'-the-wisp, " promotion, " leading them beyond the safe bounds. But when we find that such repeated acts of indiscriminate slaughter are successively commended by the authorities, we surely have a right to demand that justice be tempered with mercy. I earnestly trust that these humble pages may draw attention to the subject, that some more Christian-like course may be adopted, and that to the Chinese themselves, shall be secured the privileges of British law, if they are to suffer by British might. Surely no Englishman would attempt to justify the wholesale slaughter of the unfortunate victims in Canton. Our surprise is therefore great when such acts as the Hong-Kong *Gazettes* relate, with reference to the

proceedings above commented upon, meet with such un-
qualified approbation. The proceedings of the mandarins justified a revolution ; the country required a
change ; the manner in which the change has been
attempted is greatly to be deplored, but it was no affair
of ours to prevent it.

It is a pity that brave and daring acts should draw
down such remarks, but it must be remembered that the
rebellion is still rampant, and that though the coast is
at present comparatively tranquil, it may again become
the refuge of one of the contending parties who will seek
to preserve its existence in the same way as their predecessors.   Shall British ships of war repeat their former
course, and become the executioners of the cruel orders
of the mandarins ?

If we can believe the *Pekin Gazette*, the Government
must have had an alarming force against it.   In 1854,
the Chinese *Moniteur* reported the number of rebels
killed in action at 123,890, and in 1855 the number was
14,000, not including such expressions as " heaps of
slain," the " rivers filled with corpses," " the road for
twenty miles covered with bodies," &c. ; but the *actual
numbers given*.   This does not include the executions
in Canton city, where above 100,000 were beheaded.

In these remarks I wish rather to bring the system to
public notice than to condemn any one.   While we are
so deficient in interpreters, and really know so little of
the actual state of affairs in China, from the Plenipotentiary downwards, it is dangerous for our civil authorities to call upon the naval and military officers to make
attacks when we are not in an actual state of war.   I
remember one instance when upwards of seventy men
surrendered to H.M.S. " Niger," and claimed to be set
free because they were rebels, and had only attacked

mandarins' junks. After an examination, and without any regular trial, they were sent over to Cow-loon, the mandarin station opposite to Hong-Kong, and there in rebel dress, and with the long hair as worn by the rebels, the chiefs and others were politely handed over, by the Hong-Kong civil authorities, to the mandarins, and to the certain fate of being either beheaded or cut into pieces while alive. And this too happened when we were at war with Yeh! I saw them given over; for being unable to believe the report of such being the intention, I set off in my little yacht, and by dint of cracking on, arrived at Cow-loon in time to see the police boats land and deliver up the men. I felt interested in the matter, having been told that the leader was brother to the chief who attempted the insurrection at Go-swa, and whose wife had blown herself and family into the air when the soldiers appeared to seize her, as related in another chapter. Probably the men, like others who pretended to be rebels while we were at war with Yeh, were no better than pirates ; but as I have witnessed the horrors of a rebel execution, I was sorry for them, especially as their dress and long hair would be terrible evidence against them.

I think that the instances related will suffice to condemn the system of acting upon the old saying, that " dead men tell no tales."

CHAPTER XXIII.

CHINESE EMIGRATION.

Chinese in California and Australia—Travelling corrects prejudices—
Hard usage of Chinese insurgents—Cheerfulness at sea—Horror of burial
at sea—Sharp dealing of a Yankee captain—Unfair treatment of coolies
—Difficulty of procuring them at present—Description of coolies on
board—Effect of good and of ill treatment upon them—Traits of character—Chinese prejudices not corrected by what they see abroad.

THE thousands of Chinese that have been attracted
to the gold fields of California and Australia, and who
return with some slight knowledge of foreign nations
and customs, must eventually have some influence in
changing the stereotyped ideas long prevalent in China
regarding the might and power of other countries.
They have had an opportunity of seeing free government, some enlightened institutions, and some of the
advantages of civilisation and science. However, we
cannot give them credit for having observed all these
things, their minds were doubtless bent rather on making
money than troubling themselves with public matters.
We can easily suppose, too, that the treatment they
received while abroad would go farther in determining
their opinions than could any political problem. They
were almost expelled from California by invidious taxa-
tion, and we cannot expect that the jealous diggers and
Californian rangers gave them a high idea of American
civilisation. In one of the Australian colonies, laws

were made in contradiction to all ideas of the British Constitution, to prevent the immigration of Chinese, and every difficulty was thrown in their way. They were " stuck up," were almost driven from some of the " diggins," and their very industry and sobriety became sins in the eyes of dissolute and drunken colonists. They kept themselves aloof, and associated only with each other ; and statistics show that among the 20,000 Chinese at one time congregated in the colony of Victoria, there was far less crime than among half the number of English and others that were there. In California, when the acts of the Senate had brought the raid against the Chinese to such a crisis that few were left in the country, the people found that they could not do without them.

The worst feature in Chinese emigration is, that it is confined almost exclusively to males ; as families are not formed, they do not become settlers, but each man generally returns to his native country when he has earned capital sufficient to be useful at home.

They return with an average of about five hundred dollars, clear profit, generally in the course of a couple of years. They pay their own passage there and back, and sometimes join in cliques, some of the members probably being hired.

As *passengers* (those who pay their own passage), I have heard many captains say, that they are the best that can be carried, give less trouble, and are the most cheerful. They pass their time in gambling, eating, and sleeping, often losing on their homeward voyage all the gains made in their absence.

Some who die abroad, arrange for their remains being sent to their ancestral tombs. A smart Yankee captain bringing over about two hundred Chinese from San

Francisco lost one of his passengers, and buried him at sea ; the others complained of this, and said that they would have paid a large amount if the body had been taken to their port of destination.　Another dying, the skipper gave the order, " Heave him overboard."　The passengers protested ; no use ; he repeated, " Heave him overboard ;" until he worked up their feelings to the extent of three hundred dollars, got his money, and as he was close to Hong-Kong, brought in the body.　One ship came from California freighted with dead Chinamen.

If the Chinese could be induced to become *bona fide* emigrants, taking their families with them, they would prove invaluable additions to many of our colonies, especially in the West Indies, where labour is so much wanted.　In Ceylon too, and the Mauritius, they would be most useful.　Quick to learn, steady in their habits, and moderate in their wants, few better colonists could be found than the industrious Chinese.　The difficulty in getting them to bring their wives is hard to be got over ; even to Hong-Kong, the Chinamen are chary of bringing their females.　The proportion of the adult population on shore in 1857, was 32·711 men to 7·851 women ; the dearness of house rent may partly account for this, as houses with apartments exclusively for the females are very expensive ; out of all proportion to what the Chinese are accustomed to pay in China.

There is another kind of emigration from China : that of coolies or labourers, whose passage is paid for them, engagements being made to employ them for five, or sometimes eight years, and part of the wages paid in advance.　These men are sent to the British West Indies, Havanna, and Peru.

This system, when properly carried out, might be

very advantageous to both the foreigner and the Chinaman, but there have been cases in which it has been
so grossly abused, that the trade should be entirely
stopped until it be put upon a better footing.[1] As it at
present exists, it is little better than a legalized slave-
trade.

When the contracts are made with ·a guarantee of
the authorities at the place of destination, for their
being properly carried out, then all well and good ;
but when the contracts become matter for competition
where the coolies are disembarked, and the man's services become an article for sale, without the purchaser
guaranteeing to fulfil the terms of the contract, it is a
sort of temporal slavery. When the men are treated on
board ship like slaves, and as it were imprisoned, with
sentries with loaded fire-arms constantly over them, who
shoot them when they make an attempt to escape, the
trade becomes so thoroughly disgraceful, that the sooner
it is ended the better.

The men are engaged by native brokers. At first,
fine hale strong men came forward voluntarily as emigrants. They had it fully explained to them where
they are going—or rather the length of the voyage, what
they would have to do, &c., and no difficulty was found
in having a choice of good men. Those sent to the
British West Indies, Trinidad, and Demerara, were
particularly fortunate; there were few deaths on the
voyage, and those who have seen the men there, speak
highly of their usefulness and their satisfaction. The
cost of sending them, and caring for them properly,
exceeded the amount of Government bounty, and the
emigration to that quarter has ceased. To Havanna,
however, it still goes on, though there have been severe

1 Some improvements are now being made by Mr. Austin at Canton.

losses by mortality, arising from disease or bad management on board of some of the vessels, and the men are worked too hard when they arrive. To Peru, large numbers were sent when the slaves there were emancipated a few years ago. Those taken to that country are carried on speculation, and their services sold with their contracts ; some may be fortunate in getting good masters, others the reverse. There is now a clause in the contracts that men shall not be sent to the Guano Islands, but as the contracts are sold, it is doubtful whether this clause is always adhered to. Those Chinese who were basely inveigled away, and sent by hundreds to slave in working the guano, lived in misery the most horrible, were treated with the utmost severity, many ending their intolerable sufferings by throwing themselves over precipices into the sea. Shame on the heartless wretches implicated in this horrible atrocity ; shame on them too for the disgraceful treatment of the coolies on board ship ! Some vessels lost hundreds on the voyage, and yet to this day, no punishment has been inflicted on the guilty perpetrators of these gigantic murders.

I have said that at first the coolie emigrants came forward voluntarily, and were fine hale men. It is now difficult to get any, and most of those that are got, are poor miserable wretches compared with the first emigrants. I have been on board vessels at both periods : the first men looked even better than the average class of emigrants who pay their own passage. Many are now mere lads, beggarly-looking fellows, some covered with disease. On board of one ship that was going to Peru, as a receptacle for *prisoners*, I found a most admirable state of cleanliness and discipline. Over the hatches were iron gratings, on the decks were water-tanks provided with reeds, inserted perpendicularly into them, from which the prisoners could drink at will, thus preventing waste of water. About a dozen men marched about with loaded muskets, and well supplied with other arms and ammunition. The crew had their quarters aft; out of the bulk-head, which separated them from the rest of the deck, four large cannons protruded ready to rake the deck. On the poop above, there was another tier of guns, and above them, on high stanchions, were several swivels! All this, of course, showed the Chinese they were really prisoners; they were not allowed to communicate with the shore. Each was ticketed, all were mustered every day, and when any attempted to escape they knew what they had to expect. They were, of course, perfectly idle, but those who slept during the day were " stirred up," as it prevented them sleeping at night.

When the coolies are well treated on board they are quiet, and good passengers; but where harshness is exhibited, they have been known to rise and murder the crew. When they are managed with firmness combined with kindness, and made to understand the reason for, or the justness of the captain's acts, all goes well. Get up a laugh or a joke, and they are all in good humour. No men are easier to govern than the Chinese; even when roused almost to fury, they are readily subdued.

It is only justice to the Chinese that arrangements should be made for their return at the expiration of their time of contract-service, if they wish. No stipulation of this kind is made, and if a proprietor chooses to get a labourer into his debt, the time of service only ends with the coolie's life; besides, who is there to care for the interests of the Chinese if the governments of the respective countries do not take care that provision is

made for them ?   There have been some most melancholy instances of loss of life from want of proper care.
One ship lost nearly all her passengers and crew by
disease brought on by the vessel being ballasted with
mud ; another lost some hundreds by suffocating them
in battening down the hatches ; and a third lost several
men by a fever brought on by allowing the coolies to
buy quantities of green food, and giving an unlimited
quantity of rice to men that had been accustomed to a
supply only sufficient for their existence before they
came on board.

Taking emigration as one of the sources from which
the Chinese are to form a higher standard of the merits
of foreigners, we cannot congratulate ourselves upon the
results.   Neither California nor the West Indies, Australia nor Peru, are good fields for them to learn a
fair estimate of the " barbarian," nor should I wonder
if their experience of foreigners had ied the Chinese to
think better of their own " celestial kingdom."

Slow but sure.

CHAPTER XXIV.

CRISIS OF THE INSURRECTION.

Leaning of the English authorities to the mandarins, and to the maintenance of the Imperial government—Gross error of the English in not
recognising the Christian element that animated the Chinese rebellion—
Lord Elgin's policy biassed by the one-sided view of his interpreters—Sir
J. Bowring's policy determined by the belief that British commerce with
China depends on the maintenance of the present dynasty—Difficulty of
promulgating Christianity—Mr. Wade's animosity to the rebels con-
trasted with the opinions of others—Improbability of Lord Elgin's expedition up the Yang-tsze-Kiang being useful at present—A convincing
proof given of the non-existence of the neutrality which had been proclaimed.

FOR the last four or five years, while the cause of
Tai-ping-wang has apparently been on the wane, the
Imperial Government found strong supporters, and the
insurgents as strenuous opponents, among foreigners,
especially among British officials. In the chapter devoted to " Events on the Coast," I endeavoured to show
the kind of support the Imperial Government derived by
the direct assistance of foreign power. There was, however, another, and probably more efficient description of
aid organized at Shanghai, in the first instance, by which
the assistance of some of our best interpreters was given
to help the Chinese in collecting as large a revenue as
possible from the foreign trade. The Chinese authorities
at the different ports, either on account of their farming the customs' revenue, or being liable for only a
certain amount of duty to the Imperial Treasury, showed

no anxiety to secure full payment of duties on foreign trade. Some places, such as Foochow and Amoy, made actual reductions on the tariff, so as to induce an extension of trade, and a consequent increase of duties to their own profit. At Ningpo, the Taou-tai lost money by his post, because the trade there in the first year when Chusan was occupied, was larger than for some years afterwards, and he was accountable for an amount of duties equal to that collected when the port was first opened to foreign trade. At Canton, a rivalry among different custom-house linguists or brokers, often led to sometimes considerable reductions in duties to the benefit of foreign trade. But at Shanghai, a system of smuggling came into practice owing to the laxity of the Chinese officials, and at last was taken advantage of to such an unwarrantable extent, that for the protection of the more honest merchant, some interference became necessary.

It was, therefore, arranged that the three Treaty powers, England, France, and the United States should each furnish an officer to assist the Chinese in the proper collection of the revenue. Strict measures were enforced, and, so far as the merchants were concerned, as all were thus put upon the same footing with regard to trade, the system worked well, the foreign custom-house officers did their duty to their Chinese employers most thoroughly, and must have been very useful to the mandarins. As the trade increased, a very large revenue was collected, and the Government being in urgent necessity for funds to carry on the war against the insurgents, no doubt the Taou-tai of Shanghai was thus enabled to contribute largely to the Imperial requirements. The foreign inspectors of Customs took no cognizance of the opium trade, so, in spite of their strictness, opium was im-

ported as usual, and the revenue derived from it did not
pass through their books.   They, however, prevented the
export of rice and pulse coastwise, though a large trade
in grain was going on from all the other ports to Canton,
when prices were high there.   The export from Shanghai
might have interfered with the wants of the army, and
the supply for Pekin.   They provided all the munitions
of war for the Imperial Government, and, in fact, were
apparently so interested in the maintenance of the
empire, that they winked at prohibited articles of import that brought a revenue to the mandarins, and
strictly enforced the prohibition on exports that might
be needed by the Government of the province.   They did
not even prevent Chinese troops being sent in a British
ship to the province of Canton, when we were at war
with Yeh.   However correct they may have been in thus
assisting the mandarins, their position naturally gave them
a strong bias in favour of the Government, in whose pay
they were.   Each received £1500 a year for his services.
Mr. Wade was the active head of the department, and
chief moving power.   He had long been an interpreter
in the service of the British Consulate, and when he was
appointed Chinese Secretary to the British plenipotentiary, he retired from the inspectorate, and was succeeded
in it by Mr. Lay, who was already strongly predisposed
to the Imperial cause, and thus became a valuable
assistance to the mandarins.[1]   I am well acquainted with
both of the above gentlemen.   Few men are better informed regarding Chinese affairs, but they view them
entirely from one side.   It would be difficult to find a more
pleasant companion than Mr. Wade, full of anecdote and
humour.   He was, in a social point of view, a great acqui-

[1] As I have frequently argued against Mr. Wade's opinions personally
with himself, I feel less hesitation in disputing them now when he is absent.

sition to Lord Elgin's mission. He knows Chinese well, though he does not speak it fluently ; and his deficiency was well supplemented by Mr. Lay. Mr. Wade has for several years been the chief informant of the British Plenipotentiary regarding Chinese affairs. That Lord Elgin should have been guided by Mr. Wade is natural, as his position of Chinese Secretary to the Plenipotentiary would naturally make him interpreter to the Embassy ; but when another interpreter was required to act with Mr. Wade, it seems unfortunate that the services of Mr. Lay were made use of when his views were so identically the same, and especially, as he was at the time employed by the Chinese Government. We shall see how these circumstances influenced events. But, irrespective of the influence Mr. Wade's opinions may have had upon Lord Elgin, they have, for some time previous to his Excellency's mission, had the effect of determining the principal features of British policy in China.

The success of the foreign inspectorate at Shanghai led to the idea of showing to the Chinese Government, by it, the positive advantages the Imperial treasury would gain from foreign trade.

Since the death of the Rev. Dr. Medhurst, most of the notices published regarding the movements of the insurgents have been from the pen of Mr. Wade, and consist almost entirely of translations from the Pekin Government Gazette. This will account in a great measure for the gradual falling off of all interest in the rebellion ; nothing but defeats were reported, their religion was never mentioned,—no doubt they were losing power. They lost many cities that had been in their possession ; and quarrels among their leaders, resulting in the death of Yang, the eastern king, and many of his followers implicated in a conspiracy, became known, and confidence in the stability of Tai-ping-wang's power was considerably shaken. Many reports were current of Tai-ping-wang's death. Ching-Kiang-foo, considered one of his greatest strongholds, fell into Imperial hands with the usual amount of *éclat;* but the other story was, that the Imperial General was threatened with death if he did not recover the place by a certain day. He could not take it by force, but arranged for its purchase from the rebels; the amount stated was 300,000 taels of silver, and he had to provide boats for the conveyance of the insurgent garrison to Nankin. Some of the boatmen employed gave this account of it at Ningpo.

Mr. Consul Meadows, whose work on the "Chinese and their Rebellions," gives the most detailed account of the insurrection, was absent for some years after he visited Nankin with Sir George Bonham in 1853; and on his return to China, as Sir John Bowring and he were not on good terms, his opinions had no influence on British policy. Sir John Bowring's policy was, that the British trade with China depended upon the present dynasty being maintained. All his acts during the revolution in the Kwang-Tung province proved this; and I believe that even in the dispute with Yeh, had Sir John Bowring been allowed to carry out his own views, and not been superseded by Lord Elgin, the Canton affair would have been settled on the spot, and the indemnity for losses been secured *before* any attempt was made to disturb or harass the Government at Pekin or Tien-tsin, with imposing forces to exact new treaties. One of the greatest difficulties with which the British Government has now to contend, is the danger that exists of our acts in the coming war causing the overthrow of the dynasty which they would rather uphold.

Suppose a contrary policy had ruled the plans of the British Government in China for the last six years. Suppose an attempt had been made to set the insurgents right where they were wrong in the matters of the Christian religion, which they certainly did preach. Suppose that they had had as much assistance given them as the British Government gave to the mandarins, by preventing the rebels in Canton enforcing blockades. Suppose we had *not* protected the coast for the Chinese Government against rebels and pirates. Suppose we had, as neutrals, prohibited the sale of any description of munitions of war, *and enforced* the prohibition.[1] Any one, even unacquainted with Chinese affairs, will understand what a vast difference there would now be, both in our relations with China and the position of the Government with which we are now at war, had a different line of policy been adopted—had we remained strictly neutral.

It is unfortunate that a great nation, whose ruler bears the title of the Defender of the Faith, would do nothing to defend the Christian faith from errors when they were apparent, or to help the advancement of that faith in China when a splendid opportunity offered. Even if commerce were for a time jeopardized, it seems inconsistent that a Christian nation should look to its commercial interests only, and neglect the interests of religion. I doubt if commerce would have suffered, and am disposed to think, that whatever might have happened, the inherent trading tendencies of the Chinese would always have kept open some good channels of trade. The chance was offered to improve and promulgate a really Christian religion, emanating from the Chinese themselves. Aid might

---

[1] Arms, &c., were ordered from Hong-Kong by the Chinese Government at the time we were at war with Yeh ; and there was no check to the purchase, except laws which were never enforced.—See Cooke's *China.*

have been given upon the condition of the religion being kept free from error and presumptuous assumptions ; and one general doctrine would have obtained a good footing in a straight path, instead of, as we see now, a number of different denominations of Christians stumbling forward in divers directions, with but indifferent success. As Lord Elgin well says in his despatch to Lord Clarendon of 31st March 1858, when forwarding copy of an address presented to him by the missionaries at Shanghai :—" It is to be regretted that the existence of profound divisions among ourselves should be one of the first truths which we Christians reveal to the heathen whom we desire to convert." This shows so clearly the difficulties we have now to surmount on account of our refusal to acknowledge and assist anything that was good in the Christian religion published by the Chinese, that it is needless remarking further on the subject, except to say how many evils might have been prevented, and how much good might have been done, had the religion of the insurgents been guided by the counsels and support of enlightened Christians. India was nearly lost by pandering to expediency and supporting caste, which is a species of religion opposed to Christianity ; and how much we suffered from it ! Our difficulties in China may be commencing from our neglect of Christianity there also.

Far from endeavouring to countenance the insurgents or their religious notions, the reverse has been the case. In another chapter I have stated how Lord Elgin treated them when he visited the Yang-tsze-kiang ; and to show how much his Excellency's conduct may be attributed to the feelings of Mr. Wade, we shall notice what Mr. Wade reports of the insurgents to Lord Elgin, and contrast his remarks with those of Mr. Consul Meadows.

These will show that I have good reasons for bringing the subject to public notice.

Mr. Meadows thus relates the account of one of his meetings with a rebel leader at Chin-kiang-foo, when he was sent to look for British deserters :—

" We were ushered through one or two more halls into the presence of Commandant Lo, who received us in his full yellow and red uniform. He at once recognised me as the person who, two months before, had landed from the " Hermes " to speak to him, after we had been firing at each other. He said no foreign deserters had come within his position, nor had any foreigners been observed directing the guns fired from the Imperial camps against the city. After this formal matter had been discussed, we had some conversation on other matters, military and religious. I inquired how it was that the Tai-pings did not make greater use of the smaller firearms, muskets and pistols,—the former of which, I said, were, with the attached bayonets, our chief arms. I was induced to ask this, because,

Mr. Wade at Woo-hoo (*Blue-Book*):—

" Hau is chief theologian, as well as chief mandarin ; a dirty but not ill-looking man, in a yellow robe, with a handkerchief about his head. He was immediately joined by another Cantonese, and the hall was soon filled with a number of men speaking the dialect of Canton. All, however, high and low, without distinction of province or degree, crowded in to look at us. They became a dense mob, and paid not the slightest attention to the commands of Hau, or other chiefs.[1] There was not the semblance of order in the house or out of it. A young boy, the son of one of the leaders, rebuked the intruders in the unmistakable slang of the south, but without avail. Hau stared much when we replied to his questions, that we were merely *en route* to Han-kow. On our inquiring for supplies, he desired

[1] In the presence of the highest officers and princes of the blood, Lord Amherst, when at Pekin, was subjected to the same annoyance. " The room had filled with spectators of all ages and ranks, who rudely pressed upon us to gratify their brutal curiosity, for such it may be called, as they seemed to regard us rather as wild beasts than mere strangers of the same species with themselves."—*Embassy to China*, p. 178.

At Soo-chow, where Mr. Oliphant went to deliver a letter from Lord Elgin to the minister of state, the attendants crowded round the mandarin, and read the letter over his shoulder.—*Narrative of Lord Elgin's Mission*, vol. i. p. 202.

This sort of proceeding is quite usual in China ; and even when forced out, the people will try to peep in at the windows. But Mr. Wade brings this in evidently to tell against the insurgents.

while there was a great demand among the Tai-pings for swords, they seemed to take little interest in guns. Lo said, that his people did not understand the use of them, and that they were valueless when the supply of ammunition ran out, or the springs went wrong. Swords and spears, he said, seldom got out of order, and he found that his people could always beat the Imperialists with them. . . . He said, ' I am beginning to get old now, but give me a good spear, and I am still not afraid to meet any ten of them.' There seemed to be a very intimate relation, almost a filial relation, between his black-clothed followers and himself. Some fifty to a hundred of them were standing in the hall opposite to where I was sitting, and Lo, casting a glance over them, asked if I thought they looked like men who could ' conquer the rivers and the mountains.' . . . He volunteered the statement, that the Tai-pings had not advanced to Soo-chow and Shanghai, because they wished to avoid as much as possible whatever might cause interruption to the commercial operations of the season. In saying this there was no pretence of extreme friendly feeling. It simply meant, ' You see, where we can avoid it, we are willing to spare your countrymen loss.' He and all his people received us as persons in no way hostile to him, and with a civility that appeared to cost them no effort. Lo appeared to be about fifty years of age : he was middle-sized as to height, and square built, without, however, being remarkably broad."[1]

that a list should be taken of what we wanted. This was done by a particularly dirty Fuh-kien man, who took down Mr. Mainprise's demands with an air of great self-complacency. He wrote an execrable hand, and was evidently of no higher caste than his fellows, whom, after many years' experience at Hong-Kong, I should have, at first sight, pronounced a gang of opium-smoking pirates. The prices put upon the articles we named were not exorbitant ; but the chiefs said some days would be necessary to collect the larger quotas in our list. This part of our errand done, we took our leave, glad to escape from the pressure of this most disorderly mob, and the offensive atmosphere they created. I have seen no Chinese community in a theatre or market-place less respectable."

---

[1] *Chinese and their Rebellions,* p. 307.

Mr. Meadows thus describes a crowd of Tai-ping-wang's men:—

"They were without exception dressed in the plainest and simplest clothing, viz., black Chinese jackets and trousers.

"Amidst all the variety of figure and feature, there was invariably the grave and earnest demeanour and expression naturally to be expected in men, who had for three years been engaged in unremitting fight for their existence."

Mr. Meadows remarks as follows, upon a letter of the insurgents :—

"I subjoin the substance only, for, though carefully prepared, it is, in a literary point of view, somewhat deficient, so much so, that a translation is less likely to be informing to the English reader than an abstract. Lo-ta-kang, the commandant of Chin-Kiang, has been mentioned as originally a Triad society rebel leader, who joined the Tai-pings in Kwang-si. Though one of their best generals, and, therefore, placed in charge of a position at once so exposed, and so important, as Chin-kiang, his literary attainments were of the scantiest, and there were, in consequence, manifest signs of confusion in the Chin-kiang secretariat." On page 278, Mr. Meadows says, "The tone of these letters, as well as of the language and personal bearing of Lo-ta-kang himself, was perfectly courteous, without being in the slightest degree mean."

Mr. Wade, at Ngan-king, could not say so much against the generality of the rebels, but *picks out one specimen* to bring the others more into contempt.

"The crowd, generally, seemed to me to be in better case than the Woo-hoo rebels, more healthy looking, and better dressed. One of them, who was much the reverse, however, pushed himself forward, and addressed me in Canton English. He volunteered the information that he came from Whampoa, and bore other marks, besides his acquaintance with our language, of subjection to our influences. He looked, what I have no doubt he was, an opium-smoking coolie."

In translating a rebel document, Mr. Wade remarks :—

"The writing within is mostly in Hephthemmimer verse, of small literary pretension, and in indifferent handwriting — singularly indifferent, when it is borne in mind how generally the educated Chinese are found to write decently if not well."

Very few of the merchants in Canton can speak the mandarin, and the few who attempt it use provincialisms.

Most of the native merchants we meet with are illiterate ; they write indifferently, and if called upon to write a letter of the commonest description, hesitate and bungle over the characters. Those who write well are exceptions. After two months' travelling under the charge of various officers, Mr. Ellis says, "Our present mandarin is the first officer able to read and write with facility, who has been attached to the boat ; he is, however, totally unprovided with books, and he passes his time in the same idle gaping as his predecessors ; of his philosophy, he truly makes no use."[1]

Mr. Meadows gives the following account of his interview with one of the chiefs at Nankin in 1853.

"The northern prince listened, but made little or no rejoinder ; the conversation, in so far as directed by him, consisting mainly of inquiries as to our religious beliefs, and expositions of his own. He stated, that as children and worshippers of one God, we were all brethren ; and after receiving my assurance, that such had long been our view also, inquired if I knew the heavenly rules. I replied that I was most likely acquainted with them, though unable to recognise them under that name ; and after a moment's thought, asked if they were ten in number. He answered eagerly in the affirmative. I then began repeating the substance of the first of the Ten Commandments, but had not proceeded far before he laid his hand on my shoulder in a friendly way, and exclaimed, ' The same as ourselves ! the same as our-

At Nankin, Mr. Wade's party feeling is shown pretty strongly, for, when he has anything favourable to tell, he must find an excuse for unfavourable remarks—

"We were received by a heavy-looking Kwang-si man, named Li, in what seemed his private apartment, for he immediately called for his cap of office, the high conical head-dress, stated by Mr. Wylie to have been worn under the Ming dynasty, and led us into a really handsome hall, in the style of the Woo-hoo yamun, but far cleaner. Our host was dressed in yellow silk, and curiously embroidered shoes. His costume, on the whole, was really becoming, but he himself was manifestly very ill at ease, and, I should say, at any time, a commonplace person."

[1] Amherst's *Embassy to China*, page 313.

selves!' while the simply observant expression on the face of his companion disappeared before one of satisfaction, as the two exchanged glances. He then stated, with reference to my previous inquiry, as to their feelings and intentions towards the British, that not merely might peace exist between us, but that we might be intimate friends. He spoke repeatedly of a foreigner at Canton whom he named Lo-ho-Sun (Mr. Roberts), as being a " good man.' . . . He recurred again and again, with an appearance of much gratitude, to the circumstance, that he and his companions in arms had enjoyed the special protection and aid of God, without which, they could never have been able to do what they had done against superior numbers and resources ; and alluding to our declaration of neutrality and non-assistance to the Mantchoos, said, with a quiet air of conviction, ' It would be wrong for you to help them ; and what is more, it would be of no use. Our Heavenly Father helps us, and no one can fight with him ! ' "

Mr. Wade appears to have taken little pains to gather information about the religious opinions of the insurgents. The information he got on this point, from one who wished to desert, is given, as it well accorded with the view in which he wished to exhibit the insurgents.

It is very unfortunate that so little interest was taken with regard to the religion of the rebels, that the gentlemen of Lord Elgin's mission could not wait[1] to get some of the new books promised to be given next day by the insurgents. All that is reported on the subject shows with what different feelings Mr. Wade viewed it to those which influenced Mr. Meadows' remarks.

In describing one of the rebel leaders, Mr. Meadows says :—
"The man who used this lan-

Mr. Wade says:—
" Li was apologetic, but without servility ; he seemed more anxious

---

[1] "So much of the day has been consumed by our long ride, that we were unable to stay more than *a quarter of an hour* with Li."—*Blue Book*, page 451.

guage of courageous fidelity to the cause in every extreme, and of confidence in God, was a shrivelled-up, elderly little individual, who made an odd figure in his yellow and red hood; but he could think the thoughts and speak the speech of a hero. He and others like him have succeeded in infusing their own sentiments of courage and morality to no slight extent, considering the materials operated upon, into the minds of their adherents."

to take us on the religious side, beginning again and again that we were brethren of one family, as Christians; but this in a constrained way, without impressiveness or enthusiasm."

One would judge from this that Mr. Wade wished to avoid the matter being discussed on the religious side. Surely there must have been some "impressiveness" when the man began "again and again" on the subject.

Dr. Taylor, of Shanghai, who visited the rebels at Chin-Kiang-foo, says " he was struck with the calm and earnest enthusiasm that pervaded the entire body, and the perfect confidence evinced in the justice of their cause, and its final success." One of our cleverest missionaries in China, the Rev. Mr. Edkins, says :—" This movement in favour of Christianity, originated and carried on by the Chinese themselves, was injured by the political aims which were combined with it. It was the error of half-enlightened minds to believe themselves called to overthrow, by force of arms, *the government that persecuted them*, and the idolatry, which Christianity had taught them was a sin against God. Many of their countrymen have wondered at their crusade against images. When describing the mode of operation pursued by the adherents of Tai-ping-wang, they *praise them for their discipline and their avoiding petty thefts and other excesses* commonly practised by the soldiers in the pay of the government; but, they add, they show an extraordinary hostility to idols. They do not put the priests to death, as has often been incorrectly stated, but they show no mercy to the images of the gods."[1] " After making

[1] *Religious Condition of the Chinese.* 1859.

all the necessary deductions for imperfect instruction, the mingling of Christianity with political designs, &c., there still remains good reason to hope that not a few of the Kwang-si insurgents may deservedly be called Christians. At any rate, when they die by the sword, if such is to be their fate, there will be many sincere, brave, and stalwart upholders of *what they believe to be Christianity*, who will meet death with an unflinching courage worthy of the name, and by the hands of far worse men than themselves."[1] Both the American and French missions agreed[2] " in attributing the arrogant pretensions of the chiefs to ignorance and pride," to their ignorance respecting the importance of western nations, and the sense of their own relative power." The Rev. Mr. Martin, of Ningpo, gathered much information favourable to the rebels : he states that he has spoken to men who have been in the garrison of Nankin, and they fully bear out all former statements with regard to the religious observances of the Tai-pingites. I have authentic accounts from tea-men who passed through the rebel districts, they and their money being examined, and then permitted to pass without annoyance. One man reports having seen a brigade drawn up in line, with spears erect, and an officer preaching to the soldiers. This was on their Sunday.

Much has been said about the destruction caused by the rebels : a civil war will always lead to that result, and especially in China, as I show in many other parts of this work that it is the system of the Imperialists to destroy places that have been in rebel possession. Mr. Oliphant's narrative bears out this assertion, for in all the towns he saw which had been taken from the insur-

---

[1] Edkins' *Religious Condition of the Chinese,* page 284.
[2] *Chinese and their Rebellions,* page 315.

gents, great destruction is described; but, with the exception of Woo-hoo, which was the first town visited by the mission, the places in rebel possession are comparatively in good preservation; the suburbs, of course, have suffered from the cities being besieged. At Ngan-king, Mr. Oliphant saw the country people, on both sides of the city, running in before the Imperial soldiers, who were attacking the place, and though, like others who are guided by Mr. Wade's views, he attributes all destruction to the hands of the rebels, he acknowledges that, " in the case of cities, the Imperialists, on driving out the rebels, generally complete the work which these latter have left half finished." I have more to say on this subject in another chapter.

With regard to Lord Elgin's mission up the Yang-tsze-Kiang, at the period chosen " for the purpose of inspecting its ports, and determining which of them it will be most advisable to open to foreign trade," it seems extraordinary to suppose that during a time of civil war any proper opinion could be formed either of the places suitable to trade at, or the nature of the trade likely to be carried on. We find the Imperial Commissioners hinting that Nankin would be a favourable place for the British Plenipotentiary to be settled at.[1] Upon Lord Elgin intimating his intention to proceed up the river for the above purpose, they appear to have been well pleased, and offered letters to the different authorities, and officers to accompany his lordship, doubtless looking forward to some advantage being gained by the foreigners forcing an entrance into the rebel districts, and coming into collision with the insurgents.

It is very strange, that neither Lord Elgin, Mr. Wade, nor Mr. Oliphant, ever express any regret, that no good

---

[1] *Blue Book*, page 406.   A hint that we might assist in taking it.

emanated from the Christian doctrines first proposed by
Tai-ping-wang, and though the insurgents may have
changed since Mr. Meadows visited them, any change
for the worse is not deplored.   In fact, the mission
appears to have been predisposed against the foes of the
mandarins.

The results of an expedition so promising are very
disappointing.   In all the previous visits of foreigners,
the insurgents had distinctly stated, that if a boat was
sent in to communicate, there would be no danger of a
collision ; but notwithstanding this, Lord Elgin insisted
on passing without sending in to explain, though *his
ships came out of the Imperial fleet investing the place,*
and even when opposition was shown, still made no
attempt to prevent bloodshed, but was prepared to force
a passage, and, not contented with that, returned next
day to destroy the rebel defences.   Surely there has been
enough of blood spilt lately in China, without our seeking
opportunity to add to the sanguineous stream !   I have
shown in another chapter that Lord Elgin well knew
how to secure a peaceable passage, when he had not the
power, whatever his inclination may have been, to force
one *vi et armis.*   His lordship's conduct in this case
deserves to be condemned in much stronger language
than I choose to use.   As for learning more about the
religion of the rebels, it seems to have been lost sight of
in a fruitless attempt to look for commercial openings in
ports which were closed ; and had it not been for the
constant friendly disposition of the rebels, whenever they
were communicated with, the probable result of the
expedition would have been, that the British arms would
have been profaned to quench the only spark of religion and progress that has glimmered in China since we
had any connexion with that most important country.

I will use Lord Elgin's own words, in his address to the merchants of Shanghai, and ask, if the policy that has been pursued agrees with his expressions ? " Neither our own consciences nor the judgment of mankind will acquit us ; when we are asked to what use we have turned our opportunities, we can only say that we have filled our pockets from among the ruins which we have found or made. An eminent French writer has observed that it is one of the glories of Christian civilisation that it has caused the sentiment of repentance to find a place in the hearts of nations. Let us hope that it will not be by pointing this moral, that Great Britain, when she comes to review her connexion with the furthest East, will make good her claim to the title of a Christian nation."

Whether the rebellion sinks and fails, or rises into greater importance, it has deserved more attention and consideration than has been given to it. I do not advocate any aid by arms, but would condemn all interference and opposition to it. It is a dangerous thing to meddle with the government of a nation counting four hundred millions of souls ; particularly dangerous, when we have so few men at all acquainted with the language ! We may boast of our might, but it would dwindle into insignificance when scattered over the land, in the fiery plains of the south, or frozen regions of the north of China. There is a more mighty power watching over the destinies of China, and as one of the rebels said to Mr. Meadows at Nankin, six years ago—" If it be the will of God that our Tai-ping prince shall be the sovereign of China, he will be the sovereign of China; if not, then we will die here !" All the willing assistance we gave to the Chinese Government, by protecting its coasts and by preventing the rebel blockade of Canton, told far more against the insurgents than the unwilling warfare

at the Peiho and Canton told in their favour. In proof
of my assertions that neutrality was not maintained, the
following extract from an article in the first number of
the *Cornhill Magazine*, attributed to Sir John Bowring,
should be convincing. It shows how little thanks we
got from the mandarins for the great assistance rendered,
and should be a warning for the future.

" Whatever grounds of complaint the British authorities might have against the Chinese, nothing was left
undone to conciliate the good opinion of the mandarins.
In 1854, an application was made by Yeh to this effect :
he feared a rupture of the public peace, and feeling himself too weak to protect Canton from the invasion of the
rebels, he asked for the assistance of the naval forces of
the Treaty powers. Sir John Bowring accompanied the
admiral and the British fleet to the neighbourhood of
that city, and in co-operation with the Americans, took
such effectual measures for its security, that the intended
attack was abandoned, and general tranquillity remained
uninterrupted. This intervention was gratefully acknowledged by the people of Canton ; but there is every
reason to believe that the commissioner represented our
amicable intervention as an act of vassalage, and the
assistance rendered as having been in obedience to orders
issued by Imperial authority. Notwithstanding this and
many other evidences of friendly sentiment and useful
aid on our part, Yeh did not hesitate to represent to the
court that the rebels and Western ' barbarians' were
acting in union, and he expressed his conviction that his
policy would lead to the extermination of both."

Mr. Wylie, who accompanied Lord Elgin up the
Yang-tsze-Kiang, seems to think the religious eccen-
tricities of the rebels now threaten the extinction of the
vital truths of Christianity. If we take it for granted

that the religion of the Bible, which they first proclaimed, and their enthusiasm, are passing away from
want of speedy success against the difficulties they had
to surmount, there has been a period in the history of
our relations with China that must always be looked
back upon with sorrow and regret. While there is so
much uncertainty in the stability of the Chinese empire,
and certainty with regard to the opinion its officers bear
against foreigners, I cannot understand why our officials
were so anxious that the present dynasty should be
maintained. Its worldly policy must end in decay, and
chronic revolution is tearing it asunder, causing present
misery, which probably no foreign power could prevent.
The changes that are going on may, however, lead to
such results, that it may be a nation's boast hereafter
that it assisted in sustaining the march of progress in
China, though the first footprints were marked in blood !

CHAPTER XXV.

THE DISPUTE WITH YEH.

What lorchas are—Affair of the "Arrow"—Misunderstanding occasioned by want of interpreters—Stubbornness of Yeh—Sir Michael Seymour insists on an interview—Forces his way to Yeh's residence—The latter not at home—Yeh quarrels with the American Commodore, who retaliates by destroying some forts—Author's visit to Canton—The people not against us—All against Yeh—Fort captured by the British—Goodwill of the people—Burning of the factories—Great efforts to subdue the fire— Burning of the bank—Mr. Lane of the consulate killed—One house escaped being burnt—A friendly community broken up—War confined to the Canton waters—Honest conduct of Chinese merchants—The poisoned bread—Exaggeration on the subject corrected.

So much was said in Parliament, and so much has already been written on the "Arrow" lorcha affair, that it will be sufficient if I touch briefly on this subject.

Lorchas [1] are small vessels, built much upon the model of a Chinese junk, but somewhat improved. The owners of some are Englishmen, but the majority belong to Portuguese and Chinese. Some of the latter proprietors are allowed to call their vessels " British ships," and are furnished with a "sailing letter" from the colonial authorities at Hong-Kong, if the owner or nominal owner resides there. I have no doubt that many use either the British or Portuguese flags without being properly qualified, there being little supervision of their papers. The "Arrow," however,

---

[1] The *ch* in *Lorcha* is not pronounced hard ; many of the Hon. Members in the debate regarding the dispute with Yeh, I was told, spoke of the *Lorka* " Arrow."

did possess a sailing letter; true, it was a little out of
date at the time of her capture at Canton by Yeh's
officials. She had an English master, the rule being
that the flag is not granted unless some one who can
speak English is nominal sailing-master. Her crew
were Chinese. Yeh said they were pirates, and sent to
seize them. The master was not on board, but the
men were taken away; when he returned, his presence
was of no avail. He states that the British flag was
hauled down. The acting-consul, Mr. H. Parkes, was
informed of the proceedings of the Chinese officials, and
having to act as his own interpreter, went to the spot.
He was insulted, and the affair thus became more serious.
I am assured on the best authority that he represented
the seizure of the crew as the chief complaint, and made
light of the personal insults to himself. Yet I have no
doubt that the affair would never have been so serious
in its results, had not the ruinous scarcity of interpreters,
which is the bane of all our official intercourse in China,
placed the acting-consul in a position to be insulted.

No satisfactory communication could be had with Yeh.
The men were kept prisoners, and diplomacy being of
no avail, Sir Michael Seymour was called upon to obtain
redress by force. With the most consummate patience,
and a high-souled humanity which never deserted him
throughout the whole of these arduous proceedings, the
worthy admiral commenced his difficult task. At an
early stage, he demanded an interview with Yeh, but
that stubborn specimen of Chinese diplomatists refused
the request. Pressure had to be exercised. To avoid
injury to the population of Canton, forts on the river
were captured, in hopes that Yeh might accede to
terms before the city itself should be menaced or injured.
Sir Michael threatened to visit Yeh in his own palace if

an interview were not granted ;[1] and to show that his threats were not mere empty words, after giving ample notice to the people in the neighbourhood of the attack, a clear line was made through the houses to the city wall, adjacent to the palace. The wall was breached, and the admiral paid his promised visit, but Yeh was " not at home." The admiral's object being accomplished, the force returned to their ships.

Different forts were taken, and some occupied. Correspondence still went on ; inflammatory proclamations were published, offering rewards for foreigners' heads, &c. &c. The crew of the lorcha had even been sent to the consulate, but as the mandarins had been called upon to put them on board the " Arrow," they were sent back to the city for that purpose, and, I believe, were never heard of again !

Yeh was evidently determined to do battle against all foreigners in his own way, which was certainly neither dignified nor dashing. He managed to quarrel with the Americans also ; and the United States' Commodore attacked and destroyed some of the forts which had been re-manned and armed.

When the first symptom of the disturbance began, I went up to Canton to relieve my senior partner. I remained until the factories were destroyed, and afterwards resided as a guest of Commodore Elliot in the Dutch Folly, so that I had ample opportunities of seeing all that was going on. The *people*, I felt sure, were not against us ; they certainly did not wish foreigners to enter the city, but they had very little enthusiasm even on that point. All were against Yeh ; but his " reign of terror" during the Kwang-Tung rebellion prevented any open or pronounced opposition to his wishes.

[1] As a general rule, when interviews are obtained, disputes can be settled.

Dutch Folly.- Canton

Fr. Schenck 50 Geo. St Edin.

" Braves" were collected with difficulty, and it was chiefly on the political patriotism of certain committees of *literati* and ex-mandarins, who attempted to carry on a war of assassination, kidnapping, and burning, that the Governor-General had to depend.

Business being almost entirely suspended, most of the foreign residents at Canton left the place. Many removed their furniture and effects to Hong-Kong or Macao. The factories wore more the air of barracks than of places of trade. A few of us, however, still continued to visit the Chinese merchants, whose warehouses could be approached by water. The Chinese soldiers repaired the French Folly, one of the forts which had been taken, and seemed determined to show an active resistance, flanking batteries being built to protect it. A boat expedition was sent to retake the place, but fortunately the moral courage of the commodore, in directing a timely retreat when the nature of the defences was discovered, saved many valuable lives, for few men could be spared. Eventually the " Encounter," " Baracouta," " Coromandel," and the boats of the squadron, were thought necessary to secure the ready capture of the fort, and notwithstanding the fire from the large steamers, and from a battery in the Dutch Folly (an island-fort in our occupation), the Chinese stood to their guns, until the boats pushed in to the cannon's mouth. One gun was fired right into Captain Cochrane's boat as he reached the fort; luckily the Chinese had been in such a hurry that they had forgotten to put in any shot, otherwise our casualties would have been more serious.

Accompanied by a friend we pulled in after the boats in a small punt, just as the last of the soldiers retreated ; we were astonished at the strength of the place. The marines kept up a sharp fire on the neighbouring houses, from which we were now and then favoured with a Chinese rocket, but soon all resistance ceased. We left the force in possession, and pulled back to the factories in the punt.

The whole line of the river was crowded by thousands of what some people call the fierce and turbulent population of Canton. The tide was against us, but as I had confidence in the people, we pulled our boat most of the way close along shore. Not a stone was cast at us, nor any bad language used. In some places the people even seemed inclined to run away from the little boat. At last when we had to row more into the centre of the stream, where the soldiers on the city wall could see us, we were favoured with their attention, several shots striking the water close to us.

If it were true that the *people* of China were against foreigners, as some believe, we should have been driven out of the country long ago, or had to maintain our position in well-garrisoned forts.

To protect the factories from fire, several of the surrounding houses had been pulled down, and the ruins in great part removed. Many people must have been serious sufferers, but the passive nature of the Chinese prevented them from offering resistance at the time, and though the factories were eventually destroyed by fire, I would not attribute the destruction to any act of the *people*.

I shall never forget the night when we were burned out! All was quiet; I was just retiring to rest when I heard the alarm of fire; in a moment the whole heavens seemed to be in a blaze. All the uncleared ruins of the houses on the north side were burning. The flames spread in all directions towards the factories, and the most energetic efforts to subdue them on our side were of no avail. The Chinese kept the fire from encroaching in their direction. We had had no rain for six weeks; everything was as dry as tinder. The tide was low. An attack was looked for; the men were under arms, but no attempt was made. The fire raged all night; house after house was consumed, and where the old *hongs* existed, the flames roared down their narrow-arched passages with irresistible force. It was a magnificent sight. Standing on the top of the Oriental Bank, we had a panoramic view of the wide-spreading destruction. But there was not much time for looking at the awful prospect. Every one had to work hard, the engines began to fail, the supply of water from the wells gave way. It seemed possible to save the British factory, by far the finest pile of buildings. The parsonage was blown up, but still it did not leave sufficient space. The house next the Consulate caught fire, but by determined exertions it was saved for the time. The men began to tire, some even broke the buckets, some took to plunder. I saw one man drink off a bottle of eau-de-cologne as if it had been water. Still there were many who worked till they dropped. All sorts of articles were used to convey water to keep the fire down; even the admiral might be seen carrying his share. His quiet determined manner, his words of encouragement and noble demeanour, though he was evidently suffering severely from the effects of the smoke, made many strive hard to gain the day against the fierce element with which we were engaged. For a time success seemed to crown our efforts, and we rejoiced to think the British factories were saved from ruin, though several of the next adjoining houses were in flames. At last, however, the heat, which was almost unbearable, set fire to the soot in the main chimney of the Oriental Bank. Water could only be procured in small quantities; the com-

modore poured all that could be obtained as fast as it
was brought directly upon the fire. We had at last
almost to drag him from his dangerous post, the roof on
which he stood being in flames. A rapid dash down
the narrow staircase, now filled with smoke, brought us
safely out of the house. All hope was over! In a few
minutes we had to rush past the Bank to avoid the
falling, burning planks, as we moved off with the few
articles that could be saved from other houses. Poor
Lane, of the Consulate, had been killed by the fall of part
of a house; no good could be done by attempting to
arrest the further progress of the fire, and the admiral
ordered all into the garden to prevent further casualties.
The factories were all destroyed by a fire which raged
two nights and one day. A single house escaped the
flames, but it and the ruins were soon ransacked by the
Chinese, many of whom suffered for their temerity.
Rarely was there ever a happier community than that
which had occupied the houses whose destruction I have
attempted to describe. Every foreign resident of Canton
must regret the sad event, so many happy associations
belong to the place. The semi-confinement imposed
upon us within the limits of the old factories and the
garden, had served to bring us together in close com-
panionship; we met each other every day, and there
was a general current of social friendliness unequalled
in any other part of the world.

I may be pardoned, as one of that community, for
tendering my best thanks to the gallant officers who
so nobly strove to save our houses from destruction,
though their arduous efforts were unavailing. Where
all did their best, it is invidious to mention names, but I
should be doing injustice to Captain W. King Hall,
Captain Rolland, Captain Rotton, and Commander

Curme, if I omitted mention of their noble efforts, which were so prominently conspicuous.

Our houses all destroyed, Canton was left to the tender mercies of Yeh.

With a view to open up points of attack upon the city walls, parts of the suburbs were destroyed. Sir Michael Seymour's force was too limited to venture a general attack on Canton, for, even if the city had been taken, his force was not large enough to hold it ; indeed, there were not sufficient men to hold the different points necessary for securing the river, and to maintain at the same time a footing upon the ruins of the Factory site. That post and the Dutch Folly were therefore abandoned. Our ill-fated houses were pulled to pieces, brick by brick, to the very foundations ; the trees in the garden were rooted out, and perfect desolation marked the spot. The war appeared to be growing more serious than ever, but by good management on the part of Sir John Bowring and Sir Michael Seymour, it was confined entirely to the Canton waters. The Emperor allowed Yeh to fight his own battles, and did not interfere with foreign trade in other parts of the empire.

Large quantities of cotton, rice, &c., belonging to British and other foreign merchants, were left in the warehouses of the Chinese, and excepting such small portions as were destroyed by fire, or plundered by robbers, nearly all the rest was honestly sold and accounted for by the Chinese merchants, under whose care the property was. This would not have occurred if the people had been against us. Even after the factories were destroyed, I passed through a Chinese Hong alone, through scores of coolies who were moving rice, to save it from fire, notice having been given, I believe, that part of the Hong would be destroyed by our force ; yet not a word was said against, nor an attempt made to molest me, either going or returning, though all the coolies carried their usual large bamboo sticks.

Great care had been taken to issue proclamations to the people, declaring that our quarrel was not with them, but with Yeh, whose obstinacy was alone to blame for the mischief that was done. The fleet was provisioned by Chinese contractors, Chinese pilots were employed as usual, and the trade of Hong-Kong and Macao with the mainland greatly increased, only suffering temporary interruptions when the mandarins and the committees before alluded to were particularly vigilant and exacting.

At one time threats of death were issued against all in foreign employment, and similar punishment, even to the *relatives* of those Chinese who disobeyed the mandate, cleared many of our servants, &c., from Hong-Kong and Macao, but after money had been "squeezed" out of them, the majority soon returned. An ex-mandarin, "Chin-Kwei-tsik," was very active in his opposition to foreigners. He secured a good many heads for rewards; and I believe was at the bottom of the great poisoning case in Hong-Kong. The people eventually drove his men away from the coast, immediately opposite the island, and would not suffer his interference.

With regard to the above poisoning case, which providentially proved far less serious than it might have been, a curious circumstance may be related, to show, even in such an extreme case, how reliance may be placed upon the Chinese in foreign service. The poison was fortunately first discovered in the bread at the doctor's. He at once issued a circular notice,

"THE BREAD IS POISONED!"

and briefly prescribed simple remedies, which being at once acted upon, saved many lives.

There was strong suspicion that the Chinese intended thus to make an end of the foreign inhabitants of the colony. Yet the circular notice was sent round in charge of a Chinese coolie !

No deaths occurred at the time from the diabolical attempt ; many people, however, were seriously ill, and there is reason to believe that two or three ultimately died from the effects.

I must be excused from entering into particulars of all the kidnappings, seizures, and murders of this period. Ample proof exists that Yeh and the committees were implicated in them. They can only be excused on the plea that the mode of warfare was Chinese. If there is to be safety to foreign life and property in China, there must be some punishment inflicted when such acts are committed ; and the Chinese have good reason to be thankful that Sir Michael Seymour directed his energies against the mandarins, and did all that humanity could suggest to spare the people.

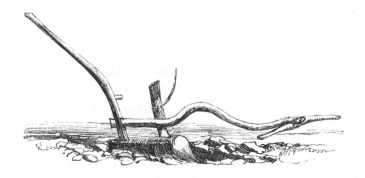

CHAPTER XXVI.

LORD ELGIN'S MISSION AND ITS RESULTS.

Troops of the Chinese expedition required for India—French Alliance—
Instructions to Lord Elgin—The Opium Trade—Proper course to pursue
in China—Lord Elgin disregards instructions, and Mr. Lay gets promotion—Correspondence with Chinese officials—Attack ordered—Successful capture of the Takoo forts—The Treaty signed—Unjust attack on
Sir M. Seymour by Lord Elgin's Secretary—Opinion of the foreign community in China—The expedition up the Yang-tsze-Kiang—Remarks
upon it—Conclusion.

Up to the date of the second attack on the Takoo
Forts, there had been little reason to regret the outbreak
of the quarrel with Yeh. On the contrary, Britain had
many reasons to be thankful for the event. The troops
destined for China, and to chastise Yeh, arrived in the
East at a most critical time. They saved India. In
May 1857, the Governor-General wrote to Lord Elgin
as follows:—"In the valley of the Ganges, between
Calcutta and Agra, for a length of 750 miles, there are
barely 1000 European soldiers, whilst there are several
towns and stations of importance containing forts, maga-
zines, treasuries, and large civil communities of Europeans, which are held by native troops alone. If
mutinous rebellion raises its head at any of these spots,
the Government of India is literally without any force
wherewith to put it down. The mutineers would carry

everything before them, and we know how they would use the opportunity. The flame would spread like wild-fire, and would rage uncontrolled."

The regiments destined for China were intercepted in the straits, and despatched by Lord Elgin to Calcutta; and subsequently, the gallant Captain Peel, with every available man that by any " contrivance or justifiable sacrifice could be spared," was sent from China to add power to that glorious band of heroes who held India against such fearful odds.

All our troubles in China thus gave place to the greater calamity in India. Lord Elgin remained but a short time at Hong-Kong, and then set off to Calcutta, to consult with the Governor-General. Sir Michael Seymour's onerous duties as admiral were increased ten-fold. New dangers threatened us at Hong-Kong when the forces were withdrawn, but no word of complaint was uttered; on the contrary, there was a general feeling of thankfulness that assistance was at hand to relieve our fellow-countrymen in India.

In October 1857, just a year after the dispute with Yeh commenced, Lord Elgin returned from Calcutta. The gun-boats and transports with marines soon after arrived, and we had some hopes of active operations being made against Canton. The French and American plenipotentiaries also reached China about this time. The latter was evidently bound down by his instructions to carry out a perfectly peaceful policy, and the force with which he was accompanied was not adapted for warfare in Chinese waters. He had a thankless office, and a most difficult position to fill, but his gentlemanly bearing and acknowledged talent made it a matter of regret that he was not more intimately associated with the other contending powers, in their endeavours to make the Chinese respect Treaty rights. Baron Gros, the minister and Plenipotentiary Extraordinary for France, was the bearer of instructions which gave the sanction of the Emperor to an alliance with the English in their war against Yeh. What the nature of this alliance was, and what specific reasons the British Government or Lord Elgin had in accepting it, are alike unknown to the public.

However beneficial an alliance with France may be in a European war, there are many objections to it in the East. The quarrel with Yeh concerned British subjects only, and could have been settled without extraneous aid. As soon as the French became associated with the English in this dispute, new difficulties arose. All action was trammelled with separate discussion and consultation. Our commanders had to act in concert with the French, instead of being left to their own unfettered judgment. The force brought by our allies to our assistance was very small in comparison with our own, though, perhaps, greater in proportion to the interest the two nations had in Chinese affairs; yet we had to act in direct conjunction, as if the force and interests of each were the same. From the first, we find Baron Gros taking the initiative. At Canton, the French were determined to be first on the walls, and rushed forward fully quarter of an hour in advance of the time appointed. I noticed many proclamations in which the name of France was placed before that of England; these were placarded over the city after it was taken. The tri-color floated most conspicuously over the highest point of the city, and in many other little ways, our gallant allies took care to bring themselves as prominently forward as possible.

The commerce of France with China, in comparison

with that of England, is as a mole-hill to a mountain. Our interests are chiefly commercial, and probably, to the disgrace of the British Government, we may say that the interests of religion have been almost entirely disregarded. Until the treaty of Tien-tsin, no provision was ever made with the Chinese Government for the protection of Protestant native converts, or the advancement of Christianity in any way.

The chief interest France has in China, is the support of her Catholic mission, and the avowed reason for taking part with us in the war, was her desire to obtain redress for the death of one of her missionaries. Now that war is again impending, this alliance with a country, whose interests in the East, it may be said, are rather to be created than protected, may be productive of many difficulties, when our own affairs are finally settled with the Chinese. The mere assembly of such a powerful French force in the East, untrammelled by either commerce or colonies to protect, might, in the event of any European complications, place us in a position destructive to our enormous commercial interests. Again, it would ill suit the policy of England to blockade the coast of China, involving, as it would, the loss of the large revenue derived from tea and opium ; but if an early termination of the war were not arrived at, France, engaged in the same conflict, but without similar risk of loss, might insist on such a blockade, with the view of crippling the resources of China ; and by such a measure, England would lose more money than the whole expense of the war, even had it been undertaken single-handed.

The alliance, however, is a *fait accompli*, and we must hope for a good ending from an apparently bad beginning.

Lord Elgin was instructed (see Lord Clarendon's despatch of 20th April 1857)—*First*, To demand reparation for injuries to British subjects. *Second*, To obtain the complete execution of the stipulations of the several treaties. *Third*, Compensation for losses at Canton. *Fourth*, To demand the assent of the Chinese Government to the residence at Pekin, or to the occasional visit to that capital of a British minister. *Fifth*, A revision of the treaties, with a view to obtaining increased facilities for commerce, such as access to cities on the great rivers, as well as to Chapoo, and other ports on the coast; and also permission for Chinese vessels to resort to Hong-Kong for purposes of trade, from all ports of the Chinese empire, without distinction.

Should the Chinese agree to the first three points, Lord Elgin was to endeavour to compass the last two by negotiation; but should they refuse to enter into negotiation, or not agree to the three demands first specified, he would be justified in having recourse at once to coercive measures.

In a second despatch, of same date, Lord Clarendon gives further instructions, containing many admirable suggestions with regard to extended fields for commerce in China; appropriation of ample extent of ground for foreigners at the various ports; revision of the tariff; right of transport, without additional duties being levied; fixed transit duties for the interior; right to purchase produce at its place of growth, &c. The instructions go on to state:—" But whatever arrangements may be made in regard to the amount of duties leviable on foreign trade, whether of export or import, I cannot too strongly impress upon your Excellency the necessity of abstaining from undertaking any obligation to protect the Chinese revenue. Your Excellency would only be laying the foundation of much future embarrassment, if you were to engage that the British authorities in China should afford any greater degree of protection to the Chinese custom-house, than that which results from the British consular officers retaining in their possession the ships' papers, until the production of a certificate from the Chinese custom-house, that all duties upon ship and cargo have been duly satisfied. It is no part of the duty of Her Majesty's consular authorities to take greater care of the Chinese revenue, than the Chinese authorities are themselves disposed to take. British subjects, indeed, are not to be protected against the consequences of any fraudulent transactions in which they may be engaged ; but the Chinese authorities, on the other hand, are not to be compelled to be more observant of the interests of the Imperial treasury, than they are when left to themselves."

Such were the instructions conveyed to Lord Elgin. He was also furnished with very full reports relative to British trade in China, by the Shanghai Chamber of Commerce, and the merchants of Hong-Kong. The latter brought to His Excellency's notice the advantages that might be gained by specific enactments being made regarding the coasting trade of China, opening it to foreign ships; also, that some settled arrangement should be made as to the nominally prohibited articles of export, rice, grain, and pulse, gold and silver bullion, and copper cash ; that the rate for inland transit duties should be *fixed*,—the amount the Chinese had a right to levy, according to the treaty of Nankin, having been *left blank since that treaty was signed*, an omission which has caused incalculable loss to British trade. " Taking a general view of the tariff as established by

the treaty of Nankin," the Hong-Kong merchants say,
" we think that it affords little ground of complaint, as
we are not aware that a much more liberal one exists in
any country of the world ;" but as a few modifications
in some articles might be beneficial, a table of altera-
tions was furnished to his Excellency. An impartial
administration of the tariff, with a uniform and equal
application of it to all parties engaged in commerce at
all the ports, was also suggested as essential. Access to
the interior for purposes of trade, some settlement regarding the currency, a decision relative to the factory
site at Canton, and a remonstrance against the Chinese
putting difficulties in the way of settling land at Whampoa, Foo-chow, &c., were also alluded to. The opium
trade was thus mentioned :—" We would finally bring
before your Lordship the position of foreign merchants
engaged in the opium trade, which might, with advantage to British interests generally, be relieved from the
peculiar manner in which it is now conducted, forbidden
as it is by the laws of China, but sanctioned and encouraged by the governing classes, as well as by the
mass of the people ; so that in the absence of any treaty
provision affecting it, the trade has been gradually
developed, without disguise or hindrance. It now exer-
cises so extensive an influence over all our commercial
relations, even when they are apparently least connected
with it, that the Chinese Government might appro-
priately extend to it recognition as well as sufferance,
though the precise mode in which this may be done is
one of those delicate questions which had best be left
to circumstances, and to your Lordship's superior
judgment."

Doubtless there are evils attending the excessive use
or abuse of opium ; but I have known many Chinese

who smoked opium for years, and never seemed to be
the worse for it. It is taken more as a sedative than
as a narcotic ; and its general effects among the Chinese
may be classed as very similar to those of either wine
or spirits in England.[1] I think, however, that much
harm has resulted from the manner in which opium has
been introduced, by the piracy it engendered by armed
boats conveying it: by the opportunity it gave the mandarins to make illegal exactions; and especially by the

[1] That the import of opium has lately been a smuggling trade, taking
that phrase in the sense in which it would be used in England, any one
who has seen its working may safely deny ; and to show how the article
is treated, I cannot do better than point to its importation at Shanghai,
where there is the strictest supervision over custom-house affairs. The
three Treaty powers (Great Britain, France, and America) each supplies a
custom-house inspector to look after the business. Opium there passed
openly before the eyes of the custom-house officers, and was the *only* article
of import that was *not* examined.

In Canton, foreign steamers brought it up to the town, and it was taken
from alongside by mandarin boats. The mandarin vessels used to take it
from the receiving-ships and bring it to Canton ; but the rebellion gave
them other employment, and put the carrying trade into the hands of the
steam-boat proprietors. The opium, per steamers, had to pay a squeeze of
$10 in addition to freight. These squeezes are nothing else than an import
duty, which goes into the mandarin's own pocket. We find, therefore, that
this opium—this prohibited article—was safely, and so far as the local
government is concerned, legally imported into Canton (even before Lord
Elgin's treaty) at a *less duty* than any other article of foreign import,
for the average rate of the tariff is equal to about 7½ per cent. *ad valorem*,
and the squeeze upon opium is scarcely 3 per cent. There was a time
when the opium was actually stored in the foreign warehouses at Shanghai,
but this told against the fees of some Chinese interested in the trade. They
therefore arranged with the Taou-tai (the intendant of customs and highest
officer at Shanghai), that they would give him so much per chest, if he
would settle that the drug should not be allowed to be landed at the
foreign ground. At Amoy the drug is stored in foreign godowns, and an
opium receiving-ship is anchored off the custom-house, in snug security,
with her masts and spars comfortably at rest, in no fear of interference
from Chinese officials. At Ningpo, Foo-chow, and Swatow, the opium
trade is equally open.

The foreign merchant pays no duty ; but the Chinese who buys and lands
the opium, is called on for a tax, which is paid upon by far the largest
quantity imported.

difficulties and troubles arising from people smoking the drug who were not able to afford it. The trade has the advantage of giving a large revenue to India, and providing a source for merchants laying down funds in China to an extent which it is doubtful British manufactures would ever have attained. If the British Government wished the trade to be carried on, it should have been legalized long ago ; if this could not be settled, it should have been prohibited altogether.

As Wingrove Cooke says, in his admirable letters to the *Times*, " The course to pursue in China is this : dare to act honestly with them, and dare to tell them truth."

The events on the Canton river, capture of the city, and reappointment of Chinese officers to govern it, are all occurrences so recent, and have already been described so well,[1] that I do not attempt to give another version. We have seen how little good has been derived from the capture of Canton. The Emperor has lost so many cities since he came to the throne, that even if he were aware that Canton had been taken, it would produce little effect on his mind. All that he knows of the affair is probably this : " That the barbarian soldiers tumultuously entered the city." But as all his officers, excepting Yeh, were almost immediately reinstated after their capture, he gets their despatches from the usual place, and replaces mandarins as he thinks proper. All that was gained by force of arms was lost by diplomacy. We certainly garrison Canton ; it saves the Chinese from having to do it, and they can employ their troops elsewhere against the rebels. The city is held nominally as a guarantee for indemnity for British losses ; but we continue to pay duties there, and all those British mer-

---

[1] *China in* 1857-58, by Mr. Wingrove Cooke. London : Routledge.

chants who suffered from the burning of the factories are still left in uncertainty whether compensation shall be granted them for the losses they have sustained.

Notwithstanding the instructions given to Lord Elgin not to interfere with the collection of the Chinese revenue, he arranged for the establishment of foreign inspectorates at all the ports; Mr. Lay is now inspector-general, with an enormous salary from the Chinese Government. Mr. Fitzroy, another of Lord Elgin's suite, also received a good appointment in the same service, and many others have joined it. Our desire to make the Chinese be as strict as possible, for honesty's sake, at Canton, must end in their being able to point to Hong-Kong as the chief place for smuggling from; we have no customs' regulations there, junks and boats come and go unrestricted.

It has been proposed to seize upon the revenues of customs at Shanghai and Canton to pay the British merchants for their losses ; but if the Chinese do not get the benefit from the duties at these ports, they will manage in some way to make up the deficiency by taxing the produce or the Chinese trader; so that eventually it is the British merchant who has to pay for his own losses. We have seen already how well this can be managed by the Chinese. The losses may be made good sooner by this method, but it is a plan which imposes a burden on the native merchants or the individual mandarins, who are interested in the customs, instead of deriving the money from the provincial authorities, and the government to whose acts the losses were attributed, and who are an entirely distinct and separate department from that of trade and customs. If we call upon the foreign inspectors of customs to collect the revenues for us, it will appear as if they had been appointed to be useful for that purpose when occasion offered ; and all the high-flown ideas of teaching the Chinese to collect their revenues honestly, may be cast in our teeth as an underhand act, by which to be the better able to appropriate the revenues they collect.

In China we never had a very clear notion of what Lord Elgin's policy was. About two months after the capture of Canton, as no good had resulted from that measure, he determined to proceed to Shanghai, in hopes of meeting there a plenipotentiary from the Emperor to settle existing difficulties, and, in event of his being disappointed, he wished as many gunboats as could be spared to be congregated at that port at the end of the month of March. No plenipotentiary was sent to meet his Lordship. The Prime Minister had refused to correspond directly with Lord Elgin ; the latter, therefore, determined on the first of April, " to place himself in more immediate communication with the high officers of the Imperial Government at the capital."

Lord Elgin accordingly arranged that the " Furious," " Pique," " Cormorant," and " Slaney" should proceed to the Peiho, and that all other available vessels arriving at Shanghai should be despatched to the same destination. His reasons for proceeding at once, without waiting for the Admiral and the gunboats, which had to make the passage against the monsoon, being, " Firstly, because the Chinese would impute delay to vacillation and weakness ; secondly, because we should lose our hold on the rice junks destined for Pekin, which are now proceeding to the north, and may yet be arrested, if necessary, at the mouth of the Peiho. Thirdly, because, if the information which I have received from Count Pontiatine on this head be correct, the season for operations in the region to which we are now proceeding terminates with the end of the month of May."

On arrival at the mouth of the Peiho, in the middle of April, Lord Elgin appears to have been disposed to avoid hostilities, and open up communications. No attempt seems to have been made to stop the grain-junks, for which service the "Slaney" alone would have been sufficient. Some days after his arrival, his Lordship wrote again to the Prime Minister, stating that "he was prepared to meet either on board his own ship or on shore, a minister duly authorized to treat with him, and to settle the several questions affecting the relations of Great Britain with China," and gave six days for the Chinese officer to arrive. In the interval, the two admirals, with strong reinforcements, arrived. Sir Michael Seymour was apprised, that, in Lord Elgin's opinion, if no plenipotentiary arrived, it might be necessary to stop the junk-trade of the Peiho, take the forts at its mouth, and proceed up the river to Tien-tsin. The Chinese Government, however, appointed a Commissioner within the time prescribed, but his powers were not sufficiently ample. Lord Elgin again, therefore, allowed him six days to communicate with Pekin. The Commissioner sent an answer within the time, but it was unsatisfactory. For some days no hostile steps were taken in consequence of a communication Lord Elgin had received from Count Pontiatine, the Russian plenipotentiary, stating that there was still some hope that full powers would be granted to the Imperial Commissioners, and Lord Elgin distinctly states this in his letter to the Chinese Commissioner,—" The undersigned *forbore for some days* " (*after the* 11*th May*), "from taking the steps warranted, *in consequence of a friendly communication which he received from the plenipotentiary of Russia, and which led him still to hope* that this deficiency in the plenipotentiary powers of the Imperial Commissioner

might be in some degree remedied by instructions
ample enough to enable him to treat upon the several
subjects detailed in the letter of the undersigned to
the Chief Secretary of State, Yu-Ching, of the 11th
February. In this hope he has been disappointed. A
later communication from Count Pontiatine has but
strengthened his conviction of the futility of any farther attempt to open negotiations at the mouth of the
Peiho."[1]

On receipt of the second communication from the
Russian ambassador on the 17th May, as it stated that
the Emperor would not receive any foreign ambassador
at Pekin, a conference was called. The allied chiefs
met on the 18th, and decided that the forts should be
taken. Next day, Lord Elgin gave his instructions to
the admiral to summon the forts of Takoo, and if the
summons was disregarded, to take them by force. On
the following day (20th May), the whole of the forts
had been gallantly captured with but slight loss; they
were first well shelled, and the men were then landed
to occupy them. "The forts were backed by a large
body of troops, supposed to be the *élite* of the Imperial
guard." The Chinese had done much to complete their
defences, and trusted to the forts and barriers keeping
out the troublesome barbarians. No preparations to
resist were made at Tien-tsin, or at other points on the
river; the Chinese evidently thought that their defences
at Takoo were sufficient; the delay in the attack doubtless helped to confirm them in this opinion. This was
the best thing that could have happened; their energies
were directed entirely to strengthen the forts, which by
good management were readily taken, and Tien-tsin
being undefended, was reached without further opposi-

---

[1] All this is omitted in Mr. Oliphant's narrative.

tion. Much harm would have resulted had it been necessary to attack that city with a small force.

It was not until the 1st June, that Lord Elgin wrote to the major-general in the south for a "respectable land force" to be sent to his assistance ; two days afterwards, Imperial commissioners, duly qualified to treat, arrived at Tien-tsin, and by the end of the week, they had agreed, with some qualifications, to most of the terms proposed by Lord Elgin, but they could not be induced to sign the new treaty until the 26th June, and the Emperor's assent was not procured until the commissioners were informed, a week later, that the reinforcements written for had arrived from Hong-Kong.

To carry out Lord Elgin's reiterated threat of going to Pekin, Tien-tsin must have been occupied, the city of Toong-chow taken and held, a land march of many miles accomplished, and then the capital of the empire besieged with a force which, even after the men arrived, who were only written for on the 1st June, would not have been at the largest computation above 1500 strong. At Tien-tsin our officers had experience how the population, naturally well disposed, could be excited against foreigners by the mandarins. What could such a small force have been able to do in an enemy's country, sixty miles from the base of operations, which must have been at Tien-tsin ? With the force that Lord Elgin had in China to support him, troubles at Canton, and the Indian mutiny unsubdued, how could he ever have expected to force an entry to Pekin, and arrive there with an army strong enough to insist upon his demands, no matter if the whole fleet of gun-boats had arrived with him at the Peiho on the 14th April.

I have been very particular in giving the dates and circumstances relative to the events at the Peiho and

Tien-tsin, as reports injurious to Sir Michael Seymour have been busily circulated, and blame has been cast upon him for not joining the plenipotentiary with the gun-boats at an earlier date. Had the whole of the official correspondence been published in the Blue Book of Lord Elgin's mission, a complete justification of the admiral's conduct would have appeared ; and Mr. Oliphant's remarks on this subject proved to be most unjust.

Even from the Secretary's own account of these transactions it is difficult to understand how the admiral had impeded the advance, or rendered it more difficult. After his arrival, Lord Elgin twice entered into communication with the Imperial Commissioners, and twice six days were given to enable properly qualified persons to be sent to treat ; and it was not until all these attempts had proved abortive that offensive operations were determined upon. Sir Michael Seymour, it was understood, held the opinion, the correctness of which was proved by the results, that, so long as the Chinese directed all their attention to the defences at the mouth of the river, the advance on Tien-tsin, after the capture of these, would be a complete success. In China, Sir Michael Seymour's high qualities as a naval commander had ere this been put to the test and fully appreciated ; and the opinion throughout the whole foreign community was, that to him was mainly to be attributed the success of our operations at the mouth of the Peiho, and the subsequent advance on Tien-tsin— successes without which Lord Elgin's treaty would never have been obtained. How far this is shown in his Lordship's Secretary's narrative the reader can judge for himself.

A copy of the letter to the commissioner (of which I have given an extract), relative to the reasons for the

delay in attacking after the second reply had been received from him, was sent to Sir Michael Seymour, so
that the admiral possesses that document to refute Mr.
Oliphant's assertion, though that gentleman studiously
avoids all mention of it.[1]   And with regard to any delay
in attacking the forts after the reply had been received
to Lord Elgin's first communication, sent on the 24th
of April with those from the other plenipotentiaries,
Mr. Oliphant evidently wishes the public to infer that
an immediate attack had been determined on, for he
says,—" The only course left seemed to be to send an
ultimatum to Tan (the commissioner), stating that the
plenipotentiaries had now placed the matter in the hands
of the allied naval authorities."   There appear to have
been no instructions given by Lord Elgin to that effect ;
there is no mention of it in the *Blue Book ;* but there
we have the following letter from the British Plenipotentiary in reply to that received from Tan :—

" May 1st, 1858.

" The undersigned begs to acknowledge the Imperial Commissioner's letter of yesterday. As that letter contained no satisfactory
answer to the question put by the undersigned in his letter of the
30th ult., he did not meet the Commissioner as he had intended
to-day. The Imperial Commissioner will presently hear more at
length from the undersigned.

(Signed)   " Elgin and Kincardine."

Lord Elgin accordingly did write more at length on
the 6th, giving six further days to the Imperial Commissioner. The circumstances after that time elapsed
have been described as above.

When it is known that no complaint whatever was
made by Lord Elgin directly to Sir M. Seymour of any
inconvenience arising from the unavoidable delay in

---

[1] *Blue Book*, p. 307.

getting the gunboats earlier to the Peiho, and that the admiral's conduct in his arduous command was appreciated by the Government, and rewarded by his Sovereign, I think enough has been said to show the injustice that has been done to one of the most gallant and judicious officers in Her Majesty's navy. The late Takoo disaster proved how necessary it is to be fully prepared before attacking even Chinese forts. This fact alone should have prevented Lord Elgin's secretary from publishing his aspersions, especially as no good can now result from trying to attach blame to the admiral,—the treaty having been concluded, however politic it might have been to be ready to throw all blame upon him, while Lord Elgin's success was still doubtful.

To show in how great esteem Sir Michael Seymour was held by the mercantile community in China, I take this opportunity to publish a copy of the address presented to him upon his retiring from command. It was eagerly signed by every British merchant in Hong-Kong :—

" *His Excellency* SIR MICHAEL SEYMOUR, K.C.B., *Rear-Admiral and Commander-in-Chief of Her Majesty's Naval Forces in the East India and China Seas.*

" HONG-KONG, 16*th March* 1859.

" SIR,—We, the undersigned British merchants, and other representatives of British trade and interests in China, do ourselves the honour of waiting upon your Excellency, to express our profound appreciation of your Excellency's public services and personal worth.

" As the period draws near which is to terminate your Excellency's arduous command in these seas, we should be doing injustice to our own feelings were we to allow it to pass without placing upon record some memorial of them, however inadequate.

" It would be travelling beyond our province and the necessary limits of this address to attempt even to sketch that extended series of naval and military operations conducted under your Excellency's auspices, and which have been instrumental in accomplishing such vast political results.

" It will suffice to say that, commencing with the demolition of every stronghold upon the Canton River in 1856, and ending with the capture of the Peiho fortresses in 1858, they materially conduce to those concessions which have been hailed with such enthusiasm by the whole western world.

" But there is one part of your Excellency's career upon which we dwell with especial pleasure. When your Excellency, uninformed of the sentiments of Her Majesty's Government, and acting mainly on your own responsibility, had to encounter the pressure of the formidable crisis which so unexpectedly occurred in the winter of 1856,—suddenly called upon, with a force ill adapted to the purpose, to assume coercive measures against a stubborn Viceroy, sheltered within a densely populated city,—your Excellency's high Christian feeling induced you to spare it at a moment when the reckless obstinacy of its own ruler abandoned it to its doom ; and, when a certain amount of destruction became unavoidable, it was confined by your Excellency's forbearance within the narrowest possible compass, and fell on that quarter alone where it was most righteously incurred.

" Let us hope that this city, so long the stronghold of irrational hate and intolerance, taught by the disastrous and humiliating lessons it has received, will henceforth entertain a wholesome respect for that power which it has hitherto affected to despise and defy.

" When we were driven from it upwards of two years ago by the burning of our houses—when a price was put upon your Excellency's head, as well as our own—when assassination took the place of war, and poison and incendiarism became its familiar weapons, —we remember your Excellency's great and untiring exertions, not only in guarding against a descent upon this island from the sea, but in preserving the river approaches to Canton from permanent obstruction, and so keeping them open for the access of that peaceful commerce which is now returning to it.

" We, more than any other section of the British community in China, are in a position to estimate the protection rendered by your Excellency to the trade of these seas, both in the prompt despatch of succour to ships in distress, as well as in the energetic repression of piracy ; and we take this opportunity of recording our warmest acknowledgments for the benefits thus conferred.

" To mark our sense of these great services, and the respect we entertain for your Excellency personally, we now do ourselves the honour to request your acceptance of a Service of Plate, commemorative of the benefit you have conferred on foreign interests, and the lustre you have shed on British arms in China.

" For this purpose we shall remit to a committee in London, by the outgoing mail, the sum of Two Thousand Guineas, with instructions to defer entirely to your Excellency's judgment as regards the selection of our memorial.

" It now only remains for us to bid your Excellency a most cordial farewell, to wish you many years of health and happiness in less trying spheres, and to assure you that you carry with you, not merely the respect, but the personal regard of this whole community.—We have the honour to remain, your Excellency's most obedient servants,

" Jardine, Matheson, & Co.—Dent & Co.—Lindsay & Co.— Fletcher & Co.—W. H. Wardley & Co.—Lyall, Still, & Co. —Turner & Co.—Birley & Co.—Oriental Bank Corporation (P. Campbell, manager).—Mercantile Bank Corporation (John Costerton, manager).—Agra and United Service Bank (Henry Turner, manager).—D. W. Mackenzie & Co.—Holliday, Wise, & Co.—Gilman & Co.—Gibb, Livingston, & Co. —David Sassoon, Sons, & Co.—Framjee, Byramjee, Metta, & Co.—Cowasjee, Pallenjee, & Co.—P. & D. N. Camajee & Co.—Max. Fischer.—A. Wilkinson.—D. N. Mody & Co.— P. F. Cama & Co.—Ameeroodeen, Jafferbhoy, & Co.—Judah & Co.—Gifford & Co.—Walker, Borradaile, & Co.—Smith, Kennedy & Co.—Hormusjee & Rustomjee.—R. H. Camajee & Co., p.p. J. Pestonjee.—Eduljee Framjee, Sons, & Co.— Stephenson & Co.—Y. J. Murrow.—R. Macgregor & Co.— G. H. Heaton.—John Lawrence.—Henry Rutter.—A. Wilson.—W. Tarrant.—R. A. Long Phillips.—B. Kenny.— Chas. Jameson.—M'Ewen & Co.—T. Piccope.—C. S. Lungrana & Co.—Ebrahim Goomer.—Nowrojee & Co.—F. B. Cama & Co.—Dhurumsee Poonjeebhoy.—Cassumbhoy Nathabhoy & Co.—Smith & Brimelow.—Muncherjee Pestonjee Setna.—Aspunderjee Tamooljee.— D. Lapraik.—Lane, Crawford & Co.—Bowra & Co.—John Lamont."

In China we had no official information given us of the contents of the Treaty of Tien-tsin, though we were the principal parties directly interested in it, until it arrived from *England.* Some of the particulars oozed out, and in general it was considered satisfactory, *if it could be carried out ;* but most people doubted this, as we felt that it had been extorted by force rather than by argument. The article which called upon the Chinese to receive communications in English, appeared the one most unlikely ever to have been *agreed* to by Chinese. According to their letter to Lord Elgin,[1] and which confirms the first information we had on the subject, the Imperial High Commissioners gave their entire consent, " that in official correspondence the English character shall henceforth be employed, the British Government, for the present, accompanying the original with a Chinese version, which practice it will discontinue as soon as Chinese, selected by the Chinese Government to study the English written and spoken language, shall have thoroughly acquainted themselves therewith ! ! " This appeared to be such an improbable concession on the part of the Chinese, that few ever believed that the Treaty of Tien-tsin was intended to be kept in good faith. In the treaty, however, the wording was somewhat modified.

I have had occasion to notice how much Lord Elgin was guided by his interpreters, Messrs. Wade and Lay ; they did not, in fact, act merely as interpreters, but became the negotiators of the treaty, and were employed in this manner to an extent far beyond what we credited in China. By the papers furnished to Parliament, it would appear that Mr. Lay, then an officer in the Chinese service, was the principal party employed in arranging the points of the treaty directly with the

[1] *Blue Book,* page 330.

Commissioners, and at their own request. Point by point was discussed by this gentleman with these high officers. Sometimes they appear to have gained partial concessions from him by flattery ; sometimes his patience left him when he could not gain a point he wished ; the result of all being, that the Commissioners, by his representations, agreed to most of the terms stipulated, provided nothing was settled to be to our advantage at once : their concessions and the treaty became, in fact, a promissory note,- the settlement of which was to be at a future date.

Take the propositions as first agreed to. The letter of the Commissioners, it must be remembered, was written at the dictation of Mr. Lay.[1] The Commissioners agreed :

1st, " That every port along the river, from its source to its mouth, shall be open to trade ; that in every province British subjects shall be free to go into the interior with passports ;" foreigners awaiting the termination of the civil war before going into provinces which were in a disturbed state, and no definite time being fixed for the arrangements coming in force.

2d, " That between us and persons of the British (*i.e.* Christian) persuasion, inasmuch as these are not offensive, there shall be peace."

3d, That there should be a modification of the tariff, and reform of customs' administration. All to be settled hereafter.

4th, " That measures shall be concerted for the suppression of pirates." A proposition much more useful to the Chinese than to ourselves.

5th, " That the English character should be employed in official correspondence." Like all the others, " by and bye."

---

[1] *Blue Book*, page 328.

The Canton indemnity question was conveniently transferred to Canton, as no other province had any concern in it.

As to the residence of a plenipotentiary at Pekin, "there is properly no objection." "Unfortunately a collision has occurred with the vessels of war of your Excellency's Government, and as the dignity of ours would perhaps be outraged by (the minister's) proceeding at once (to Pekin), his visit might, we think, be postponed. Her Majesty's plenipotentiary might live in Tien-tsin, and an official residence could be appointed him in the capital."

In the conversation between Mr. Lay and the High Commissioner, Kwei Leang,[1] it is reported "He prayed Mr. Lay to aid in getting the proposition for a resident minister at Pekin withdrawn. To allow all nations free access to the capital would be fraught with evil to China ; and he appealed to Mr. Lay to say, from his knowledge of the country, whether what he said was not correct. Mr. Lay *could not help, to a certain extent, acquiescing in his Excellency's argument.* He explained that there would not be any objection to admitting the minister of Great Britain, though there was to the admission of the ministers of all four nations. He was an old man of seventy-four years of age ; if he did not settle this point in accordance with the wishes of his Majesty, he would be inevitably degraded and punished. He, therefore, again invoked Mr. Lay's kind offices, that some compromise might be made by which the proposal should be waived *for the time at least.*" The flattery, and appeal to Mr. Lay's sympathy, appear to have had the desired effect.

Well, the treaty was signed, and had the Emperor's assent, as I have said before. It was a mere make-shift,

---

[1] *Blue Book,* page 327.

and I believe never was intended to be carried out. Lord Elgin and all the forces left Tien-tsin. Here was the great mistake ; and the subsequent concession, that no merchant should go to Pekin to trade, explains it. Among our officials in China, especially among some of the interpreters, there exists a jealousy of the mercantile community coming into connexion with the Chinese officials. Every obstacle was thrown in the way of any British merchant being consul for a foreign state. Whether the objections arose from the British consuls not wishing merchants to have the same title as themselves, I cannot say, but there was a determination to try to keep us away from the mandarins. Even Tien-tsin was too near the capital for us ; and instead of a consul *at once* being appointed to that port, ships of war were left there to keep the river free, so that we might keep the advantage which had been gained. Tien-tsin was not to be an open port,[1] but two others, less important, in the north of China, were fixed upon before either the one or the other had been visited ! It may be said that there were only eleven feet over the bar of the Tien-tsin river ; greater difficulties exist at one of the other ports, and if such vessels as the " Cormorant" and " Nimrod" could cross the bar at Takoo, the merchants in China were quite prepared to send vessels there if permitted.

In the meantime, affairs at Canton had again become troublesome, the Chinese had threatened to retake the city, and renewed their attempts at assassination, sometimes successfully. The principal part of the force which had enabled Lord Elgin to get the treaty signed was sent to the south. The British plenipotentiary went

---

[1] The Commissioners were given the choice of fixing on Tien-tsin or New-chwang, hundreds of miles off in Manchuria : they of course fixed upon the port most distant from the capital. See *Blue Book*, p. 338.

to Shanghai, thence to Japan, and completed another treaty there, which has since been ratified. He returned to Shanghai to meet the Commissioners who were to arrange about the tariff. The particulars of that part of the negotiations, however interesting they may be to a merchant, would not claim much attention from the general reader. Great credit is due to Mr. Wade and his colleagues for the patience, tact, and discrimination with which this part of their business was conducted. Nothing had been agreed upon in the treaty regarding the legal importation of opium : by the new tariff it was settled that it might be imported upon payment of a rather higher rate than the amount previously obtained by the mandarins for sanctioning its importation.

The concession made at Shanghai, that no British merchant should be allowed to go to Pekin for the purposes of trade, may have had some influence upon the mandarins, in subsequently trying to gain their point of refusing entry of a British plenipotentiary to the capital. On this point, I think that the conduct of Mr. Bruce in not meeting the Commissioners at Shanghai to discuss the matter of his reception at Pekin, is not without blame, for Lord Elgin had written to the Commissioners requesting them to remain at Shanghai until he returned from Canton, as there were several matters still to discuss, and he again used his threat of proceeding to the capital if they would not remain to meet him. They did remain, but he never returned. They waited until Mr. Bruce arrived, some months afterwards, and then he would not meet them there, but desired that they should go to Pekin, where he was going. When it is considered that these officers were men of the highest rank in the empire, it would have been courteous to have seen them ; and had difficulties occurred, he would have been better prepared to act when he went to carry into execution the threat of going to Pekin, and in which he so signally failed. He was badly advised, when the mandarins offered to receive him at a place only eight miles distant from Takoo, in not sending to communicate with them there before having recourse to arms. The Takoo disaster would never have occurred had Tien-tsin been opened as a port when the treaty was signed; but with advisers such as Mr. Lay and Mr. Wade, who appear to have thought that it would be dangerous to the empire if foreigners obtained admission to Pekin, I am not surprised that Lord Elgin lost a golden opportunity, and that the Chinese hearing a foreigner admit that it would be dangerous if foreign merchants went to the capital, would be anxious to try to keep them out, even after the permission for their entry had been extorted.

Under a proper system of passports, I cannot see what danger there would be to the empire, if foreigners had the right of trade in any part of it, but it might prove inconvenient to mandarins if their illegal taxations on the transit of goods in some districts were discovered. I would condemn the unrestricted navigation of the rivers, and think that good might be done if the navigation on the coast were restricted also; for there is a class of adventurers who scarcely deserve any protection, who own and sail lorchas, employing them often in the most illegal acts along the whole seaboard of China, under whatever flag may be most convenient, and if these craft had the right to go at will up all the rivers of China, great harm might be done. Especially, as many mere matters of detail regarding customs' affairs are inserted in the treaty, any dispute relative to these petty matters thus becomes of undue importance as a treaty right.

It was not only in their capacity of custom-house

officers to the Chinese, that Lord Elgin's principal advisers saw affairs in a different light to most of the foreign community. Every point in Chinese has been discussed by them with their teachers, their chief informants on Chinese affairs. It is well known that any Chinaman you pay, will tell events to you in such a way as he thinks will be most agreeable to your ideas, and accordingly, the information imparted by these teachers may be taken for what it is worth. But not only this, these men have stories to tell to suit other masters, and they ply their pupils with these to serve other purposes. It has often been suspected that the teachers and informants of many of the Government interpreters, were spies in the service of the Chinese mandarins. Some light is thrown on this by an extract from one of the papers seized among official documents when Canton was taken. Among these was one reporting a conversation held between the Emperor and an ex-judge of Kwang-Tung, brother of one of the four principal secretaries of State. The Emperor asks, "How are you informed of what passes in foreign countries?" He is answered, "In foreign parts (*lit.* in the outer seas) there are newspapers. In these, everything that concerns any nation is minutely recorded, and these we have it in our power to procure, and as the barbarians cannot dispense with our people in the work of interpretation, Seu and Yeh manage to make their employées *furnish them privately every month with all particulars.* We are thus enabled to know everything that concerns them." *Emperor,*—"How is it that persons in barbarian employ, will, notwithstanding, furnish us with intelligence?" *Answer,*—"It merely costs a few hundred dollars more a year to bestow rewards on them. For these they are well pleased to serve us. Then, again, if the news received from any one quarter appears unsatisfactory, there is more sent in from other quarters, and if the reports from different quarters agree, the information is of course entitled to full credit."[1] This is too circumstantial to be false.

Just about the time the treaty was signed, one of the teachers was promoted to the rank of a mandarin. Mr. Wingrove Cooke gives some most valuable remarks upon the information and opinions the interpreters hold. Mr. Oliphant tells us, speaking of one of Mr. Wade's teachers (I think it was the same one who was promoted), " He was a not unfavourable specimen of the literary class in China, a good scholar, an efficient spy in behalf of his own Government, a gentleman in his manners, a great humbug, and a confirmed opium-smoker."[2]

I know that my opinion on this point agrees with that of many others in China ; and, however ignorant of Chinese affairs foreigners generally may be, too much weight should not be given to the political ideas of our interpreters, at least when they are so strongly biassed on one side or other. It must be borne in mind, that not only has Mr. Wade been chief informant to Sir George Bonham, Sir John Bowring, and Lord Elgin, but his leisure was employed in supplying the public with information through the press, so that most of the general opinions formed upon Chinese events have been derived *from one source*. It is a difficult work to attempt to change opinions once formed ; but I have considered it to be my duty, in the absence of any one else undertaking the task, to endeavour to show that there may be some doubt whether the opinions that have thus been formed are correct. I know all the

[1] *Blue Book,* p. 235.
[2] *Narrative of Lord Elgin's Mission,* vol. i. p. 441.

principal interpreters in China, and believe that no others would have influenced Lord Elgin's opinions in the same direction as Messrs. Wade and Lay.

Nothing shows more clearly how Lord Elgin's acts were governed by the views of these gentlemen, than the events which took place in the latter part of his mission, when he undertook the expedition up the Yang-tsze-Kiang. No immediate good could have resulted from it while the rebels were still unconquered. Yet Lord Elgin sends forward a gunboat, while his other vessels were passing through the Imperial fleet investing Nankin. There is no attempt made to communicate with the rebels on shore. The gunboat advances; the other ships follow; the former is fired upon for breaking the blockade without giving any notice. She hoists a flag of truce which is not understood; in China many of the fighting flags of the Imperialists are white.[1] Some few more shots are fired. The whole of the ships engage the forts, and force the passage. Not contented with this, Lord Elgin sanctions the return of the ships next day to "hammer the forts into ruins," and they only cease—though the rebels scarcely attempted to resist—when the Imperial fleet, with a steamer in Chinese service, came up to join in the attack. At other places, the same heartless policy was adopted; and as if there had not been sufficient bloodshed in China, Mr. Oliphant tells us that at one place "a large crowd had collected outside the gate, chiefly composed of rebel soldiers watching the proceedings. We sent them a ten-inch shell just to give them some idea of our armament."[2] When, however, the chief object to be gained was to procure supplies, Mr. Wade was sent on shore to communicate

[1] One of the banners of the eight great Tartar brigades is white.
[2] *Narrative of Lord Elgin's Mission,* p. 318.

at Woohoo, also held by the rebels. "The authorities were most anxious to do all in their power to show us civility." [1] A letter was sent in return by them, addressed "to the younger brethren of Jesus," and all such supplies as were wanted were procured. I have entered upon this subject elsewhere, but have yet another example to give of how the fleet acted even after this. At Ngan-king, where they arrived when they "knew that it was impossible" that news of what had happened at Nankin could have reached, still no attempt was made to communicate, and they determined to force a passage, even though, at the time, the Imperial soldiers were attacking the city, which was held by the rebels, *and the country people running into it on both sides for protection.* Some slight opposition was shown. "This was a piece of absurd impertinence, which involved another ten minutes' bombardment as a punishment. It came upon them too hot and strong to admit even of a third shot. The battery was speedily silenced, and after trying our range at some of the most imposing-looking public buildings in the centre of the town, *and bursting a shell or two* in the streets, by way of a warning, we left Ngan-king behind us, and with it got clear of the last stronghold of our not very agreeable friends, the rebels. On this side of the city, as on the other, country people were running in before the advancing Imperialists." Mr. Oliphant's account of the expedition up the Yang-tsze-Kiang is very interesting. Some curious circumstances, however, are brought to light in his narrative, even though written with a strong bias against the rebels, and in support of Lord Elgin's proceedings, which are strongly corroborative of my view of the question. He shows that all the cities which had been recaptured by the Im-

[1] *Narrative of Lord Elgin's Mission,* p. 326.

perialists were in a deplorable state of ruin. Chin-Kiang-foo, Kew-Kiang-foo, Hwang-Chow, Han-Yang, and Woo-Chang-foo, appear to have suffered most ; and wherever large numbers of Imperial soldiers are mentioned as collected together there is the greatest destruction, and the people have left the places to their mercy, and not ventured to return, apparently shunning their presence ; for at other places, such Hwang-Shih-kang and Han-kow, *more free from soldiers, and unprotected even by city walls,* the people congregate together in the largest numbers and carry on the most thriving trade ! Han-kow had been more than once in the possession of the rebels, and at one time had been destroyed, probably upon its first recapture. In reference to this Mr. Oliphant relates a curious fact, that the people who rebuilt the place did not erect the usual shrines in the houses,—*" there was not one to be seen, in deference, doubtless, to the iconoclastic propensities of the long-haired men."* One would rather infer from this that the houses were rebuilt when the rebels were there ! There are other incidents related which point to the Imperial soldiers being the principal agents of destruction. For instance, at Woo-Chang-foo, where he mentions that not a third of the place is built upon or inhabited, large tracts of ground being strewed with ruins, though the palace of the governor-general " had been spared by the insurgents ;" it seems probable, that if the destruction was due to the rebels, that building would have been the last they would have spared. The Imperial soldiers, as usual, may have destroyed houses occupied by the people who lived there while the rebels were in possession, but they would scarcely attempt to destroy the palace of their viceroy !

In the descriptions given of places in the hands of the

rebels, but besieged by the Imperialists, the suburbs are described as in ruins ; but excepting Woohoo, the cities themselves appear to be in comparatively good preservation, as no mention is made of ruins at Tai-ping, Che-chow, or Ngan-king ; on the contrary, some attempt seems to have been in progress to keep them in repair notwithstanding that the population was confined chiefly to the motley followers of Tai-ping-wang. At Nankin, Mr. Oliphant states, " the number of houses standing is very great." And again : " Several respectable houses are occupied by persons with high-sounding titles, members of the new nobility, and official establishments. Li said the latter had several ' myriad' yamuns (official residences), and we certainly saw some score of buildings more or less smartened with paint and gilding, some of them in very good Chinese style." The rebel city, Too-cheaou, " presented a very un-Chinese appearance of whitewash and cleanliness." At Ngan-king, when the country people were running in to the rebels for protection before the advancing Imperialists, " Columns of black smoke rising in various directions proved to us that the work of destruction was progressing, and that houses and villages were being reduced to ashes far and wide." Surely the country people would not be running in to the rebels for *protection* if their houses were being destroyed by them. This ought to be sufficient proof of who it is that creates the destruction which is so fre-quently attributed to the hands of the rebels !

Mr. Oliphant gives a most amusing account of the difficulty of getting the Chinese to answer questions upon different subjects, and the uncertainty of the information arrived at when they were not quite sure what answer is required. Lord Elgin, in his despatch to Lord Malmesbury relative to the expedition up the Yang-tsze-kiang, writes as follows :—" Chinamen of the humbler class are not much addicted to reflection, and when subjected to cross-examination by persons greedy of information, they are apt to consider the proceeding a strange one, and to suspect that it must be prompted by some exceedingly bad motive. Moreover, having been civilized for many generations, they carry politeness so far, that in answering a question it is always their chief endeavour to say what they suppose their questioner will be best pleased to hear."[1] This is especially true when the conversation is held with strangers. Now, when it is considered that all the people addressed by Lord Elgin's mission were strangers, and that the principal " cross-examination " was carried on by Messrs. Wade and Lay, it is not surprising that Lord Elgin and the gentlemen of his suite did not hear much in favour of the rebels. The appearance of foreign men-of-war, the attendance of mandarin soldiers, the visits with the high Chinese authorities, the Government notifications that foreigners were about to arrive, the news of the attacks at Nankin and Nganking, the presence of a mandarin on board the " Furious," and Mr. Wylie's residence on board the " Retribution " at the *Imperial* town of Kew-heen, all must have had some influence upon the Chinese who imparted information, and certainly would keep them from saying anything to the foreigners against the mandarins. Suppose the case to have been possible that Lord Elgin had gone up the river with a large force, in company with an army of insurgents, and commenced to clear away all the Imperial soldiers, to whose presence the people appear to have had so great a repugnance, we probably would have heard as much against the Imperialists as Mr. Oliphant and Mr. Wade have been able to relate against the in-

[1] *Blue Book*, page 442.

X

surgents. If Lord Elgin's secretary had been better acquainted with China, his opinions would probably have been very much modified.

1 judge Lord Elgin by the words of his own secretary. No attempt was made to prevent bloodshed. On the contrary, there appears to have been some anxiety to destroy human life, and fight against men who were willing to be our friends.[1] I am not stating too much when I say this ; for when Lord Elgin was deprived of the assistance of his larger vessels, and had to return past Ngan-king, close to the same batteries, only with a small gunboat, *then* he thought right to send in to communicate. His messenger, Mr. Wade, was favourably received. The rebels regretted that any collision had taken place, offered to send presents of oxen and other provisions, and bade good-bye, wishing them "good luck."[2] The chiefs at Nankin also sent a letter, stating their regret that any misunderstanding had occurred. In fact, it was well known that they would have been friendly had they been told that we had no intention to interfere with them. Would matters have been conducted in the same spirit by Lord Elgin had he really intended and wished to be neutral ? Neutrality had been enjoined by the British Government, but in this instance as well as in every other which could be made favourable to the Imperial Government, and the views of his interpreters, the general tenor of his instructions do not appear to have guided him.

It is difficult to point to any good results of Lord Elgin's mission, if the Treaty be not carried out in its integrity, or be suffered to remain a mere document, negotiated as it was—as the Imperial Commissioners sub-

---

[1] *Narrative of Lord Elgin's Mission,* vol. ii. page 364.
[2] *Ibid.* page 451.

sequently declared to his Lordship at Shanghai—when there was a pressure of an armed force,—" Weapons of war were constraining; there was a state of crackling fire and rushing water." Lord Elgin left China without having brought any point to a definite conclusion.

I think that we sometimes expect too much from the Chinese. They certainly have brought a good deal of difficulty to their own doors by endeavours to repel us, so that when we force an entrance we take the run of the house. Many of our doings in China do not present good examples of the Christian religion as explained by Lord Elgin in the Treaty. He says, " The Christian religion, as professed by Protestants or Roman Catholics, inculcates the practice of virtue, and teaches man to do as he would be done by."

Confucius has a somewhat similar precept, which might well be brought forward by the Chinese. He says, " Do not to others what you would not that they should do to you."

APPENDIX.

On the first outbreak of the great insurrection, the rumours and reports were so vague and contradictory, it is not unlikely that the chief who disturbed the districts nearest to Canton, where the name was in the greatest vogue, was entitled " Teen-teh." The districts of Tsing-yuen and Yin-teh, in Kwang-tung, were at one time in danger ; and when the disturbers of tranquillity were dispersed, there is good reason to believe that they joined with Hung-siu-tsuen at the city of Yung-ngan, on the eastern side of Kwang-si. When the rebels left that place on its being closely besieged, they went out by three different routes. One party was almost entirely cut off ; and as it was here the Imperialists made boast of taking Teen-teh prisoner, it is most likely there is some truth both in his execution and confession. The details entered into in the latter document are so circumstantial, and have in so many points been confirmed, that we see no reason to doubt the truth of most of the statements in the confession. Until the city of Nankin was taken, the rebel proclamations were dated under Teen-teh's reign. He was called Tai-ping-wang in some proclamations, where his surname was said to be Choo, a descendant of the Ming dynasty. The names of his generals[1] have not since appeared as members of the Kwang-si rebellion. Nor was that movement originated in any of the secret so-

[1] Seu-chang-pan and Ching-wan-yuen.

cieties. There is, however, a singular coincidence, which
deserves notice when treating of this point. Hung-siu-
tsuen's family name is represented by the same character
as is used to designate the Hung-clan, which is so prominently mentioned in all documents relating to the
secret societies. The Shanghai and Amoy rebels had it
in the centre of their badges of membership ; the Triads
have it in their seal : " First firmly connect the house of
Hung, and next secure the brethren." " The celestial
dynasty will be established, and Hung exalted." " The
five lodges, taking their respective parts, all engage in
full chorus, bearing on their persons the emblem of Hung,
which is unknown to others." It would be strange if
Hung-siu-tsuen went to Kwang-si to head an insurrection
of Triads, when he did not join any lodge in that province ; and we know that before he was interfered with
by the Government, the society he constituted was called
the " Shang-te-whui" (" God worshippers," as it has been
translated), and remained two years undisturbed, the
members living upon a common fund. The inter-
marriage and connexion of the families of the *chiefs* who
were all different from the Kwang-Tung Triad adventurers, proves the high standing they had over those who
joined them from other societies, and the bond of union
that existed between those of the Shang-te. We can
trace some of the Triads among the smaller chieftains
who remained faithful for a long time ; but when some
of the Fokien lodges joined, some misunderstanding occurred. There was disaffection ; and upon part of the
force deserting, the rest were put to the sword. The
Fokien men of the " Hung-kea," finding the expedition that had been sent had resulted in this way, and
dreading that they would not come in for a share of the
spoil when the empire was overthrown, organized another
revolution, and commenced by taking several cities in

the south of Fokien, Amoy among the number. On hearing this through rebel sources, the incident seemed extraordinary ; but lately seeing part of the story confirmed in Dr. Macgowan's notes, there is reason to credit it.

In one of Yang's (the eastern king) proclamations, addressed to the people soon after the rebels began their march on Nankin, he says : " Moreover, you valiant men are many of you adherents of the Triad society, and have entered into a compact that you will exert your united strength and talents to exterminate the Tartar dynasty. Who ever heard of men joining in a solemn compact, then turning their backs upon their foes ?" Had he been a Triad chief, he would have used very different terms. Lo-ta-kang, the lieutenant-general of the advance guard, and at one time commander at Ching-kiang, is said to be a Triad, and has easy communication with members of that society, who are in Imperialist pay. This man was at one time in an opium-receiving ship at Lintin ! The high post he held in the command of such an important station as Ching-kiang, shows that he was trusted and useful.

This is all we can trace of the connexion of the Taiping movement with any of the secret societies. We may therefore conclude that its whole foundation rests on an attempt of a few Chinese to propagate a religion for the benefit of their countrymen, and that religion founded in Scripture.[1]

1 In Gutzlaff's posthumous work, *The Life of Taou-Kwang*, there is mention made of the leader of the insurrection in 1849. " This pretender," he says, " promised exemption from taxes, and an entire freedom from all restraints ; and great numbers of idle fellows joined his standard ; but he *had reckoned upon the support of foreigners ;* and as he did not find it, he was obliged to fly for his life. Several hundreds of his adherents were killed on the spot (the author does not say where), and the whole band dispersed." It is to be regretted that more information was not given be-

How far this is shown by the publications of the rebels, the following translations of their verses, intended for repetition on Sundays, will serve as an example :—

" We praise and glorify Shang-te, as the Heavenly, Holy Father ;
We praise and glorify Jesus as the Saviour of the world—the Holy Lord ;
We praise and glorify the Holy Spirit as the Holy Intelligence ;—
We praise and glorify the Three Persons as the united, true God :
The true doctrines assuredly differ from worldly doctrines—
They save man's soul, and lead to his enjoyment of happiness without end.

" The wise joyfully receive them as a means of happiness ;
The foolish, when awakened, have by them the road to heaven opened.
The Heavenly Father, in his vast goodness, great and without limit,
Spared not his Eldest Son, but sent him down into the world,
Who gave up his life to redeem our iniquities ;
If men will repent and reform, their souls will be enabled to ascend into heaven."[1]

How dangerous it is to let this religion be propagated without giving it the attention it deserves, may be understood from the following circumstance which has come to my knowledge since this volume has gone to press. A native Christian convert lately went to visit his relations on the borders of Kiang-si. He had in his possession a Chinese Bible received from the missionaries. He was seized as having books similar to the insurgents, and cast into prison at Ta-po as a rebel ! In the same prison were many long-haired rebels.

fore Dr. Gutzlaff's death, as conjectures have been entertained that some of those connected with Tai-ping-wang had been pupils at Gutzlaff's Chinese school. Mr. Hamberg's *Visions of Hung-siu-tsuen* give no light on this subject at the date named, but state many interesting circumstances.

[1] Meadows' *Chinese and their Rebellions,* p. 428.